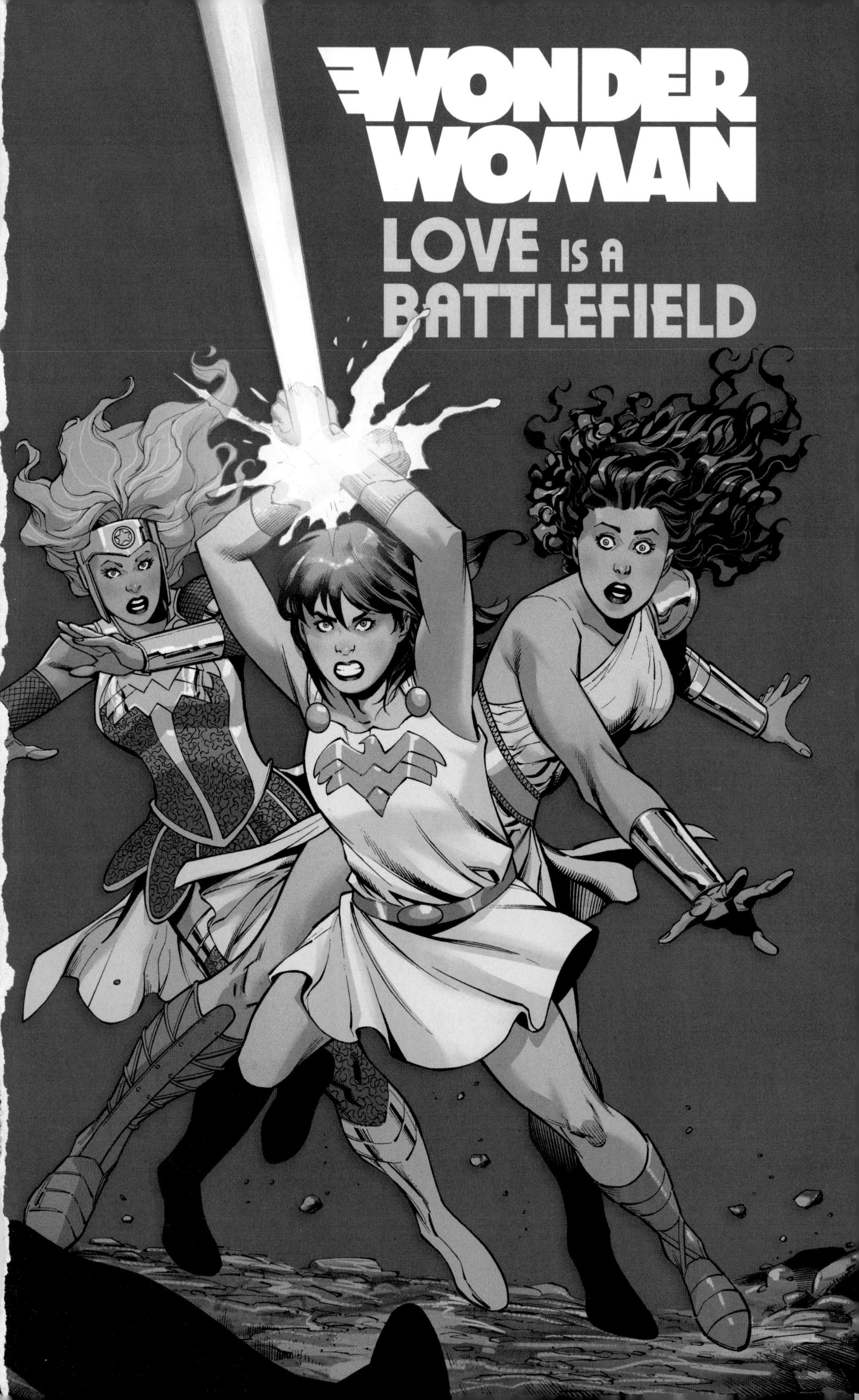
WONDER WOMAN
LOVE IS A BATTLEFIELD

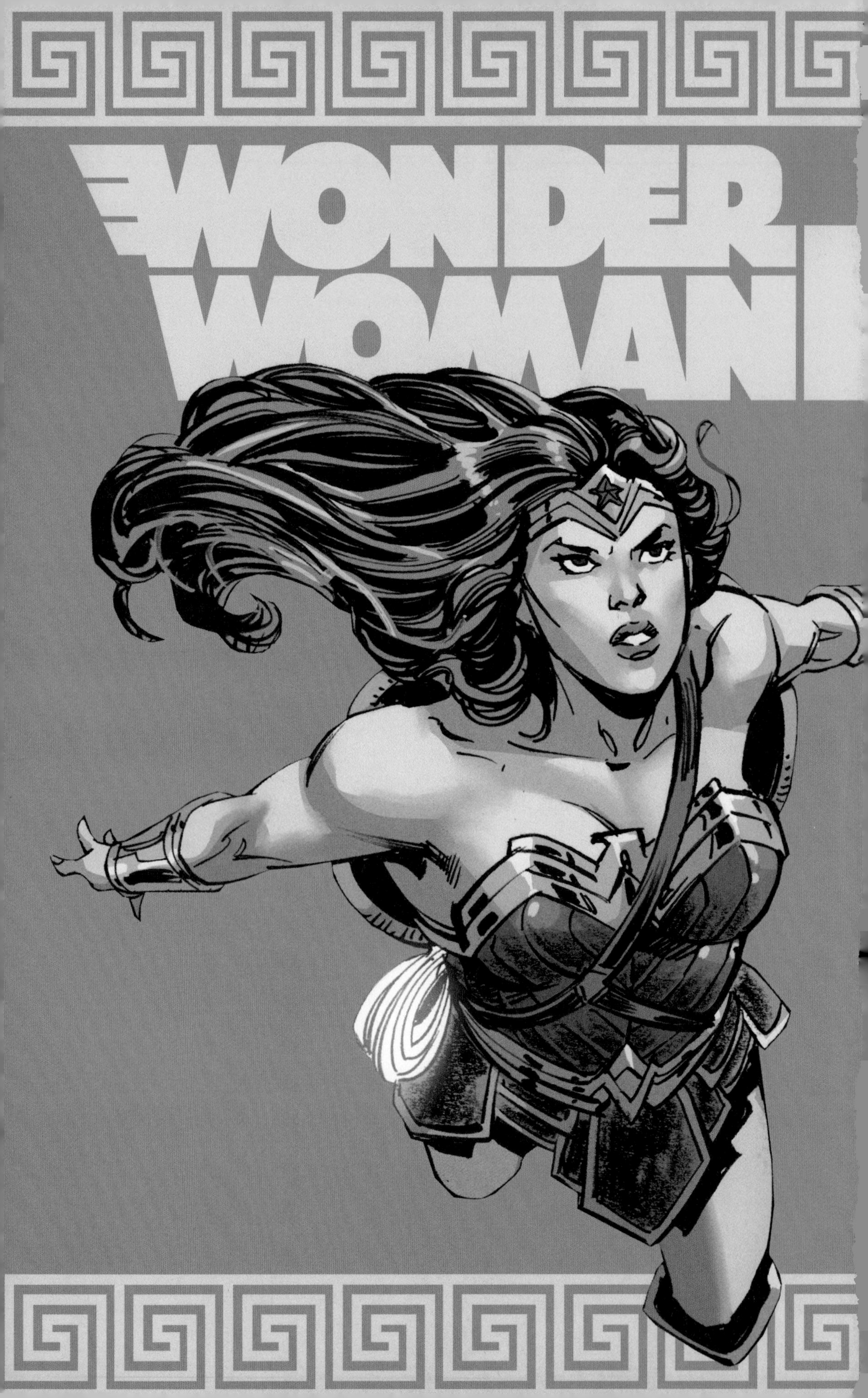
WONDER WOMAN

LOVE IS A BATTLEFIELD

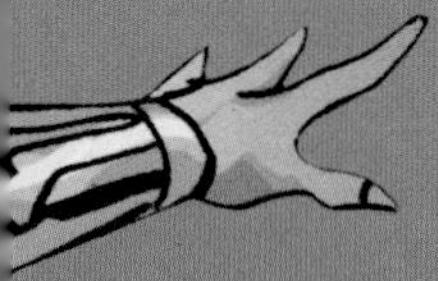

G. WILLOW WILSON
STEVE ORLANDO
WRITERS

CARY NORD
XERMANICO
RONAN CLIQUET
TOM DERENICK
AARON LOPRESTI
JESÚS MERINO
PENCILLERS

MICK GRAY
XERMANICO
RONAN CLIQUET
SCOTT HANNA
JESÚS MERINO
MATT RYAN
INKERS

ROMULO FAJARDO JR.
COLORIST

PAT BROSSEAU
LETTERER

TERRY DODSON & RACHEL DODSON
COLLECTION COVER ARTISTS

WONDER WOMAN **CREATED BY** WILLIAM MOULTON MARSTON

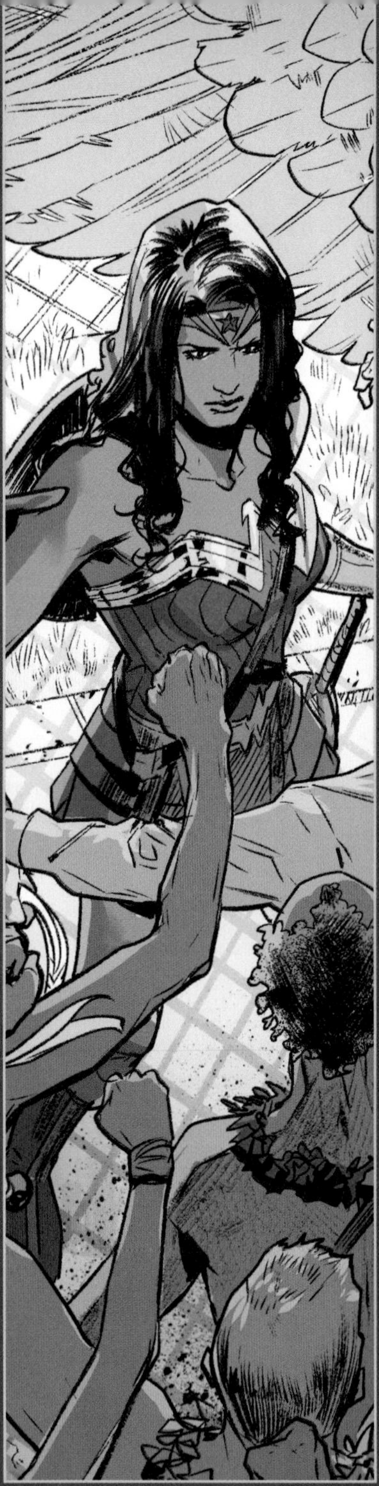

CHRIS CONROY
BRIAN CUNNINGHAM
Editors – Original Series

BRITTANY HOLZHERR
Associate Editor – Original Series

DAVE WIELGOSZ
Assistant Editor – Original Series

JEB WOODARD
Group Editor – Collected Editions

ERIKA ROTHBERG
Editor – Collected Edition

STEVE COOK
Design Director – Books

JOHN J. HILL
Publication Design

ERIN VANOVER
Publication Production

BOB HARRAS
Senior VP – Editor-in-Chief, DC Comics

PAT McCALLUM
Executive Editor, DC Comics

DAN DiDIO
Publisher

JIM LEE
Publisher & Chief Creative Officer

BOBBIE CHASE
VP – New Publishing Initiatives & Talent Development

DON FALLETTI
VP – Manufacturing Operations & Workflow Management

LAWRENCE GANEM
VP – Talent Services

ALISON GILL
Senior VP – Manufacturing & Operations

HANK KANALZ
Senior VP – Publishing Strategy & Support Services

DAN MIRON
VP – Publishing Operations

NICK J. NAPOLITANO
VP – Manufacturing Administration & Design

NANCY SPEARS
VP – Sales

MICHELE R. WELLS
VP & Executive Editor, Young Reader

WONDER WOMAN VOL. 2: LOVE IS A BATTLEFIELD

DC Comics, 2900 West Alameda Ave., Burbank, CA 91505
Printed by Transcontinental Interglobe, Beauceville, QC, Canada. 2/28/20.
First Printing. ISBN: 978-1-77950-040-3

Library of Congress Cataloging-in-Publication Data is available.

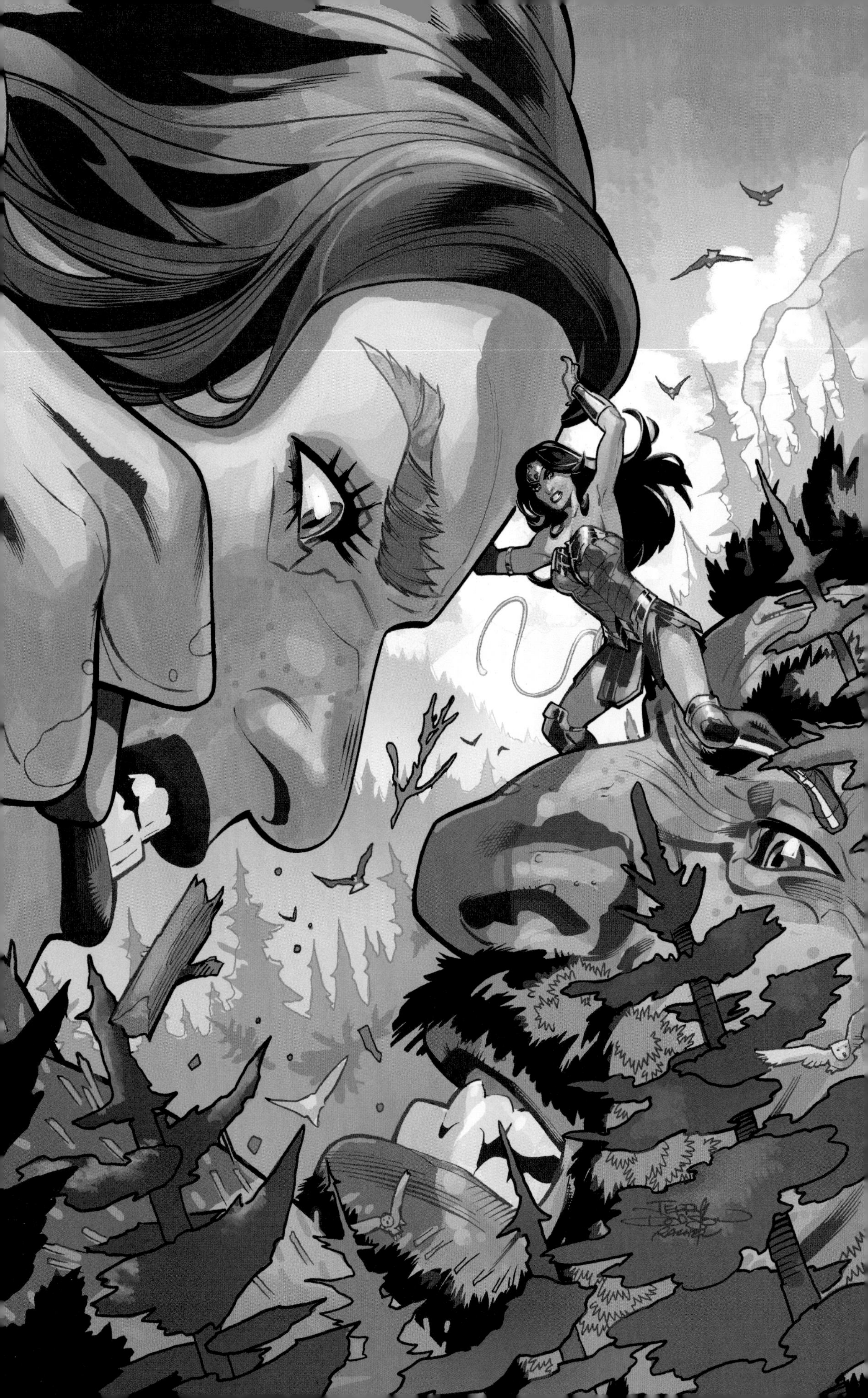

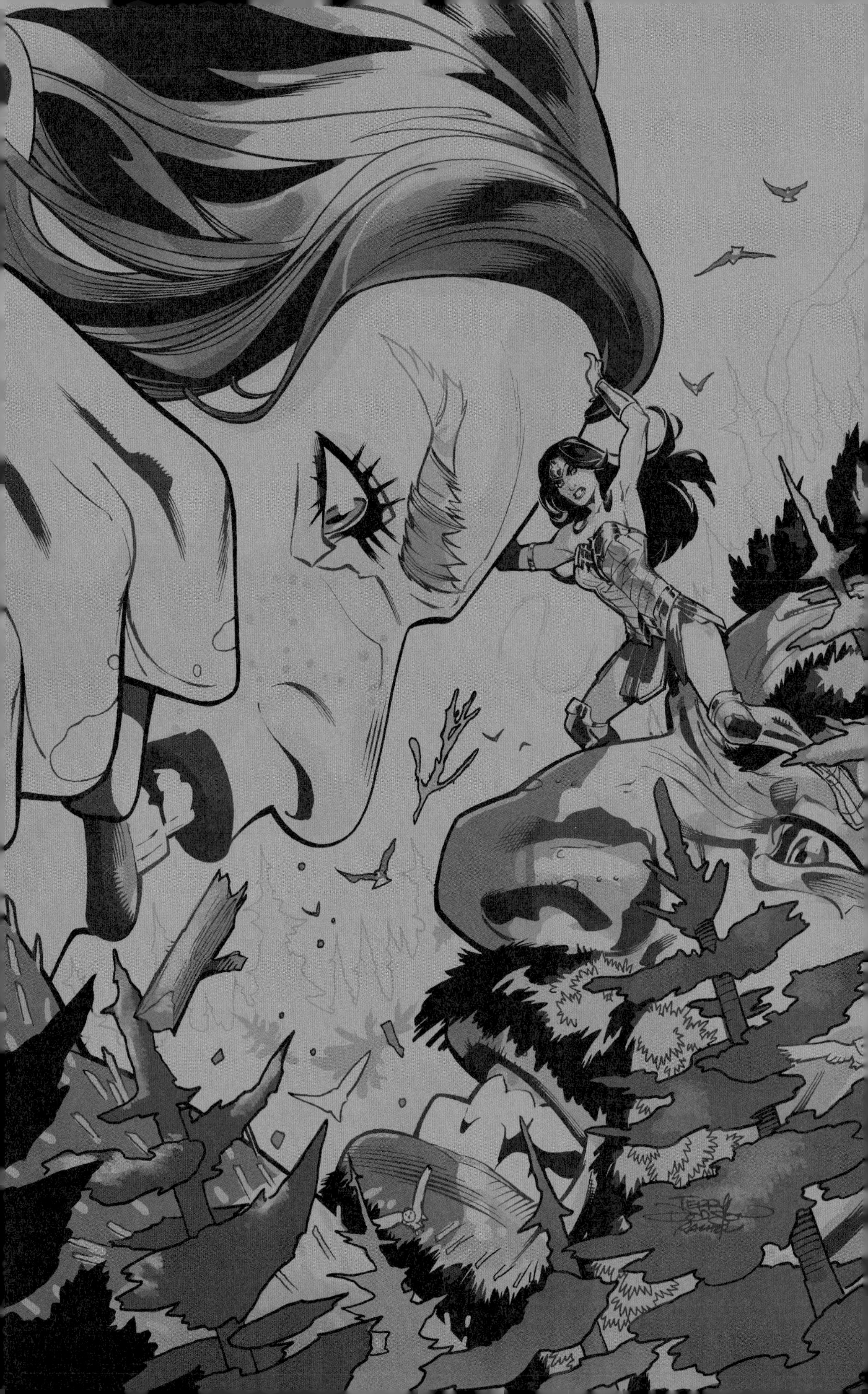

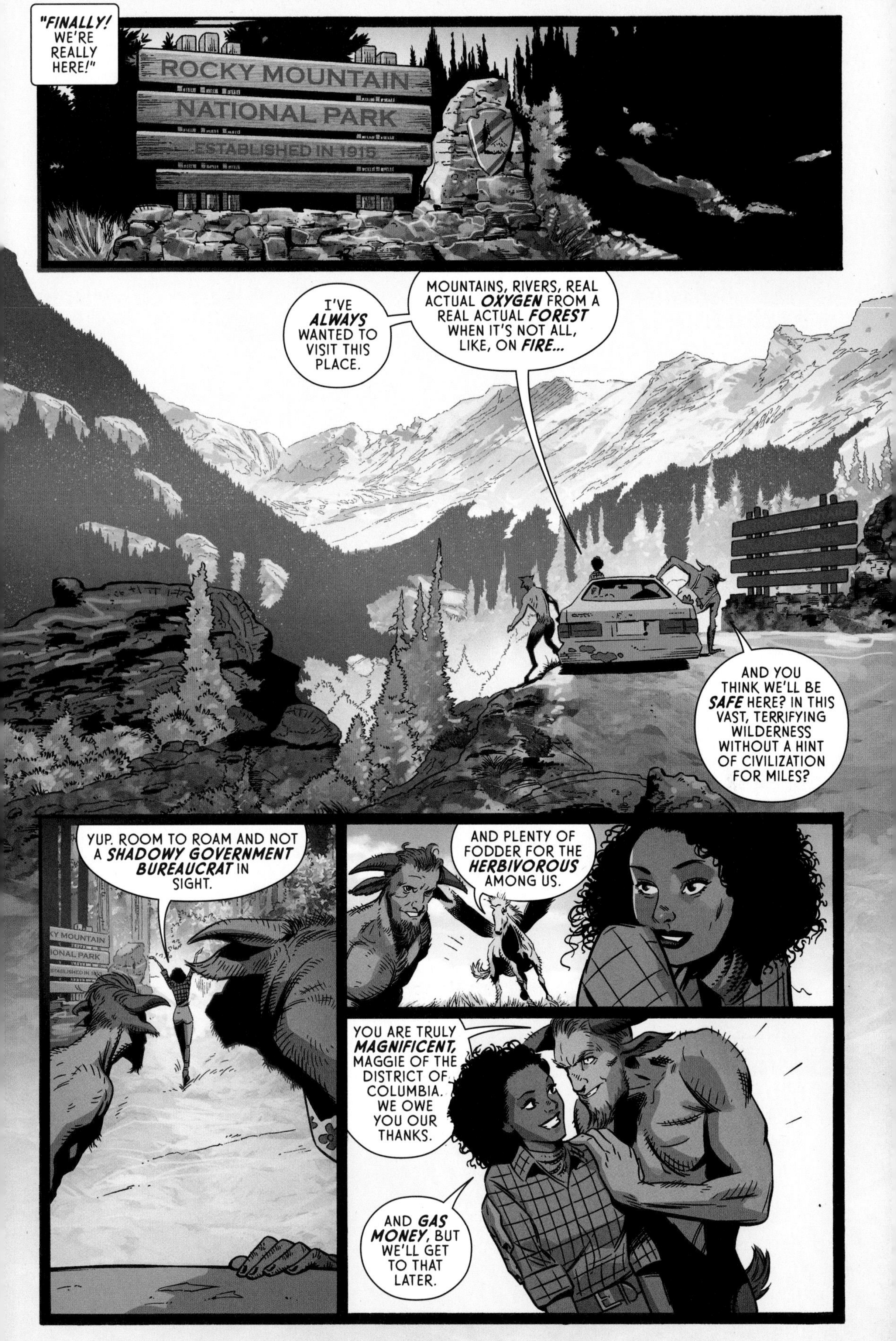
"FINALLY! WE'RE REALLY HERE!"
ROCKY MOUNTAIN NATIONAL PARK
ESTABLISHED IN 1915
I'VE ALWAYS WANTED TO VISIT THIS PLACE.
MOUNTAINS, RIVERS, REAL ACTUAL OXYGEN FROM A REAL ACTUAL FOREST WHEN IT'S NOT ALL, LIKE, ON FIRE...
AND YOU THINK WE'LL BE SAFE HERE? IN THIS VAST, TERRIFYING WILDERNESS WITHOUT A HINT OF CIVILIZATION FOR MILES?
YUP. ROOM TO ROAM AND NOT A SHADOWY GOVERNMENT BUREAUCRAT IN SIGHT.
AND PLENTY OF FODDER FOR THE HERBIVOROUS AMONG US.
YOU ARE TRULY MAGNIFICENT, MAGGIE OF THE DISTRICT OF COLUMBIA. WE OWE YOU OUR THANKS.
AND GAS MONEY, BUT WE'LL GET TO THAT LATER.

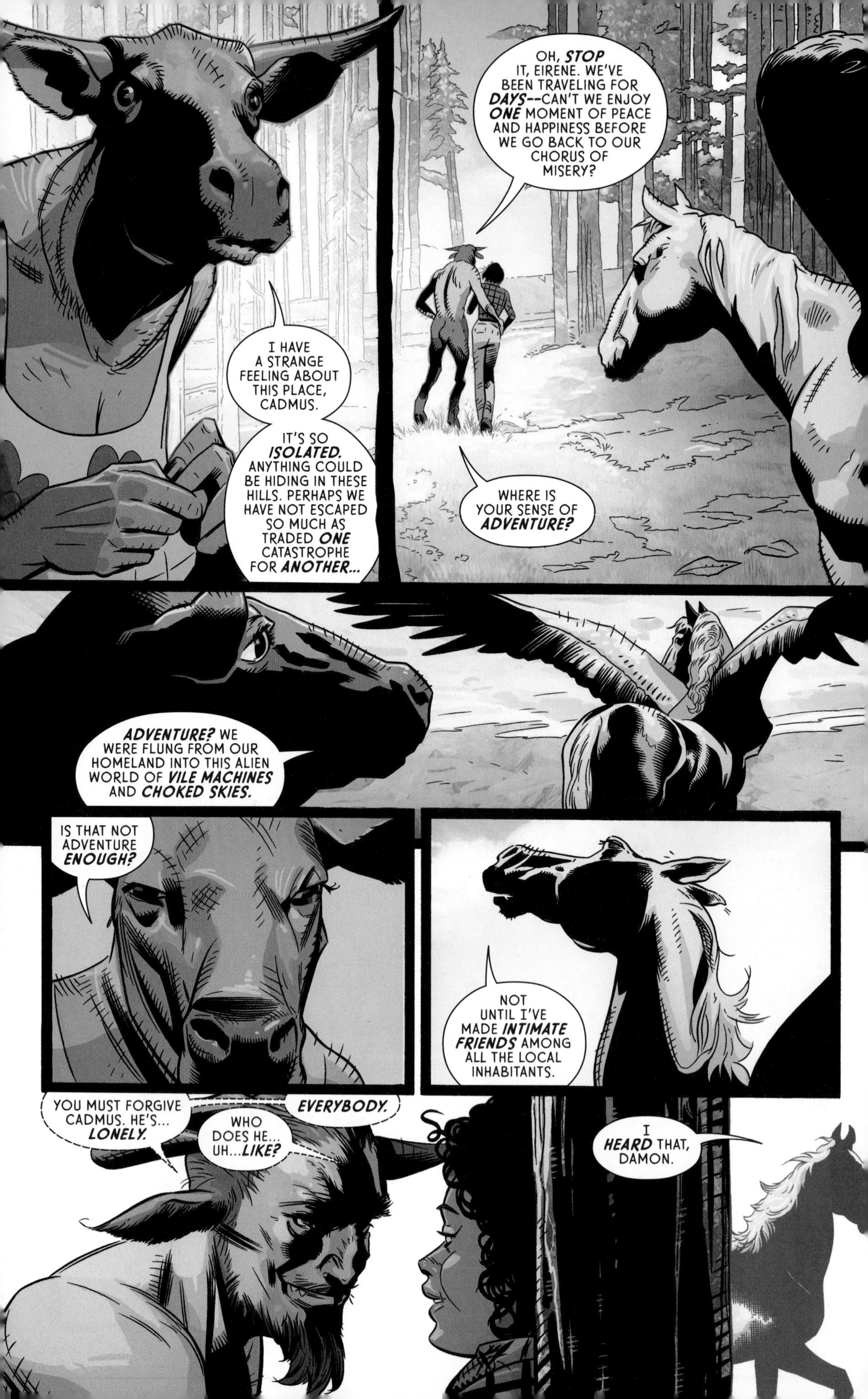
I HAVE A STRANGE FEELING ABOUT THIS PLACE, CADMUS.
IT'S SO ISOLATED. ANYTHING COULD BE HIDING IN THESE HILLS. PERHAPS WE HAVE NOT ESCAPED SO MUCH AS TRADED ONE CATASTROPHE FOR ANOTHER...
OH, STOP IT, EIRENE. WE'VE BEEN TRAVELING FOR DAYS--CAN'T WE ENJOY ONE MOMENT OF PEACE AND HAPPINESS BEFORE WE GO BACK TO OUR CHORUS OF MISERY?
WHERE IS YOUR SENSE OF ADVENTURE?
ADVENTURE? WE WERE FLUNG FROM OUR HOMELAND INTO THIS ALIEN WORLD OF VILE MACHINES AND CHOKED SKIES.
IS THAT NOT ADVENTURE ENOUGH?
NOT UNTIL I'VE MADE INTIMATE FRIENDS AMONG ALL THE LOCAL INHABITANTS.
YOU MUST FORGIVE CADMUS. HE'S... LONELY.
WHO DOES HE... UH...LIKE?
EVERYBODY.
I HEARD THAT, DAMON.

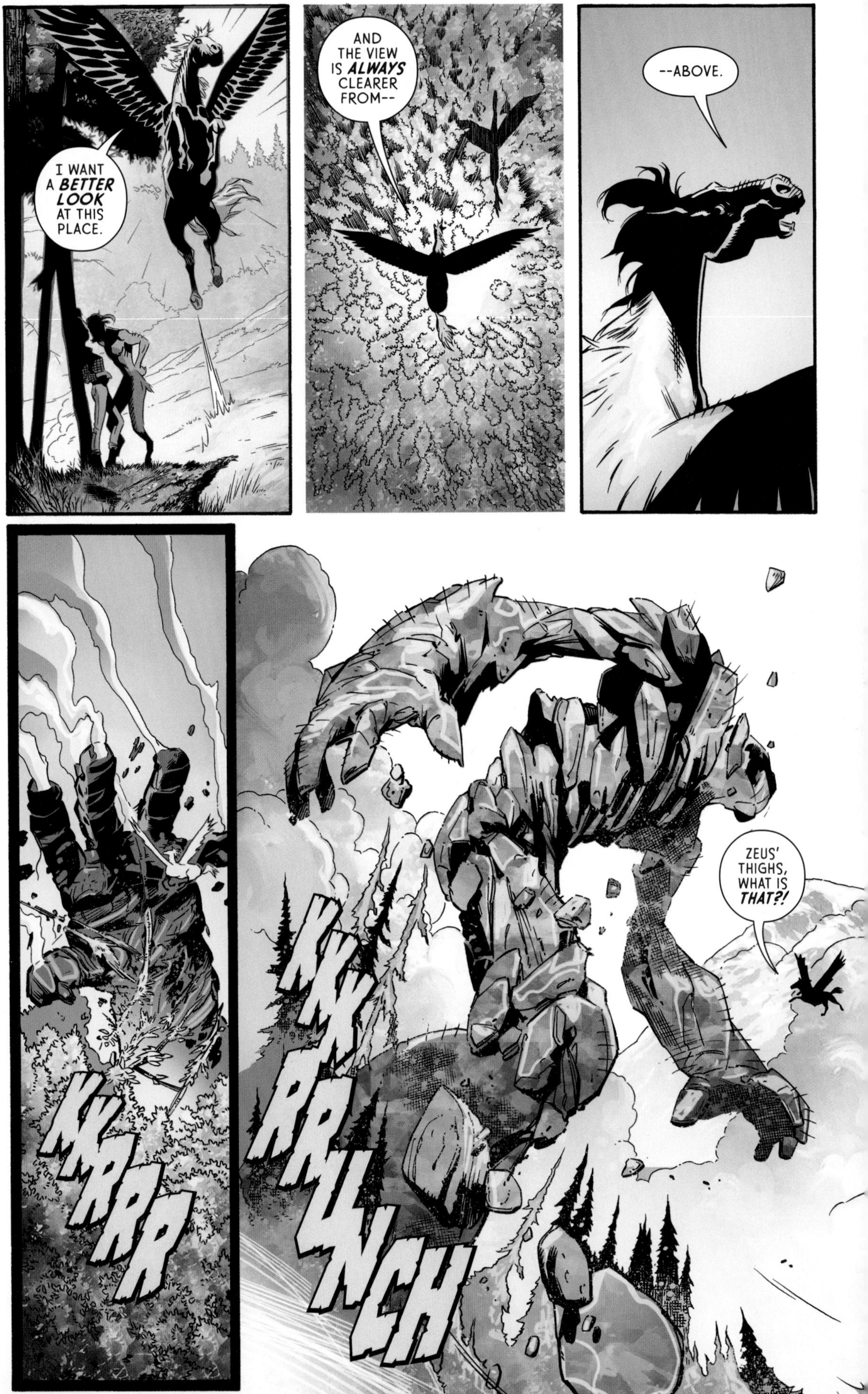
I WANT A BETTER LOOK AT THIS PLACE.
AND THE VIEW IS ALWAYS CLEARER FROM--
--ABOVE.
KKRRR
KKKRRUNCH
ZEUS' THIGHS, WHAT IS THAT?!

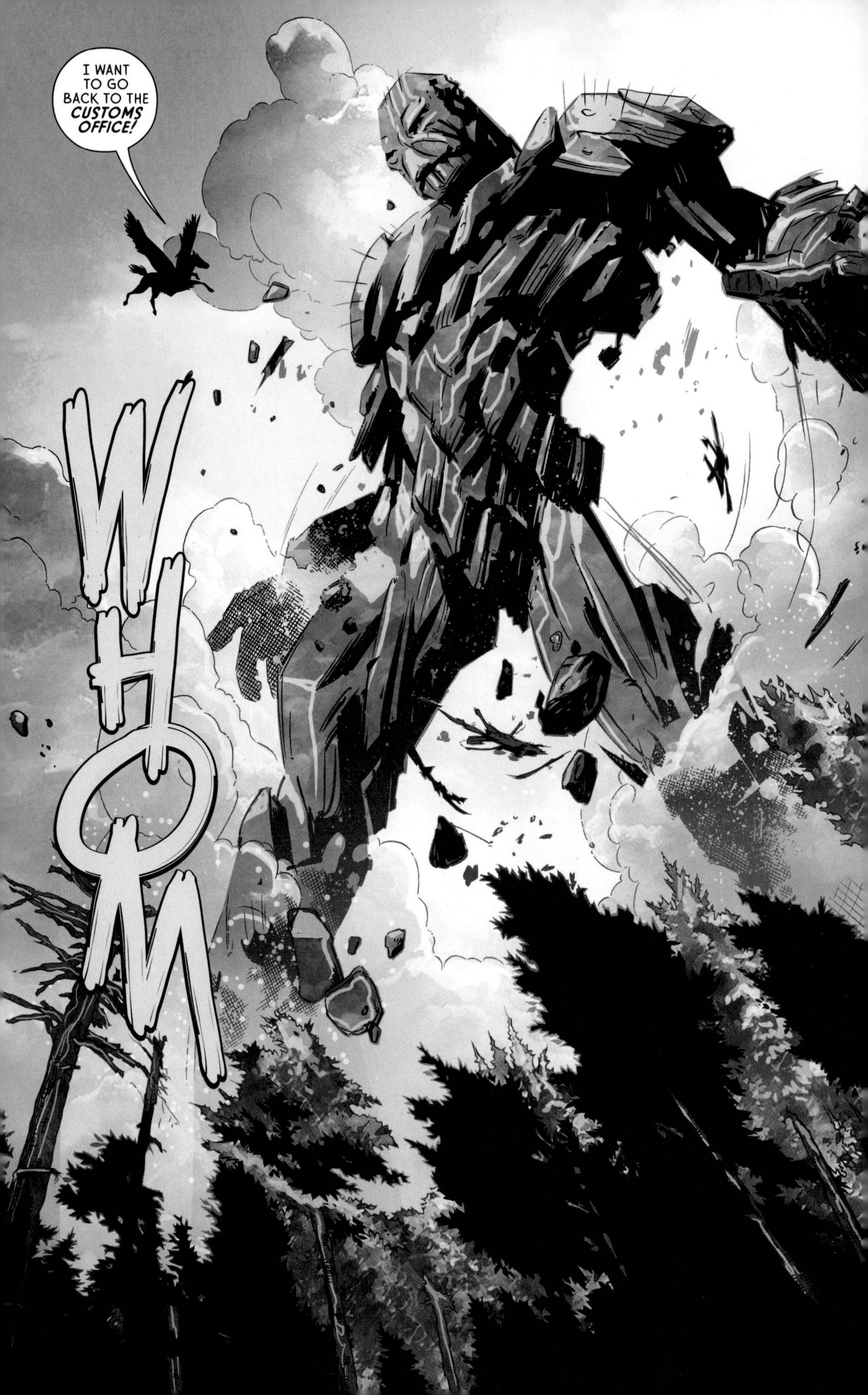
I WANT TO GO BACK TO THE *CUSTOMS OFFICE!*
WHOOM

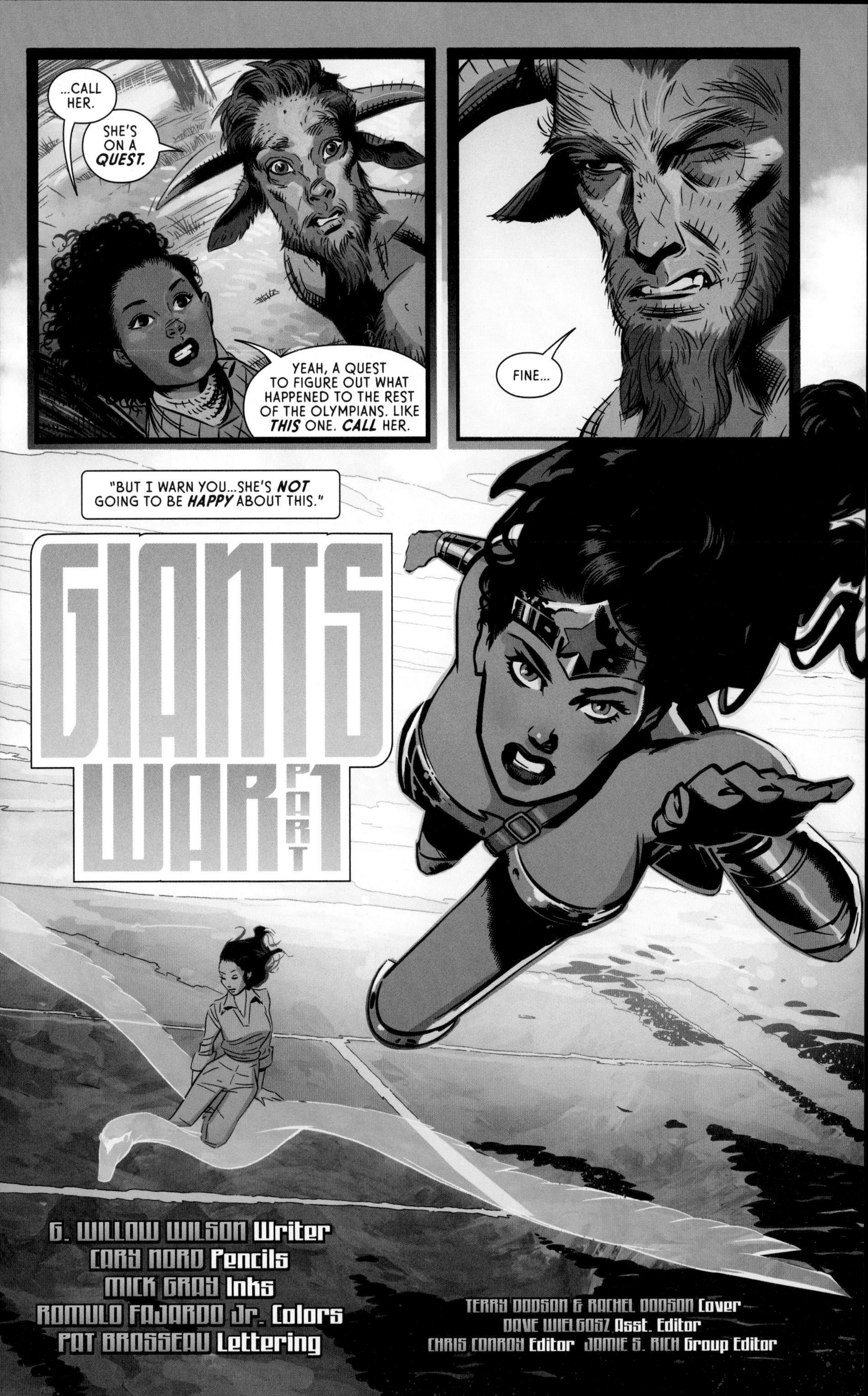
...CALL HER.
SHE'S ON A QUEST.
YEAH, A QUEST TO FIGURE OUT WHAT HAPPENED TO THE REST OF THE OLYMPIANS. LIKE THIS ONE. CALL HER.
FINE...
"BUT I WARN YOU...SHE'S NOT GOING TO BE HAPPY ABOUT THIS."
GIANTS WAR PART 1
G. WILLOW WILSON Writer
CARY NORD Pencils
MICK GRAY Inks
ROMULO FAJARDO Jr. Colors
PAT BROSSEAU Lettering
TERRY DODSON & RACHEL DODSON Cover
DAVE WIELGOSZ Asst. Editor
CHRIS CONROY Editor JAMIE S. RICH Group Editor

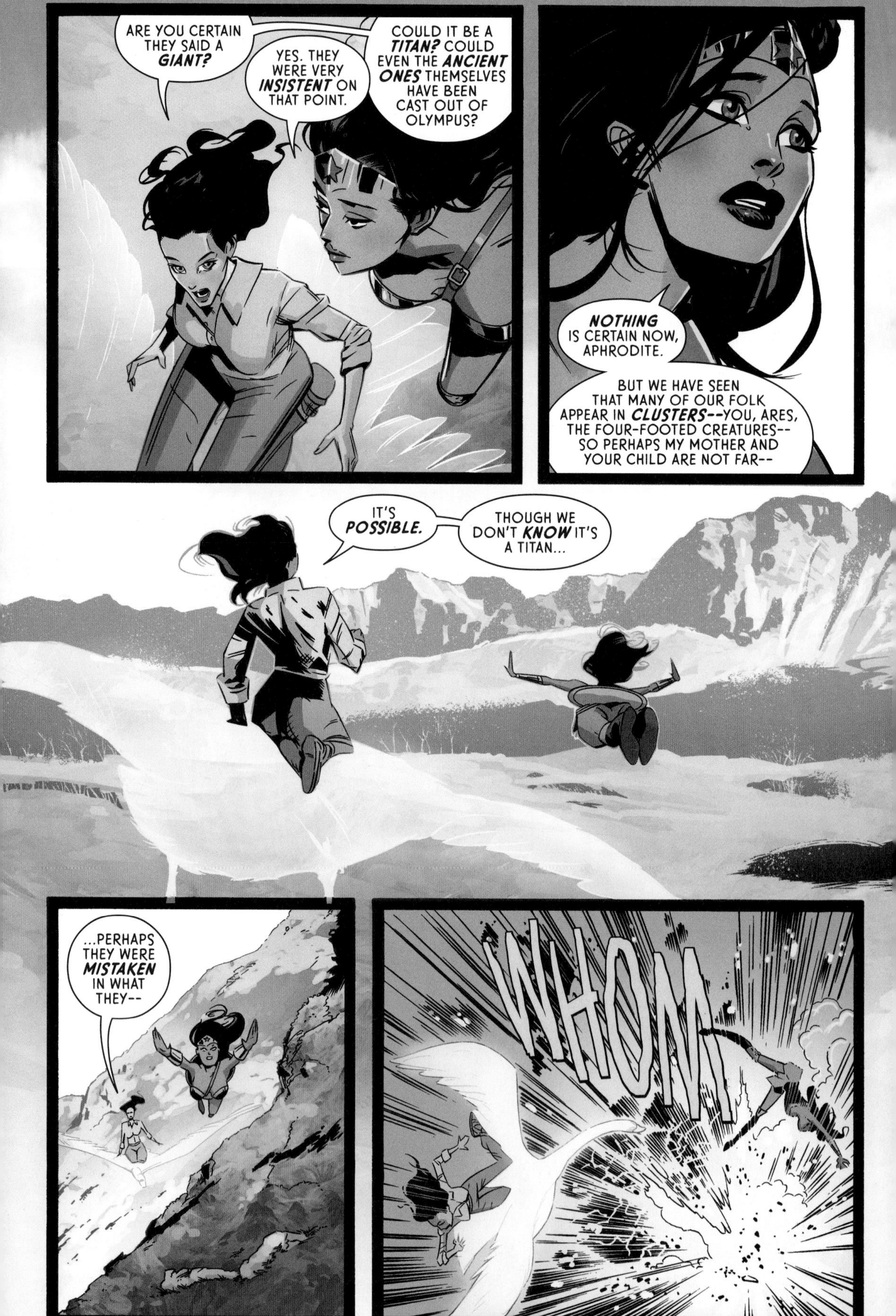
ARE YOU CERTAIN THEY SAID A GIANT?
YES. THEY WERE VERY INSISTENT ON THAT POINT.
COULD IT BE A TITAN? COULD EVEN THE ANCIENT ONES THEMSELVES HAVE BEEN CAST OUT OF OLYMPUS?
NOTHING IS CERTAIN NOW, APHRODITE.
BUT WE HAVE SEEN THAT MANY OF OUR FOLK APPEAR IN CLUSTERS--YOU, ARES, THE FOUR-FOOTED CREATURES--SO PERHAPS MY MOTHER AND YOUR CHILD ARE NOT FAR--
IT'S POSSIBLE.
THOUGH WE DON'T KNOW IT'S A TITAN...
...PERHAPS THEY WERE MISTAKEN IN WHAT THEY--
WHOM

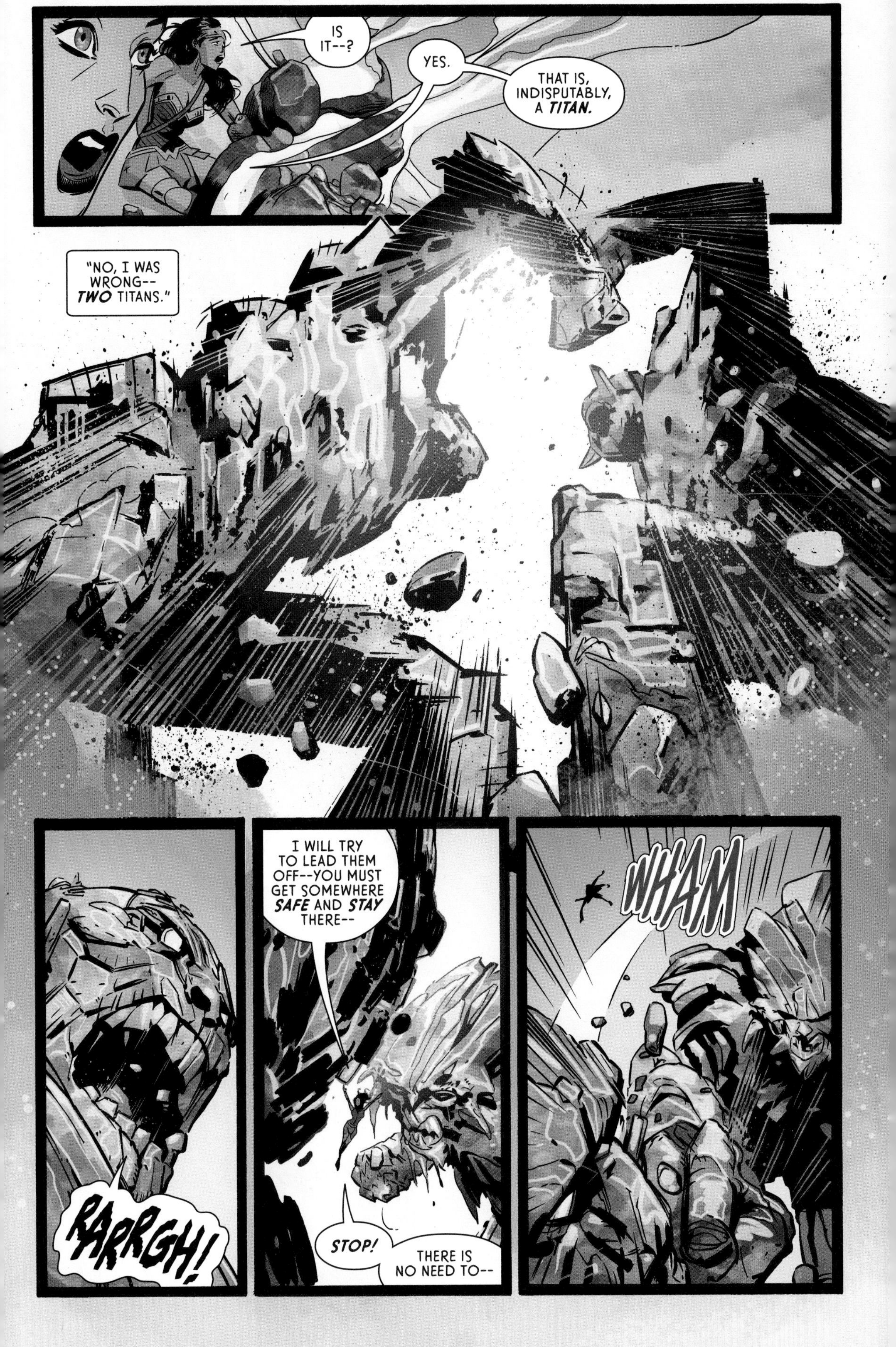
IS IT--?
YES.
THAT IS, INDISPUTABLY, A TITAN.
"NO, I WAS WRONG-- TWO TITANS."
RARRGH!
I WILL TRY TO LEAD THEM OFF--YOU MUST GET SOMEWHERE SAFE AND STAY THERE--
STOP!
THERE IS NO NEED TO--
WHAM

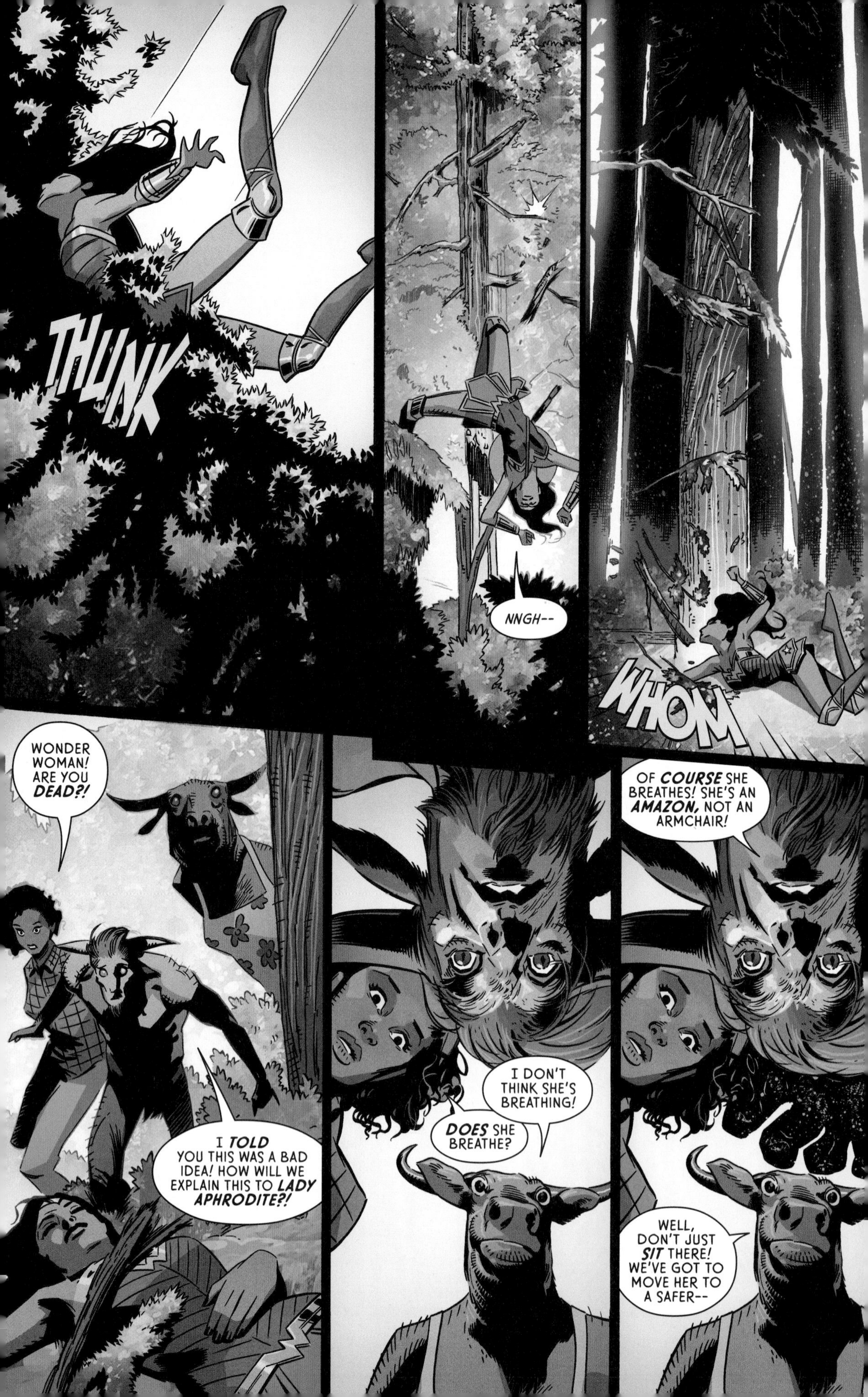
THUNK
NNGH--
WHOM
WONDER WOMAN! ARE YOU DEAD?!
I TOLD YOU THIS WAS A BAD IDEA! HOW WILL WE EXPLAIN THIS TO LADY APHRODITE?!
I DON'T THINK SHE'S BREATHING!
DOES SHE BREATHE?
OF COURSE SHE BREATHES! SHE'S AN AMAZON, NOT AN ARMCHAIR!
WELL, DON'T JUST SIT THERE! WE'VE GOT TO MOVE HER TO A SAFER--

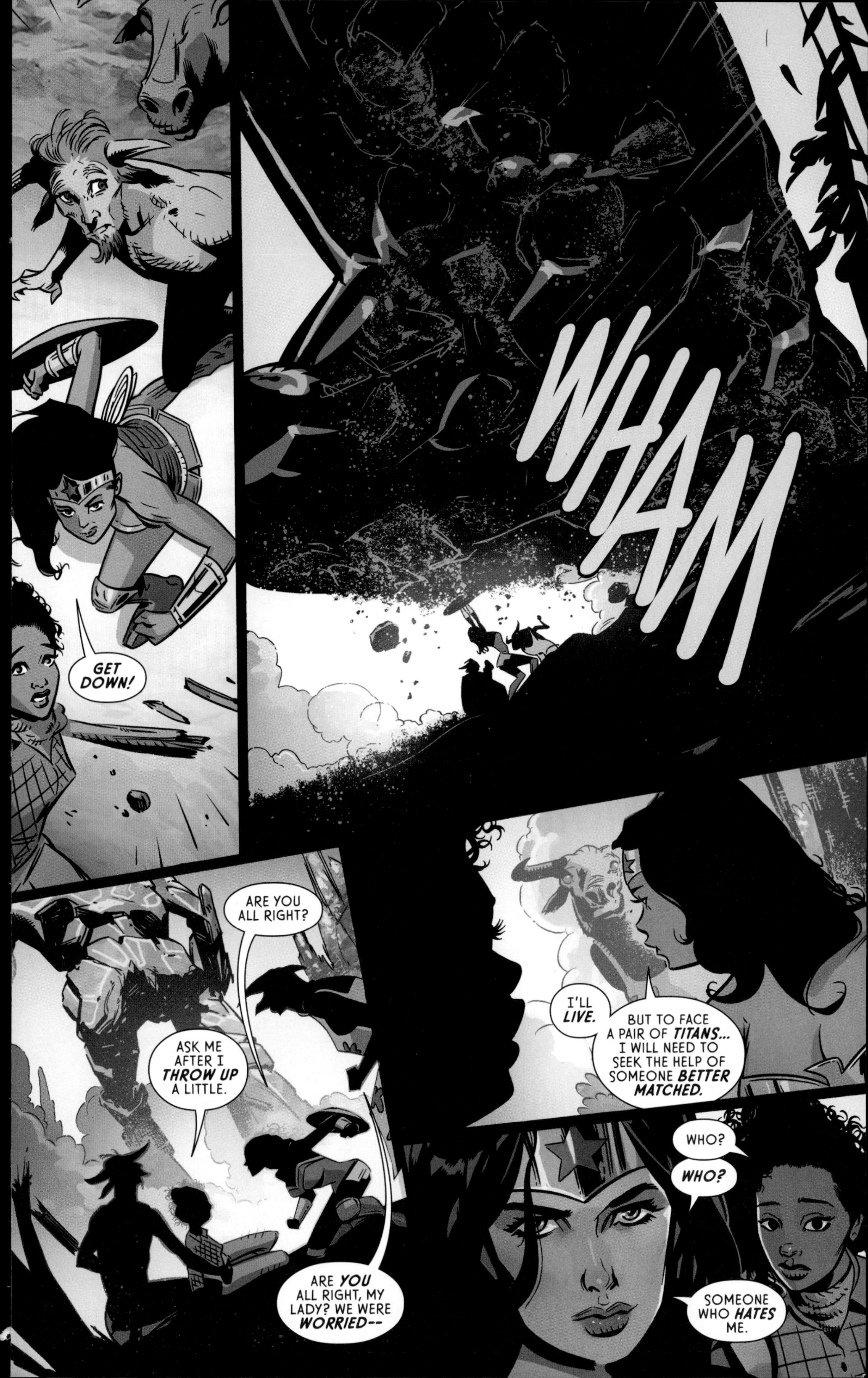
GET DOWN!
WHAM
ARE YOU ALL RIGHT?
ASK ME AFTER I THROW UP A LITTLE.
ARE YOU ALL RIGHT, MY LADY? WE WERE WORRIED--
I'LL LIVE.
BUT TO FACE A PAIR OF TITANS... I WILL NEED TO SEEK THE HELP OF SOMEONE BETTER MATCHED.
WHO?
WHO?
SOMEONE WHO HATES ME.

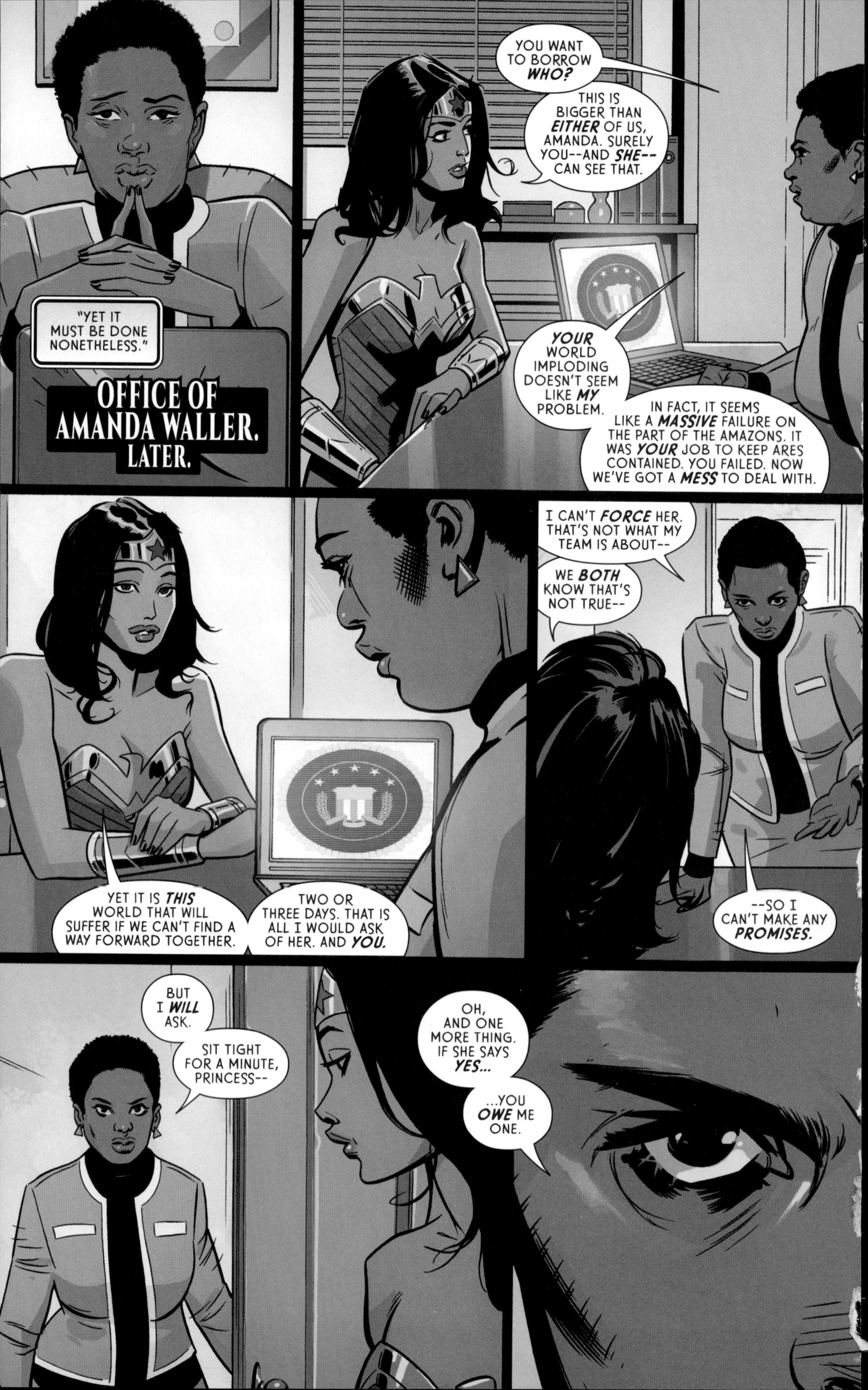
"YET IT MUST BE DONE NONETHELESS."
OFFICE OF AMANDA WALLER. LATER.
YOU WANT TO BORROW WHO?
THIS IS BIGGER THAN EITHER OF US, AMANDA. SURELY YOU--AND SHE-- CAN SEE THAT.
YOUR WORLD IMPLODING DOESN'T SEEM LIKE MY PROBLEM.
IN FACT, IT SEEMS LIKE A MASSIVE FAILURE ON THE PART OF THE AMAZONS. IT WAS YOUR JOB TO KEEP ARES CONTAINED. YOU FAILED. NOW WE'VE GOT A MESS TO DEAL WITH.
YET IT IS THIS WORLD THAT WILL SUFFER IF WE CAN'T FIND A WAY FORWARD TOGETHER.
TWO OR THREE DAYS. THAT IS ALL I WOULD ASK OF HER. AND YOU.
I CAN'T FORCE HER. THAT'S NOT WHAT MY TEAM IS ABOUT--
WE BOTH KNOW THAT'S NOT TRUE--
--SO I CAN'T MAKE ANY PROMISES.
BUT I WILL ASK.
SIT TIGHT FOR A MINUTE, PRINCESS--
OH, AND ONE MORE THING. IF SHE SAYS YES...
...YOU OWE ME ONE.

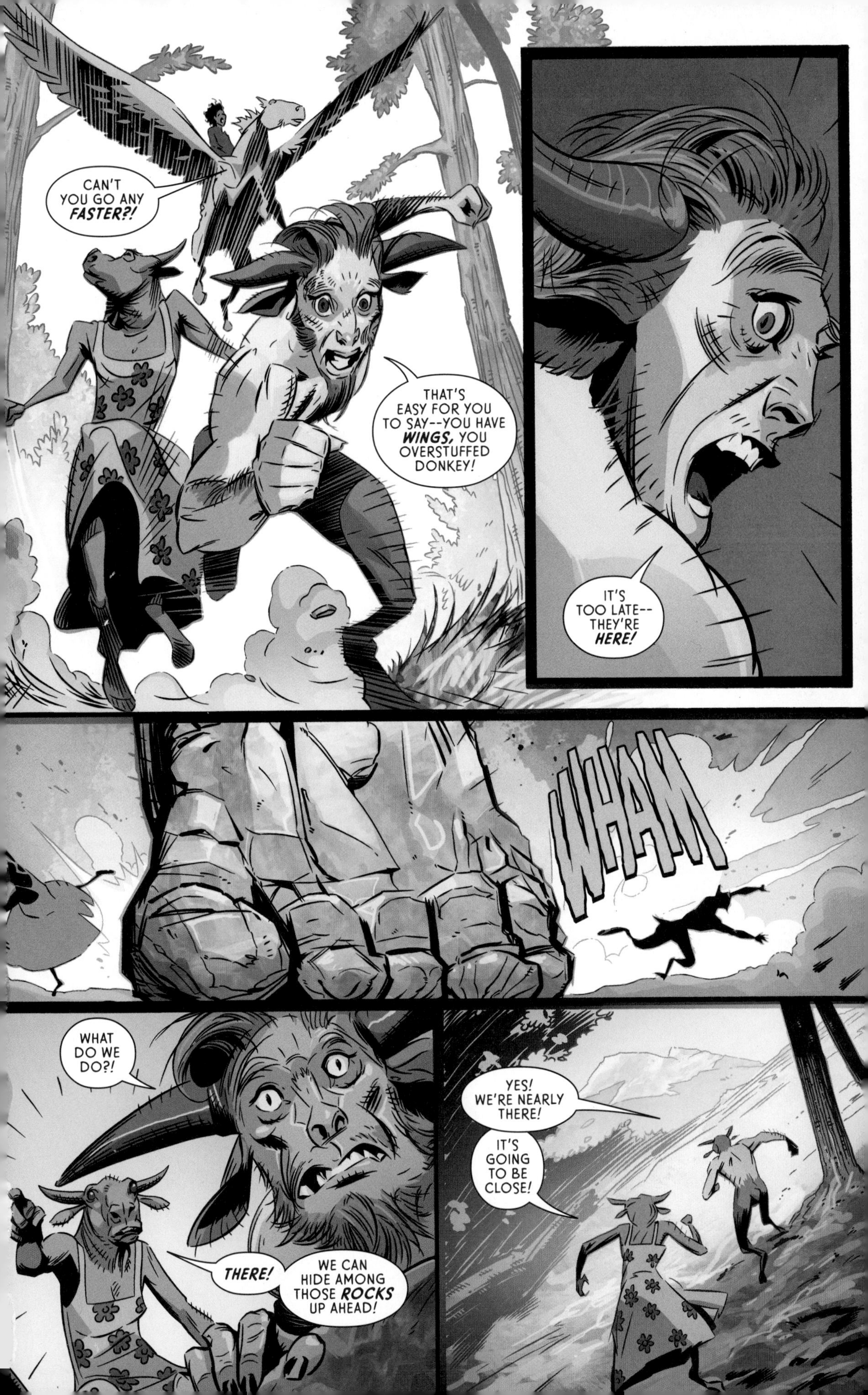
CAN'T YOU GO ANY FASTER?!
THAT'S EASY FOR YOU TO SAY--YOU HAVE WINGS, YOU OVERSTUFFED DONKEY!
IT'S TOO LATE--THEY'RE HERE!
WHAM
WHAT DO WE DO?!
THERE!
WE CAN HIDE AMONG THOSE ROCKS UP AHEAD!
YES! WE'RE NEARLY THERE!
IT'S GOING TO BE CLOSE!

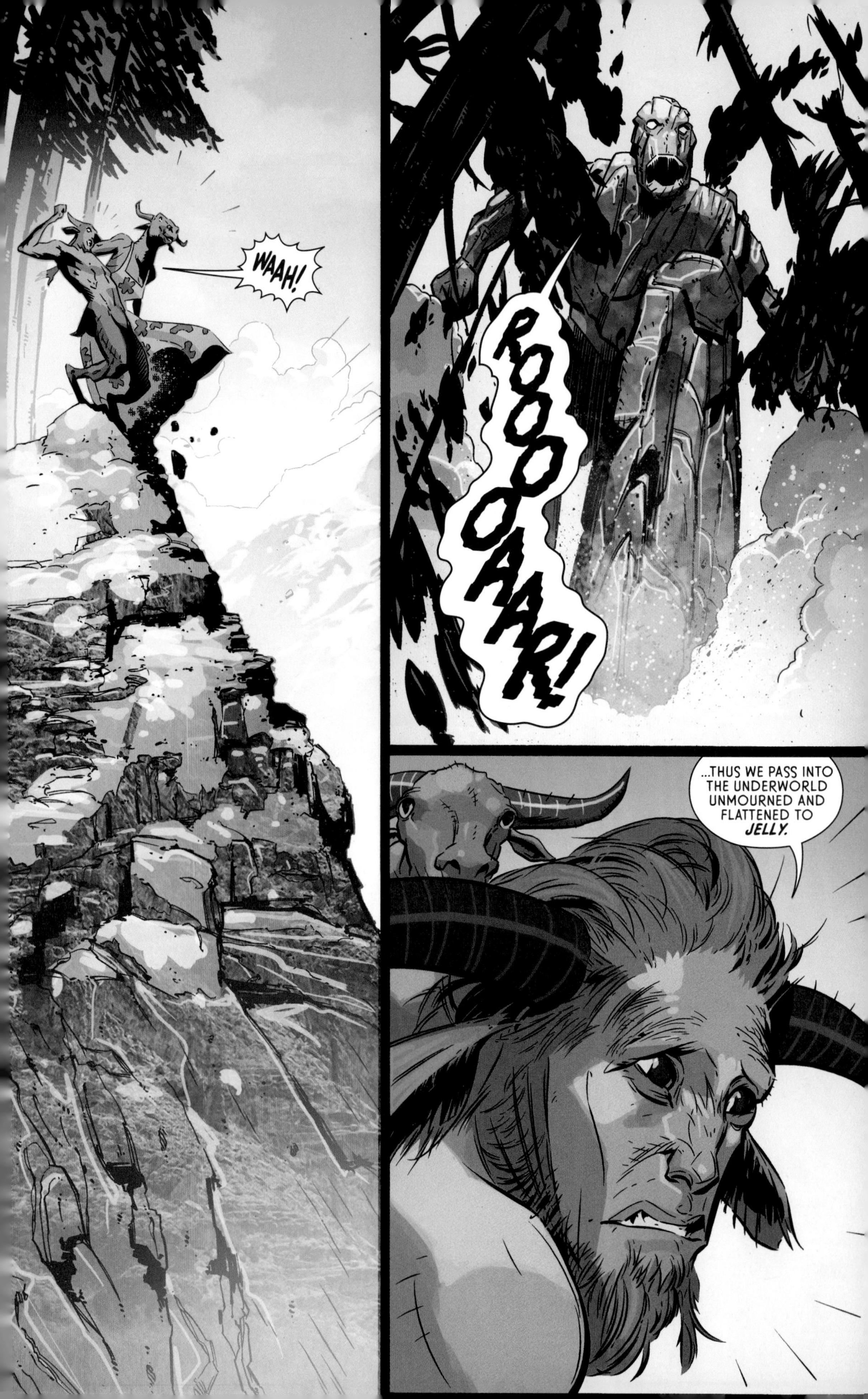
WAAH!
ROOOOAAR!
...THUS WE PASS INTO THE UNDERWORLD UNMOURNED AND FLATTENED TO *JELLY.*

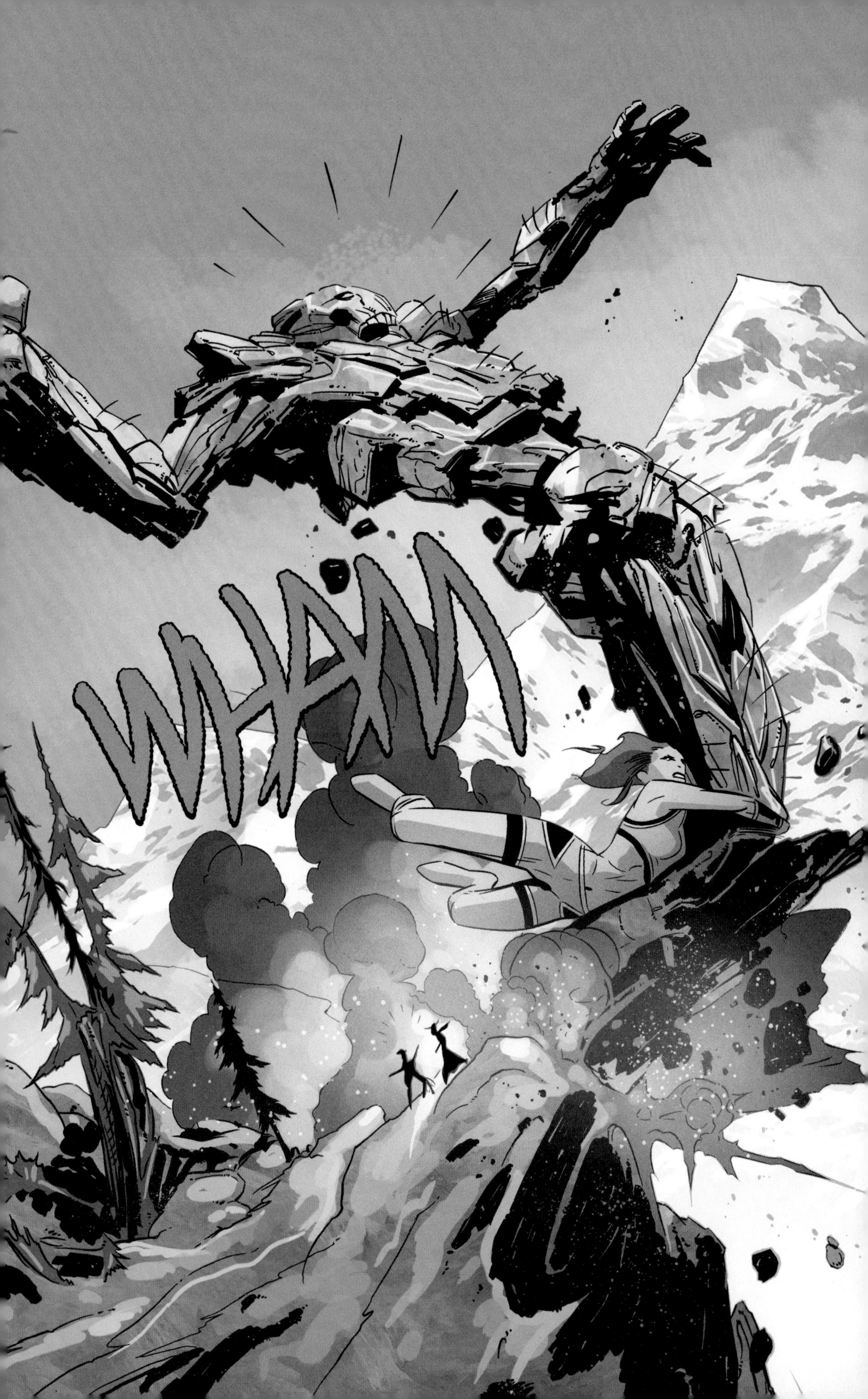
WHAM

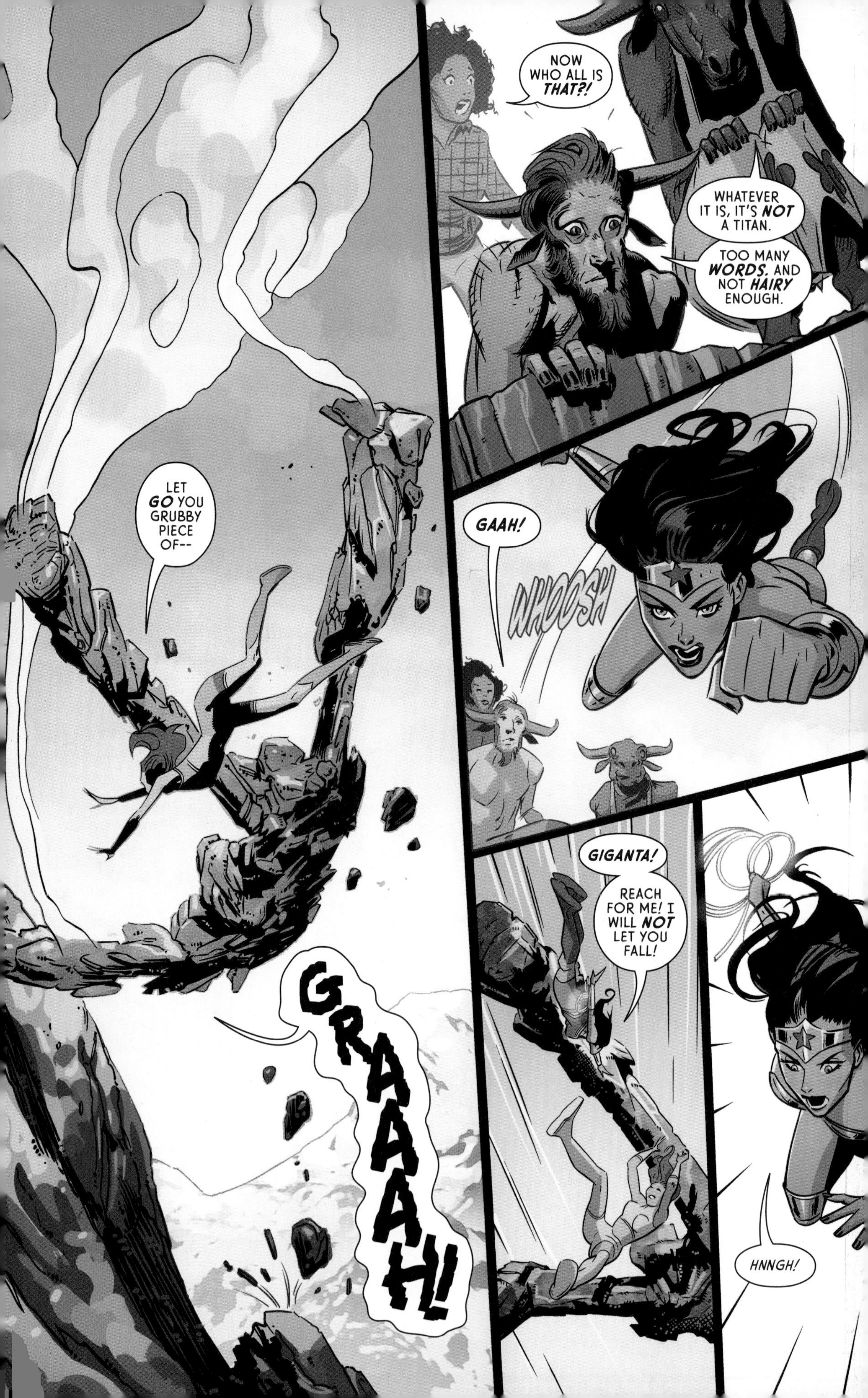

LET GO YOU GRUBBY PIECE OF--
GRAAAAH!
NOW WHO ALL IS THAT?!
WHATEVER IT IS, IT'S NOT A TITAN.
TOO MANY WORDS, AND NOT HAIRY ENOUGH.
GAAH!
WHOOSH
GIGANTA!
REACH FOR ME! I WILL NOT LET YOU FALL!
HNNGH!

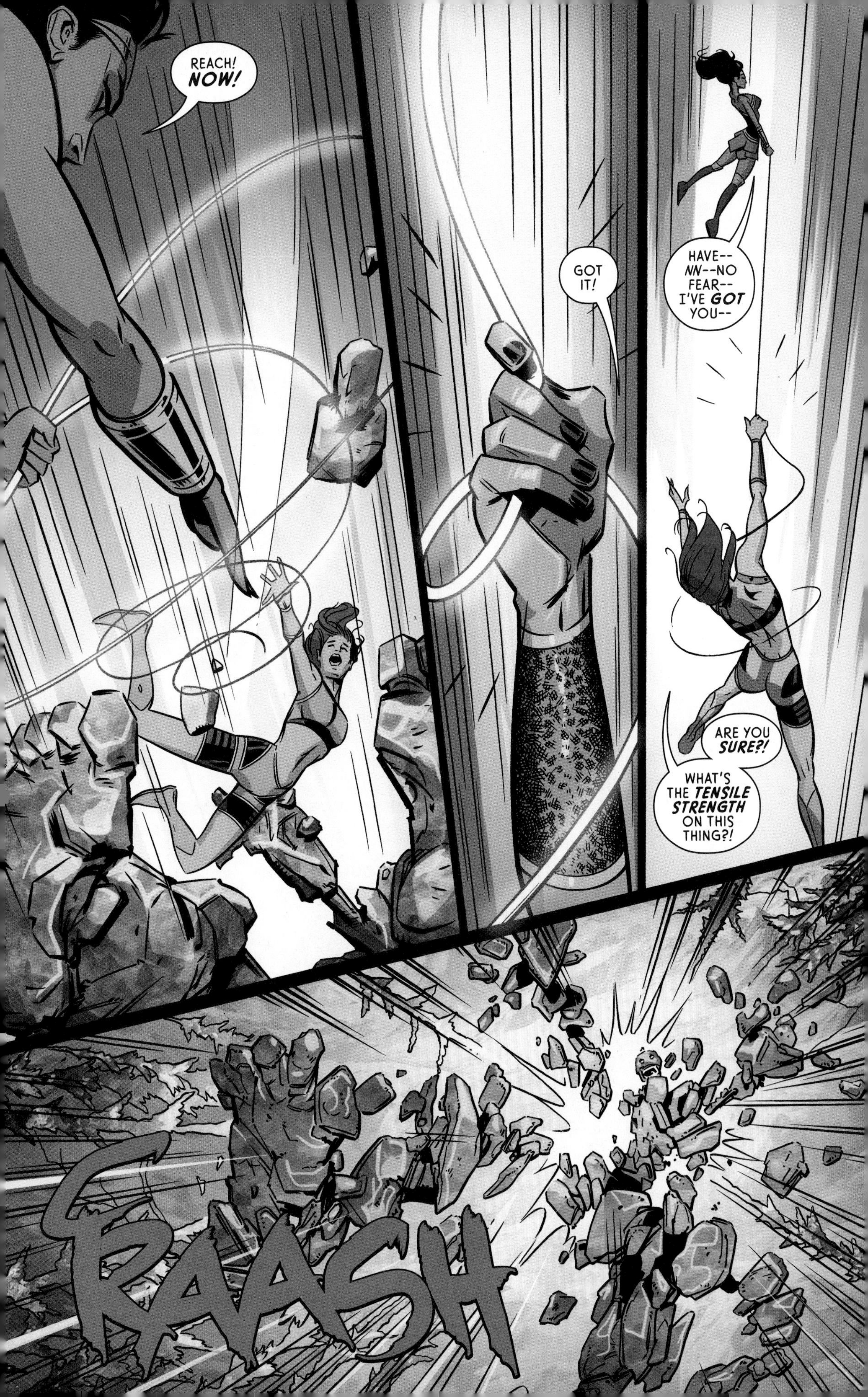
REACH! NOW!
GOT IT!
HAVE-- NN--NO FEAR-- I'VE GOT YOU--
ARE YOU SURE?!
WHAT'S THE TENSILE STRENGTH ON THIS THING?!
CRAASH

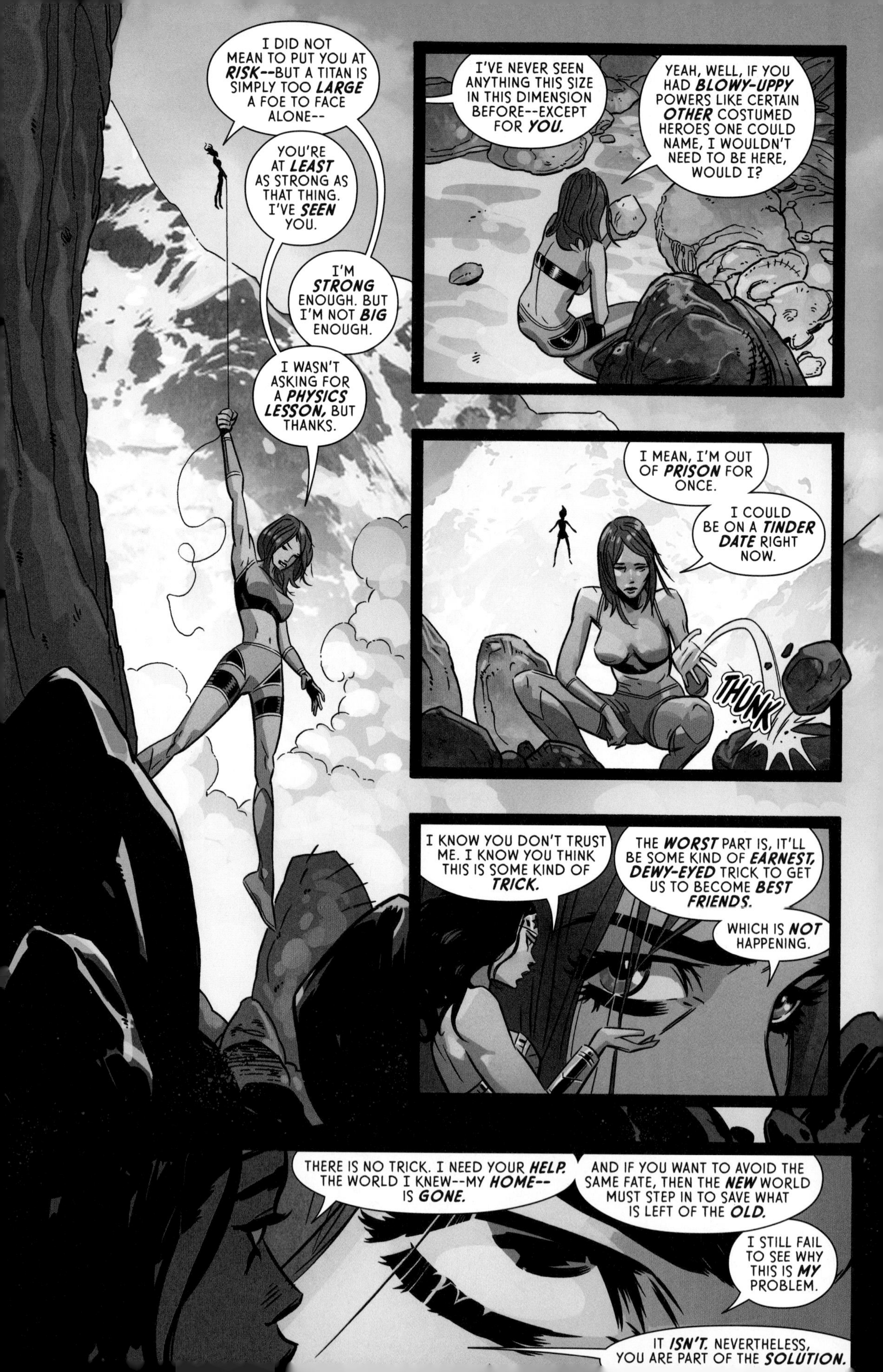
I DID NOT MEAN TO PUT YOU AT RISK--BUT A TITAN IS SIMPLY TOO LARGE A FOE TO FACE ALONE--
YOU'RE AT LEAST AS STRONG AS THAT THING. I'VE SEEN YOU.
I'M STRONG ENOUGH. BUT I'M NOT BIG ENOUGH.
I WASN'T ASKING FOR A PHYSICS LESSON, BUT THANKS.
I'VE NEVER SEEN ANYTHING THIS SIZE IN THIS DIMENSION BEFORE--EXCEPT FOR YOU.
YEAH, WELL, IF YOU HAD BLOWY-UPPY POWERS LIKE CERTAIN OTHER COSTUMED HEROES ONE COULD NAME, I WOULDN'T NEED TO BE HERE, WOULD I?
I MEAN, I'M OUT OF PRISON FOR ONCE.
I COULD BE ON A TINDER DATE RIGHT NOW.
THUNK
I KNOW YOU DON'T TRUST ME. I KNOW YOU THINK THIS IS SOME KIND OF TRICK.
THE WORST PART IS, IT'LL BE SOME KIND OF EARNEST, DEWY-EYED TRICK TO GET US TO BECOME BEST FRIENDS.
WHICH IS NOT HAPPENING.
THERE IS NO TRICK. I NEED YOUR HELP. THE WORLD I KNEW--MY HOME--IS GONE.
AND IF YOU WANT TO AVOID THE SAME FATE, THEN THE NEW WORLD MUST STEP IN TO SAVE WHAT IS LEFT OF THE OLD.
I STILL FAIL TO SEE WHY THIS IS MY PROBLEM.
IT ISN'T. NEVERTHELESS, YOU ARE PART OF THE SOLUTION.

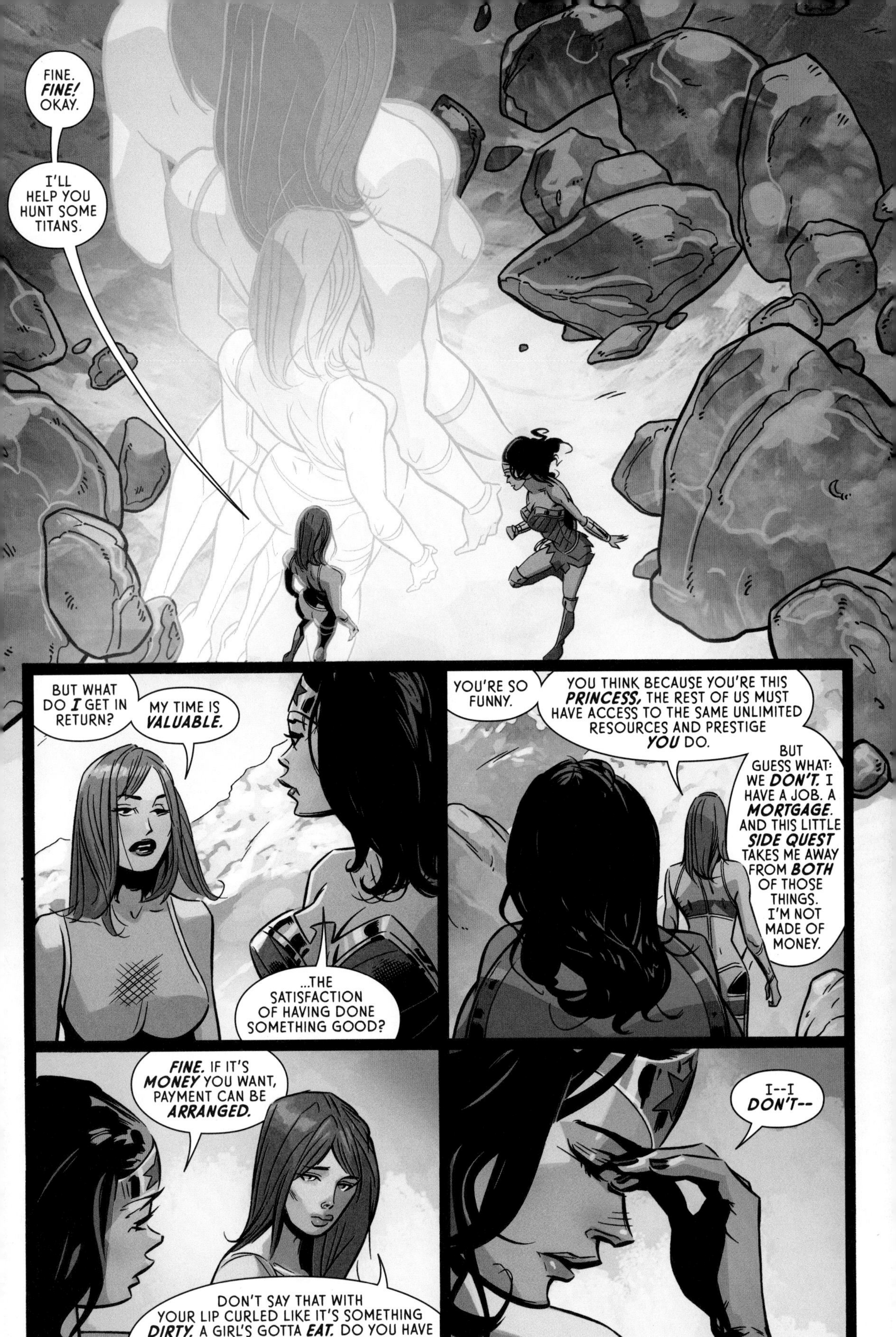

FINE. FINE! OKAY.
I'LL HELP YOU HUNT SOME TITANS.
BUT WHAT DO I GET IN RETURN?
MY TIME IS VALUABLE.
...THE SATISFACTION OF HAVING DONE SOMETHING GOOD?
YOU'RE SO FUNNY.
YOU THINK BECAUSE YOU'RE THIS PRINCESS, THE REST OF US MUST HAVE ACCESS TO THE SAME UNLIMITED RESOURCES AND PRESTIGE YOU DO.
BUT GUESS WHAT: WE DON'T. I HAVE A JOB. A MORTGAGE. AND THIS LITTLE SIDE QUEST TAKES ME AWAY FROM BOTH OF THOSE THINGS. I'M NOT MADE OF MONEY.
FINE. IF IT'S MONEY YOU WANT, PAYMENT CAN BE ARRANGED.
DON'T SAY THAT WITH YOUR LIP CURLED LIKE IT'S SOMETHING DIRTY. A GIRL'S GOTTA EAT. DO YOU HAVE ANY IDEA WHAT MY CALORIC REQUIRE-MENTS ARE WHEN I'M AT MY MAX HEIGHT?
I--I DON'T--

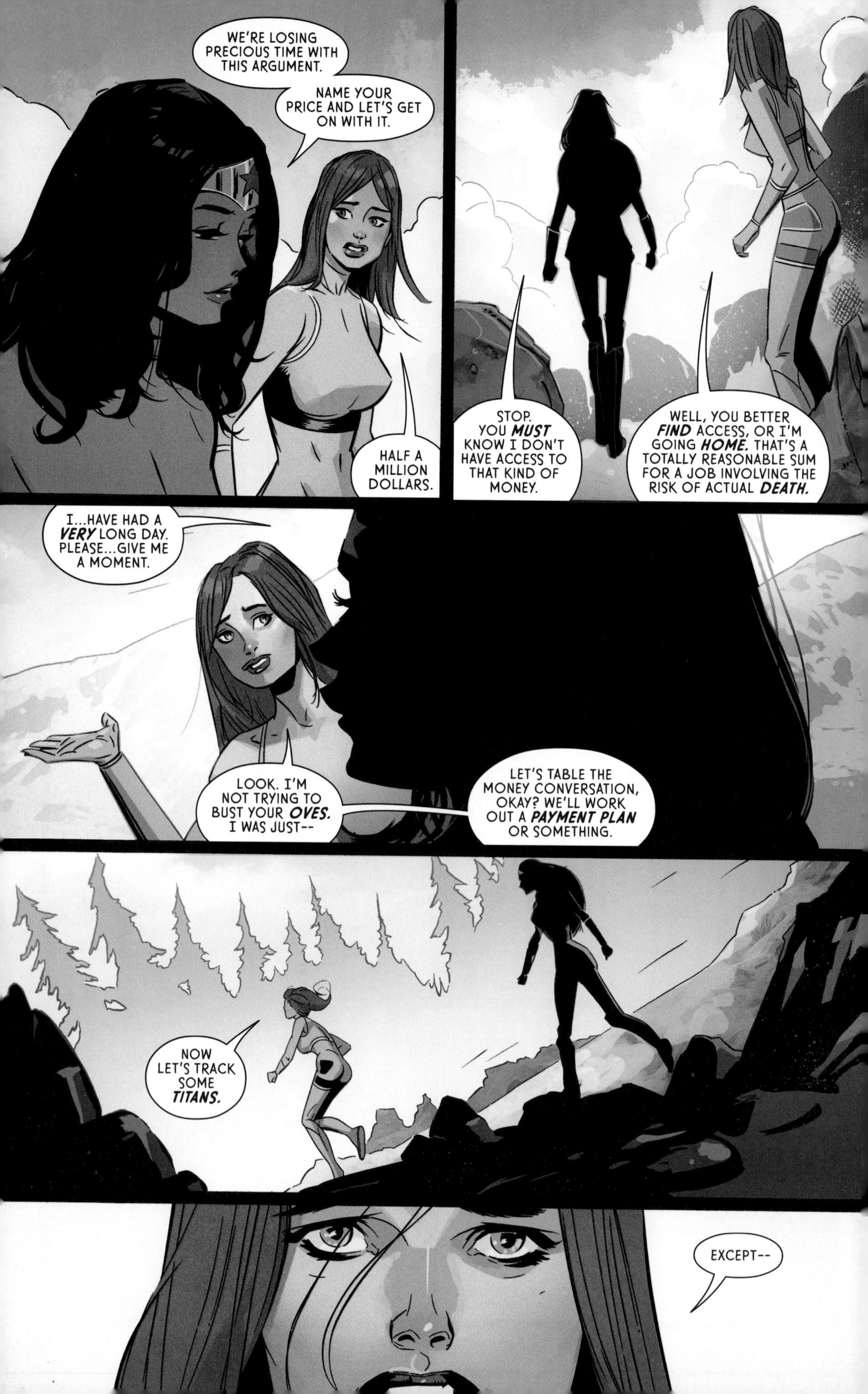
WE'RE LOSING PRECIOUS TIME WITH THIS ARGUMENT.
NAME YOUR PRICE AND LET'S GET ON WITH IT.
HALF A MILLION DOLLARS.
STOP. YOU MUST KNOW I DON'T HAVE ACCESS TO THAT KIND OF MONEY.
WELL, YOU BETTER FIND ACCESS, OR I'M GOING HOME. THAT'S A TOTALLY REASONABLE SUM FOR A JOB INVOLVING THE RISK OF ACTUAL DEATH.
I...HAVE HAD A VERY LONG DAY. PLEASE...GIVE ME A MOMENT.
LOOK. I'M NOT TRYING TO BUST YOUR OVES. I WAS JUST--
LET'S TABLE THE MONEY CONVERSATION, OKAY? WE'LL WORK OUT A PAYMENT PLAN OR SOMETHING.
NOW LET'S TRACK SOME TITANS.
EXCEPT--

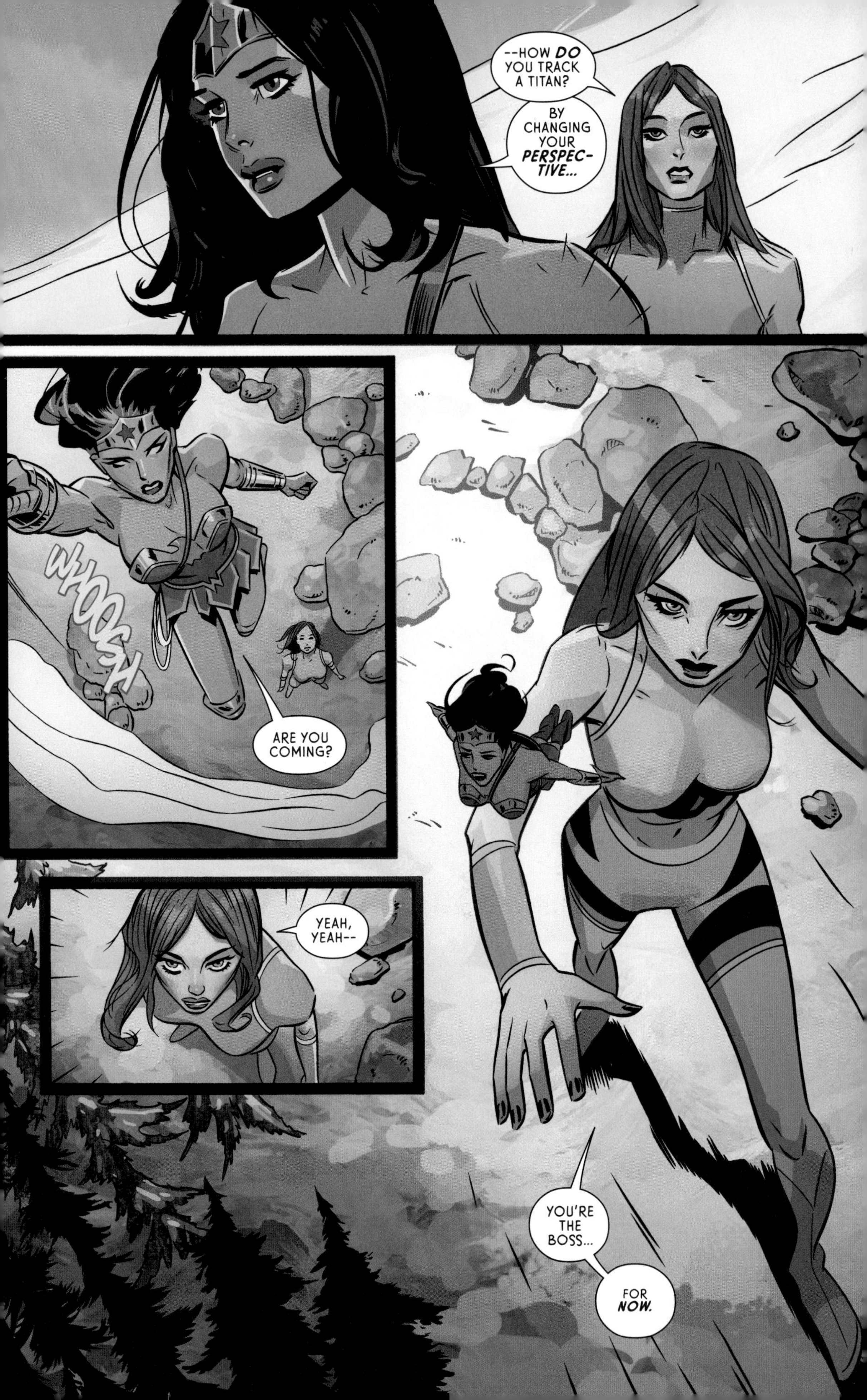
--HOW DO YOU TRACK A TITAN?
BY CHANGING YOUR PERSPEC-TIVE...
WHOOSH
ARE YOU COMING?
YEAH, YEAH--
YOU'RE THE BOSS...
FOR NOW.

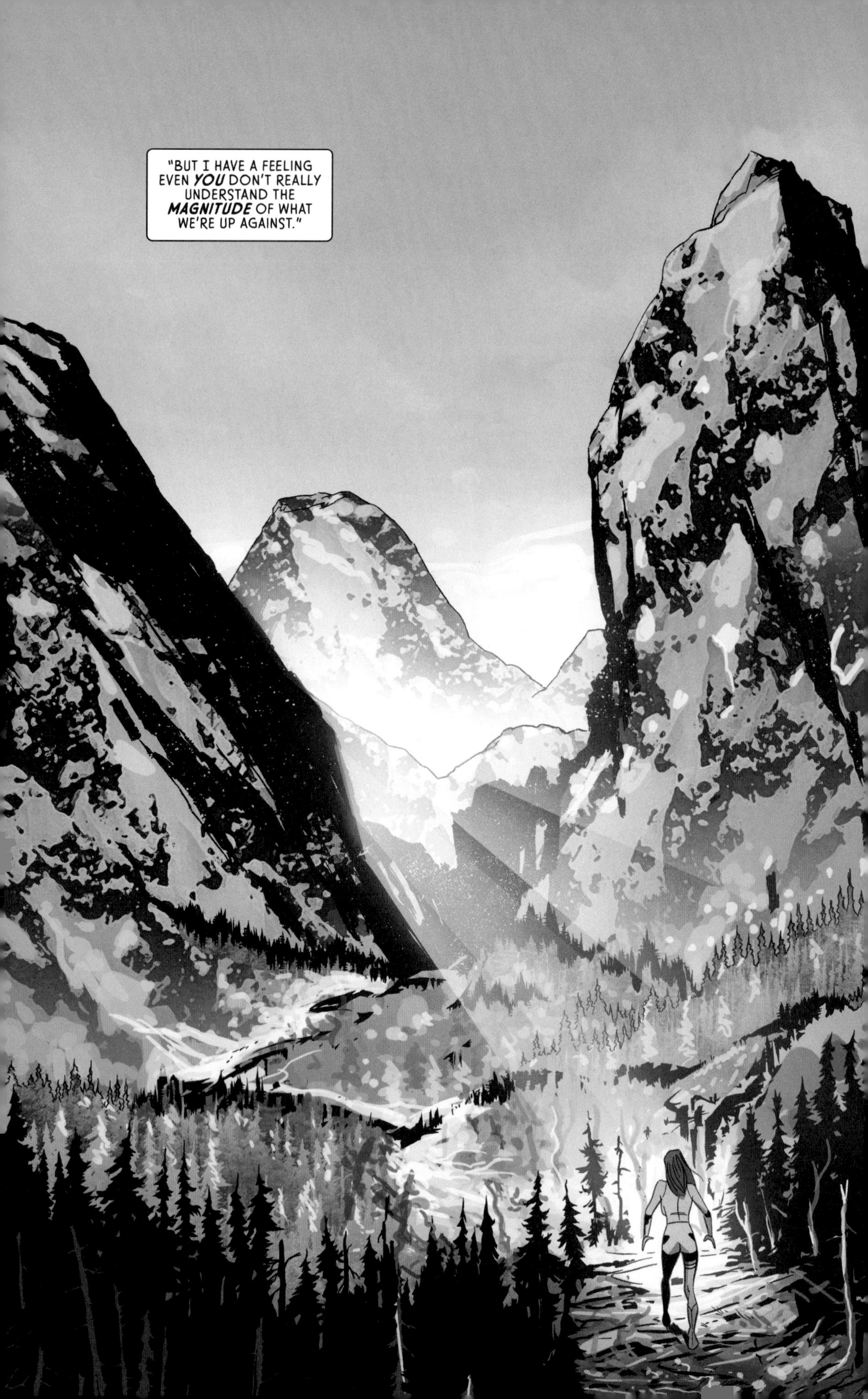
"BUT I HAVE A FEELING EVEN ***YOU*** DON'T REALLY UNDERSTAND THE ***MAGNITUDE*** OF WHAT WE'RE UP AGAINST."

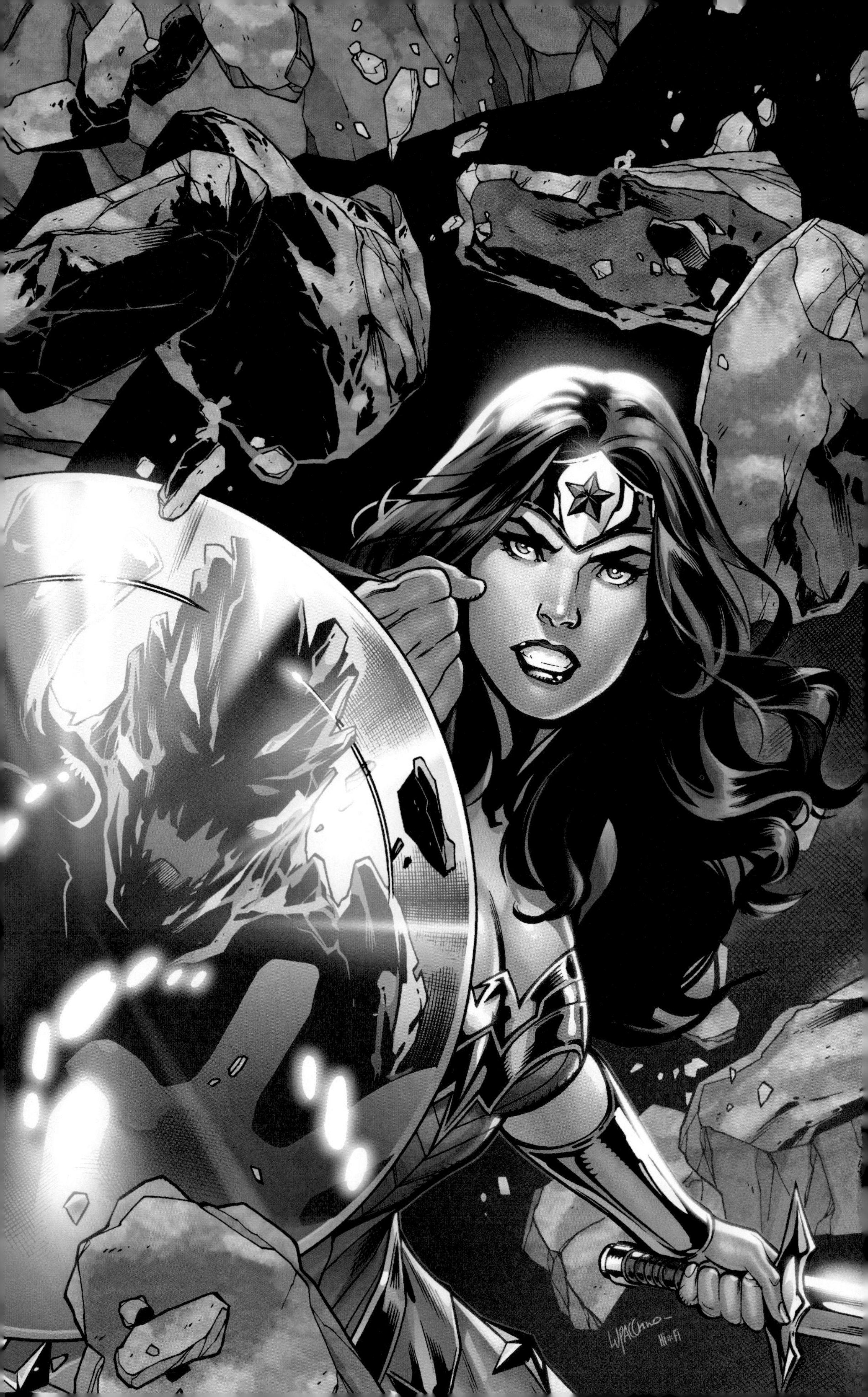

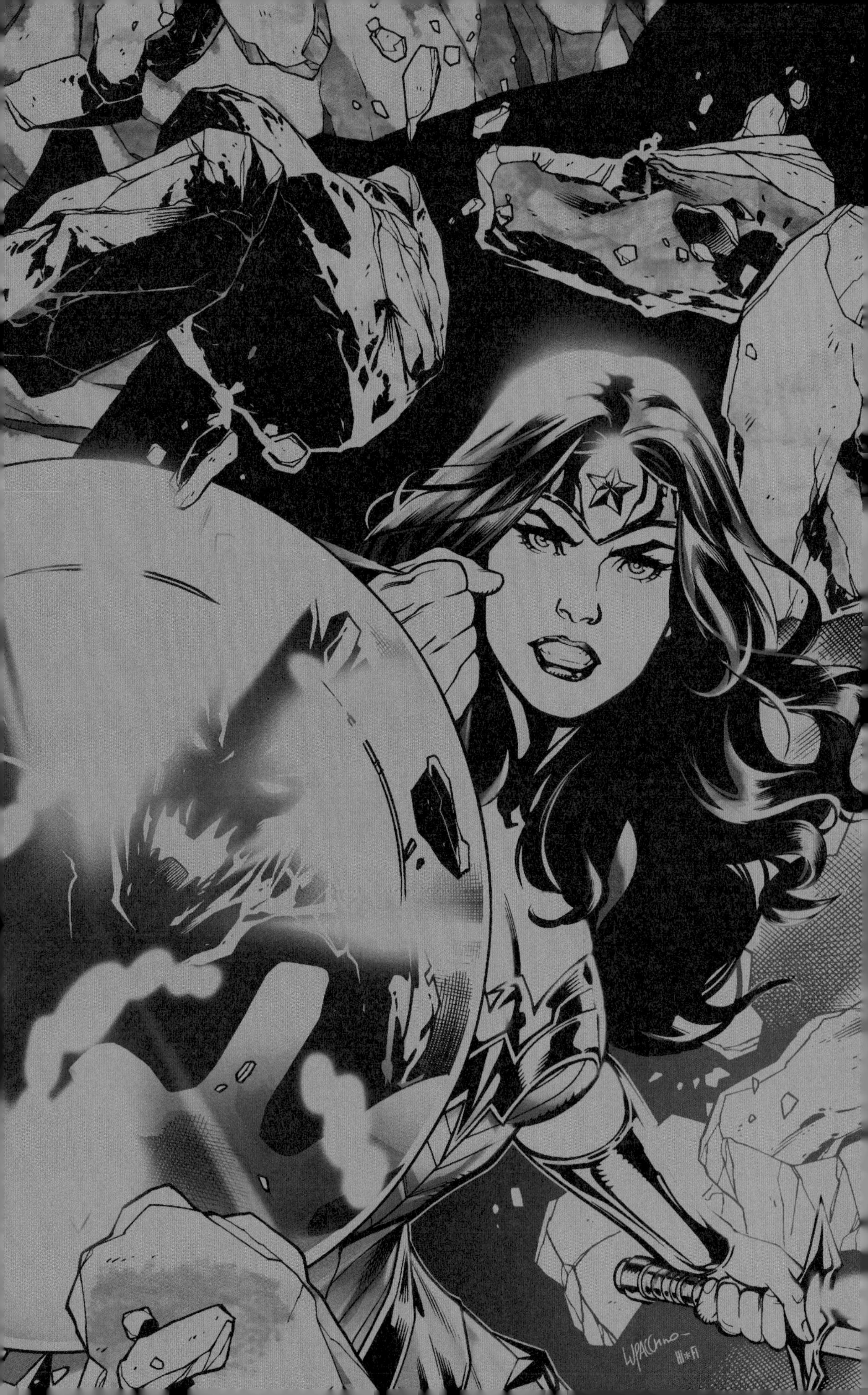

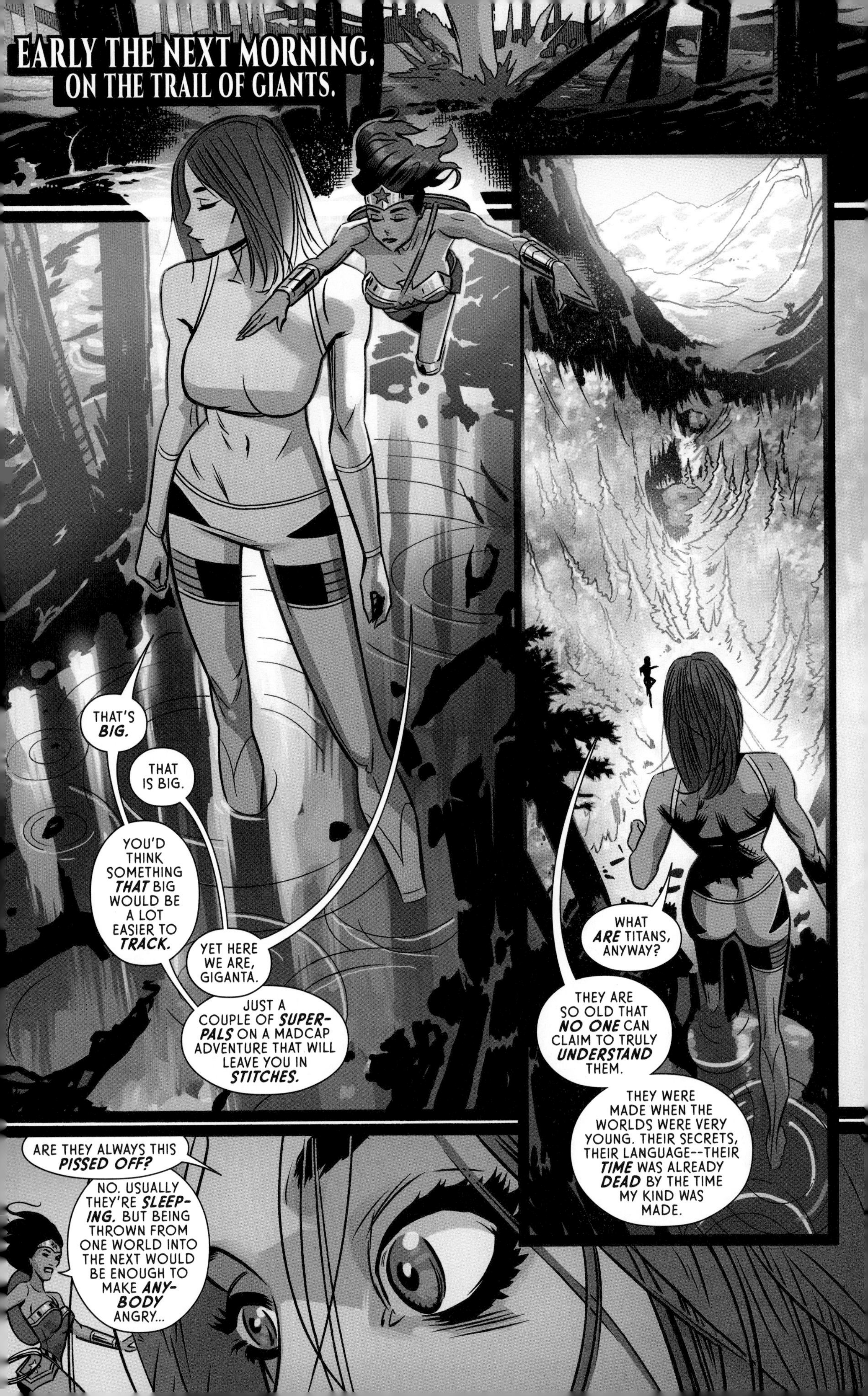
EARLY THE NEXT MORNING.
ON THE TRAIL OF GIANTS.
THAT'S BIG.
THAT IS BIG.
YOU'D THINK SOMETHING THAT BIG WOULD BE A LOT EASIER TO TRACK.
YET HERE WE ARE, GIGANTA.
JUST A COUPLE OF SUPER-PALS ON A MADCAP ADVENTURE THAT WILL LEAVE YOU IN STITCHES.
WHAT ARE TITANS, ANYWAY?
THEY ARE SO OLD THAT NO ONE CAN CLAIM TO TRULY UNDERSTAND THEM.
THEY WERE MADE WHEN THE WORLDS WERE VERY YOUNG. THEIR SECRETS, THEIR LANGUAGE--THEIR TIME WAS ALREADY DEAD BY THE TIME MY KIND WAS MADE.
ARE THEY ALWAYS THIS PISSED OFF?
NO. USUALLY THEY'RE SLEEP-ING. BUT BEING THROWN FROM ONE WORLD INTO THE NEXT WOULD BE ENOUGH TO MAKE ANY-BODY ANGRY...

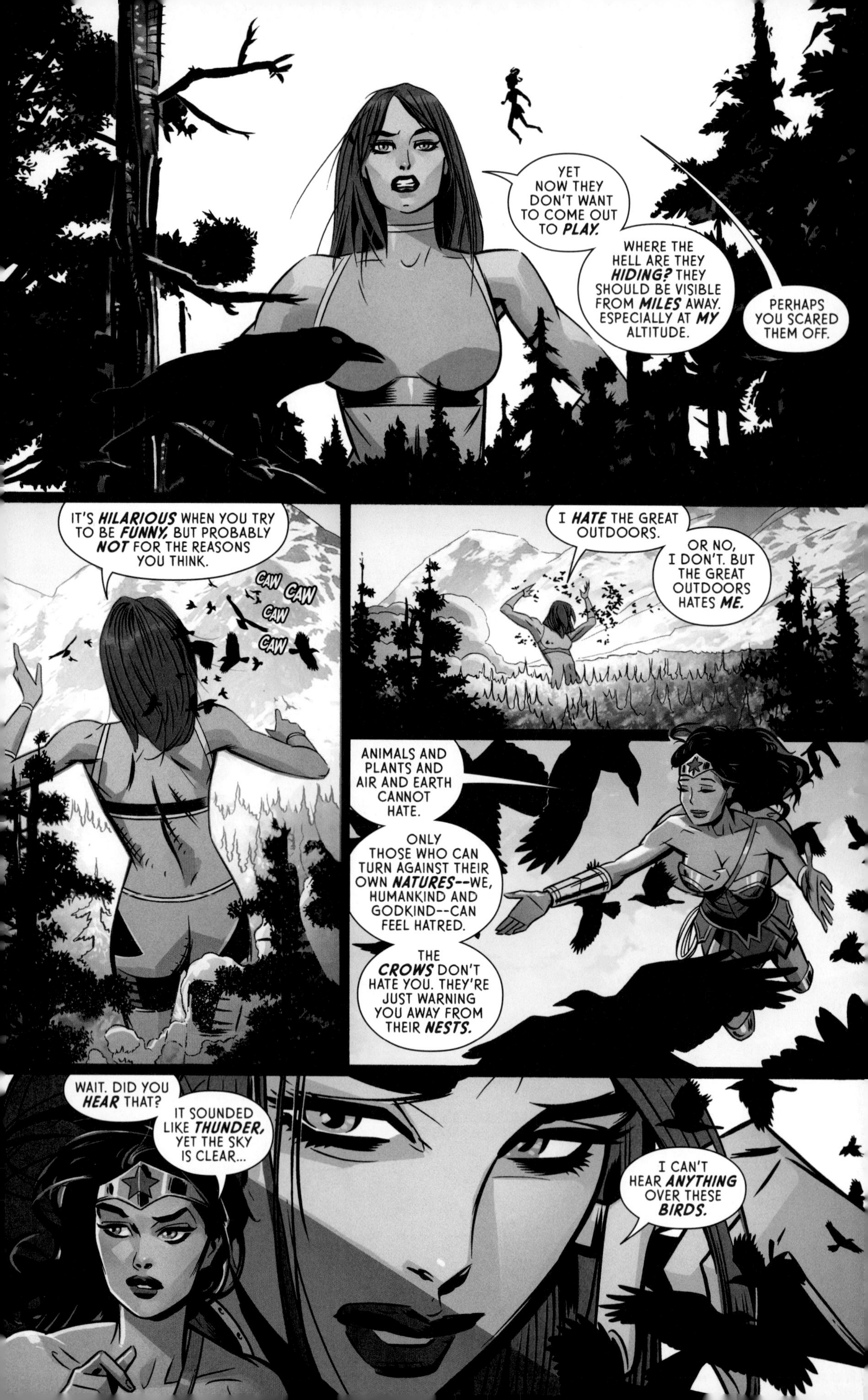
YET NOW THEY DON'T WANT TO COME OUT TO PLAY.
WHERE THE HELL ARE THEY HIDING? THEY SHOULD BE VISIBLE FROM MILES AWAY. ESPECIALLY AT MY ALTITUDE.
PERHAPS YOU SCARED THEM OFF.
IT'S HILARIOUS WHEN YOU TRY TO BE FUNNY, BUT PROBABLY NOT FOR THE REASONS YOU THINK.
CAW CAW
CAW
CAW
I HATE THE GREAT OUTDOORS.
OR NO, I DON'T. BUT THE GREAT OUTDOORS HATES ME.
ANIMALS AND PLANTS AND AIR AND EARTH CANNOT HATE.
ONLY THOSE WHO CAN TURN AGAINST THEIR OWN NATURES--WE, HUMANKIND AND GODKIND--CAN FEEL HATRED.
THE CROWS DON'T HATE YOU. THEY'RE JUST WARNING YOU AWAY FROM THEIR NESTS.
WAIT. DID YOU HEAR THAT?
IT SOUNDED LIKE THUNDER, YET THE SKY IS CLEAR...
I CAN'T HEAR ANYTHING OVER THESE BIRDS.

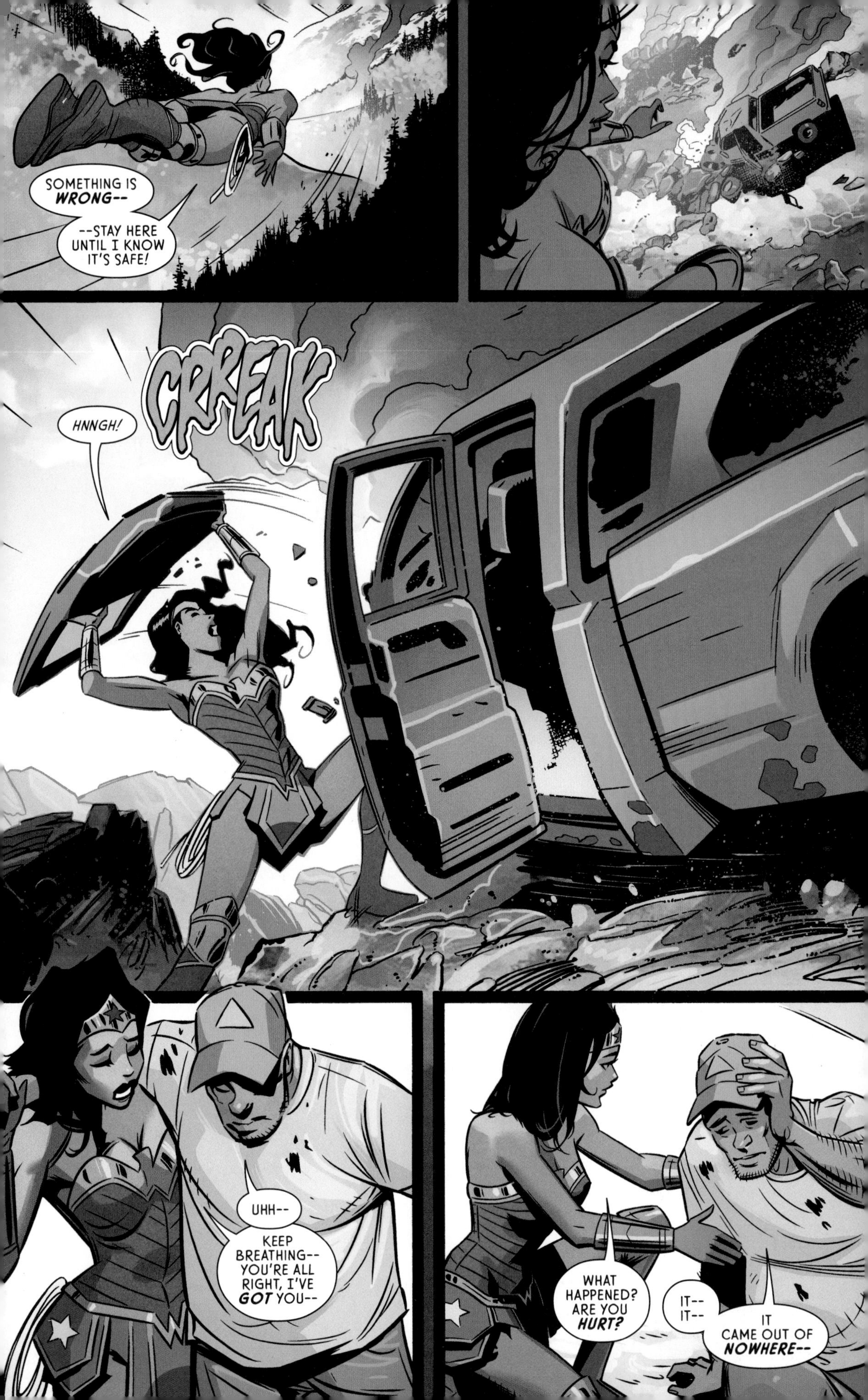
SOMETHING IS **WRONG--**
--STAY HERE UNTIL I KNOW IT'S SAFE!
HNNGH!
CRREAK
UHH--
KEEP BREATHING-- YOU'RE ALL RIGHT, I'VE **GOT** YOU--
WHAT HAPPENED? ARE YOU **HURT?**
IT-- IT--
IT CAME OUT OF **NOWHERE--**

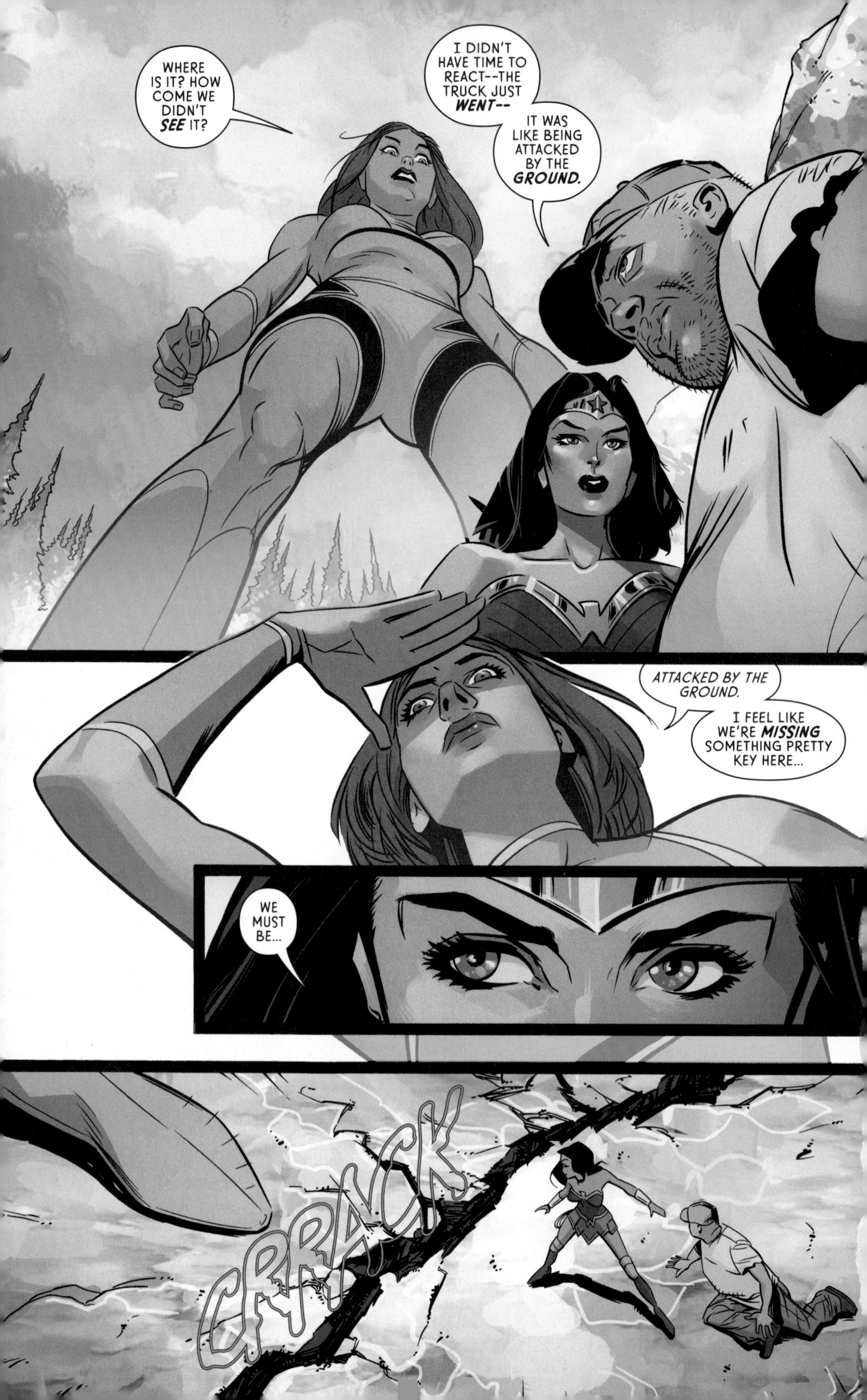
WHERE IS IT? HOW COME WE DIDN'T SEE IT?
I DIDN'T HAVE TIME TO REACT--THE TRUCK JUST WENT--
IT WAS LIKE BEING ATTACKED BY THE GROUND.
ATTACKED BY THE GROUND.
I FEEL LIKE WE'RE MISSING SOMETHING PRETTY KEY HERE...
WE MUST BE...
CRRACK

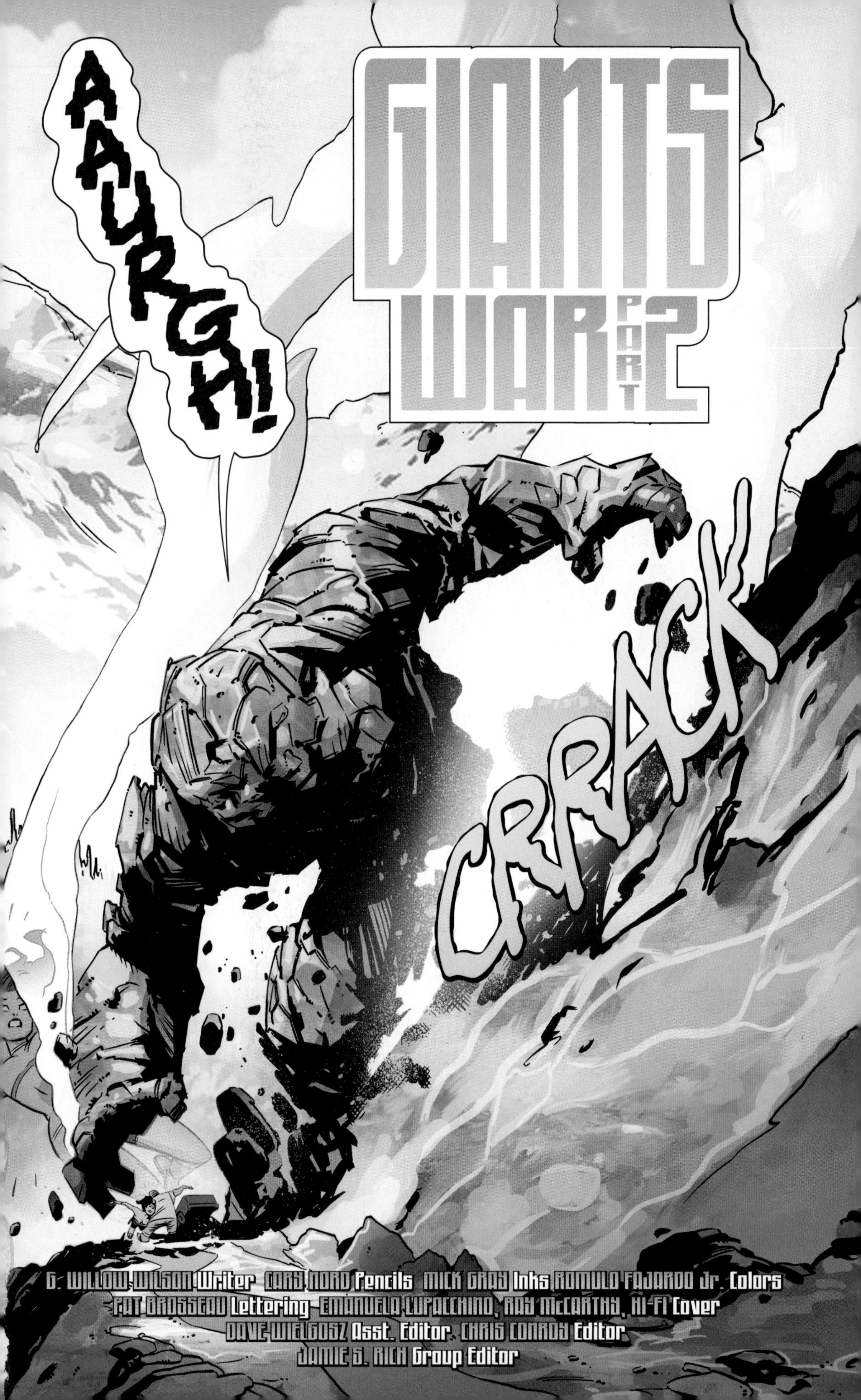
AAURGH!
GIANTS WAR PART 2
CRRACK
G. WILLOW WILSON Writer CARY NORD Pencils MICK GRAY Inks ROMULO FAJARDO Jr. Colors
PAT BROSSEAU Lettering EMANUELA LUPACCHINO, RAY McCARTHY, HI-FI Cover
DAVE WIELGOSZ Asst. Editor CHRIS CONROY Editor
JAMIE S. RICH Group Editor

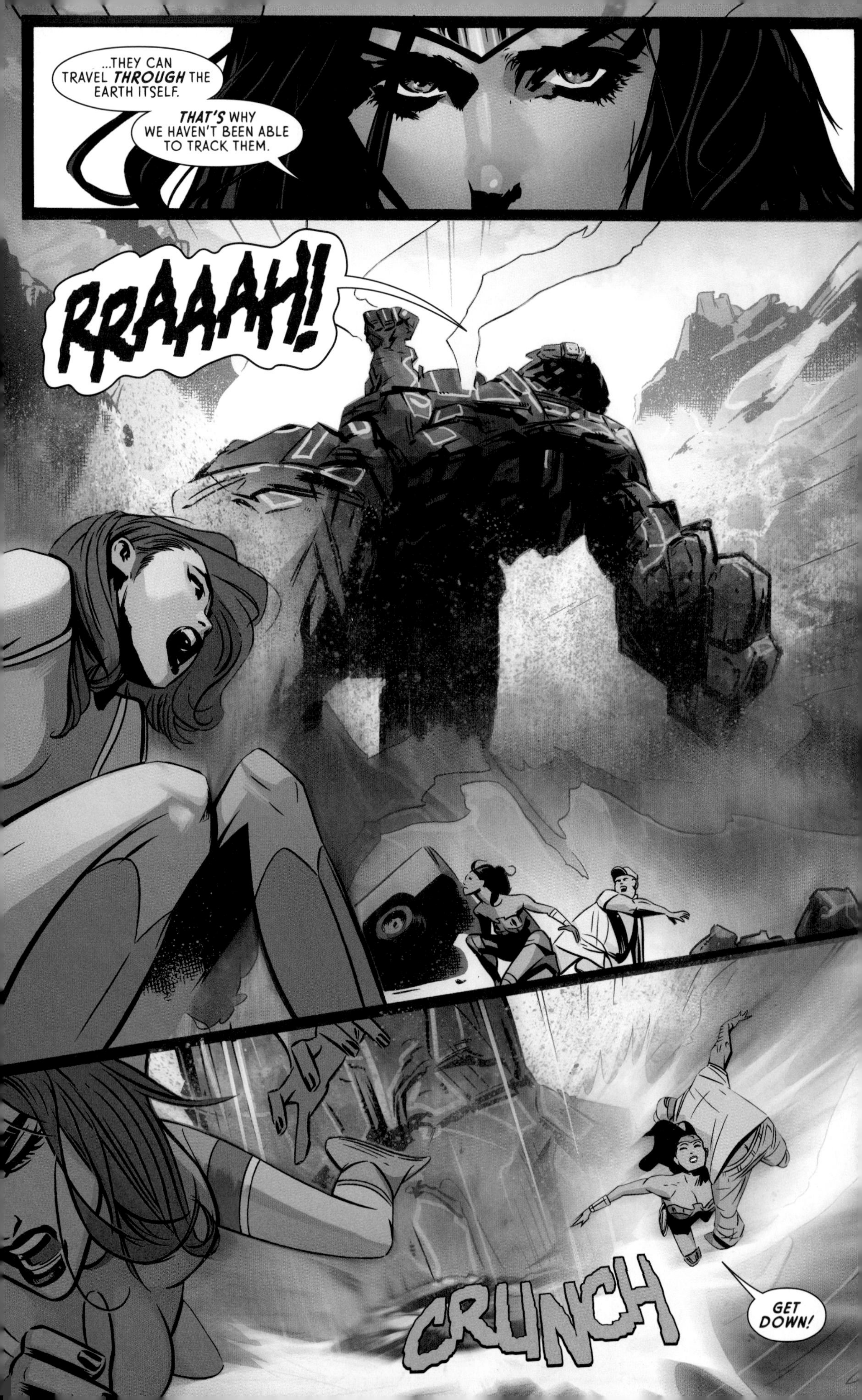
...THEY CAN TRAVEL *THROUGH* THE EARTH ITSELF.
THAT'S WHY WE HAVEN'T BEEN ABLE TO TRACK THEM.
RRAAAH!
CRUNCH
GET DOWN!

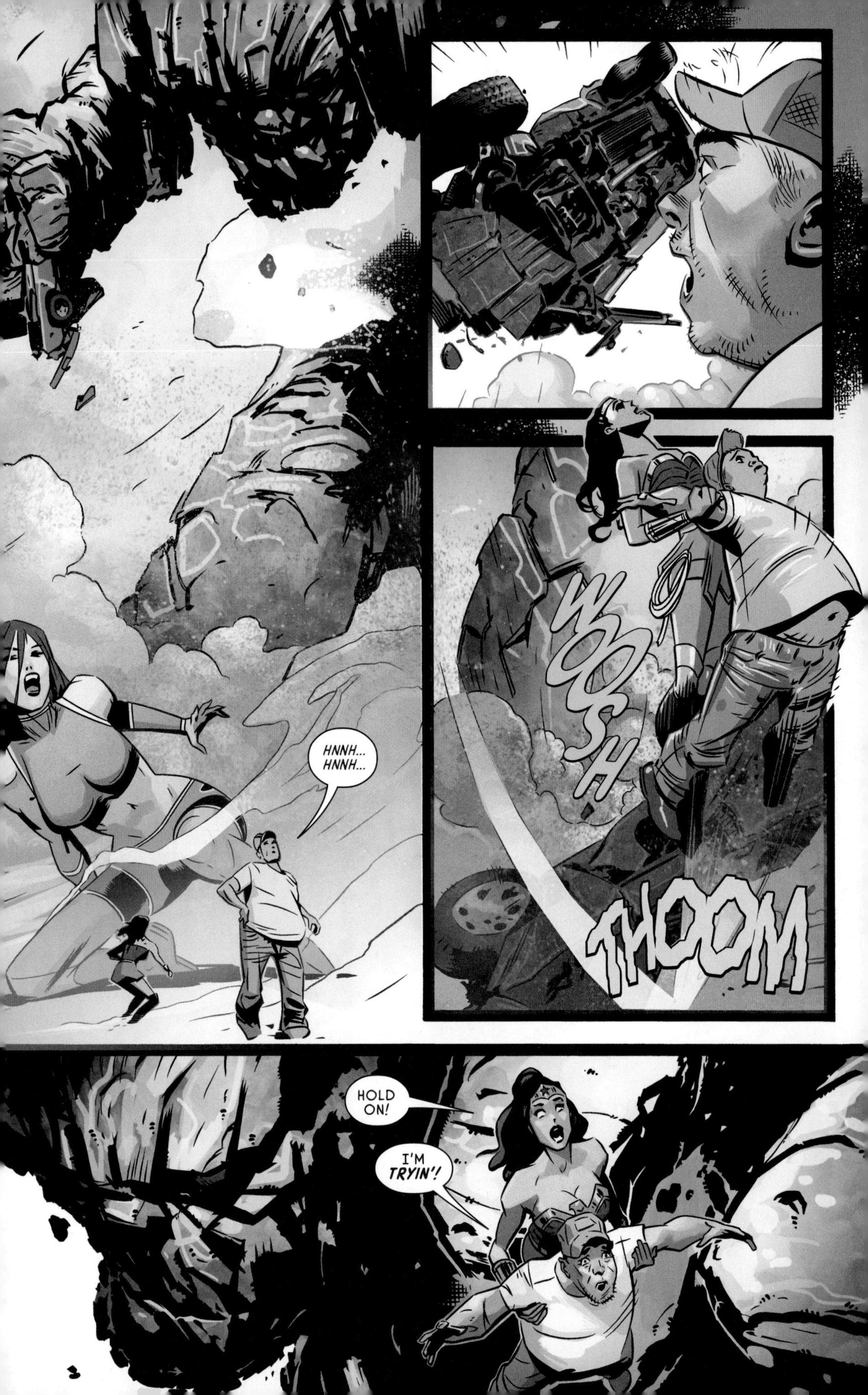
HNNH... HNNH...
WOOSH
THOOM
HOLD ON!
I'M TRYIN'!

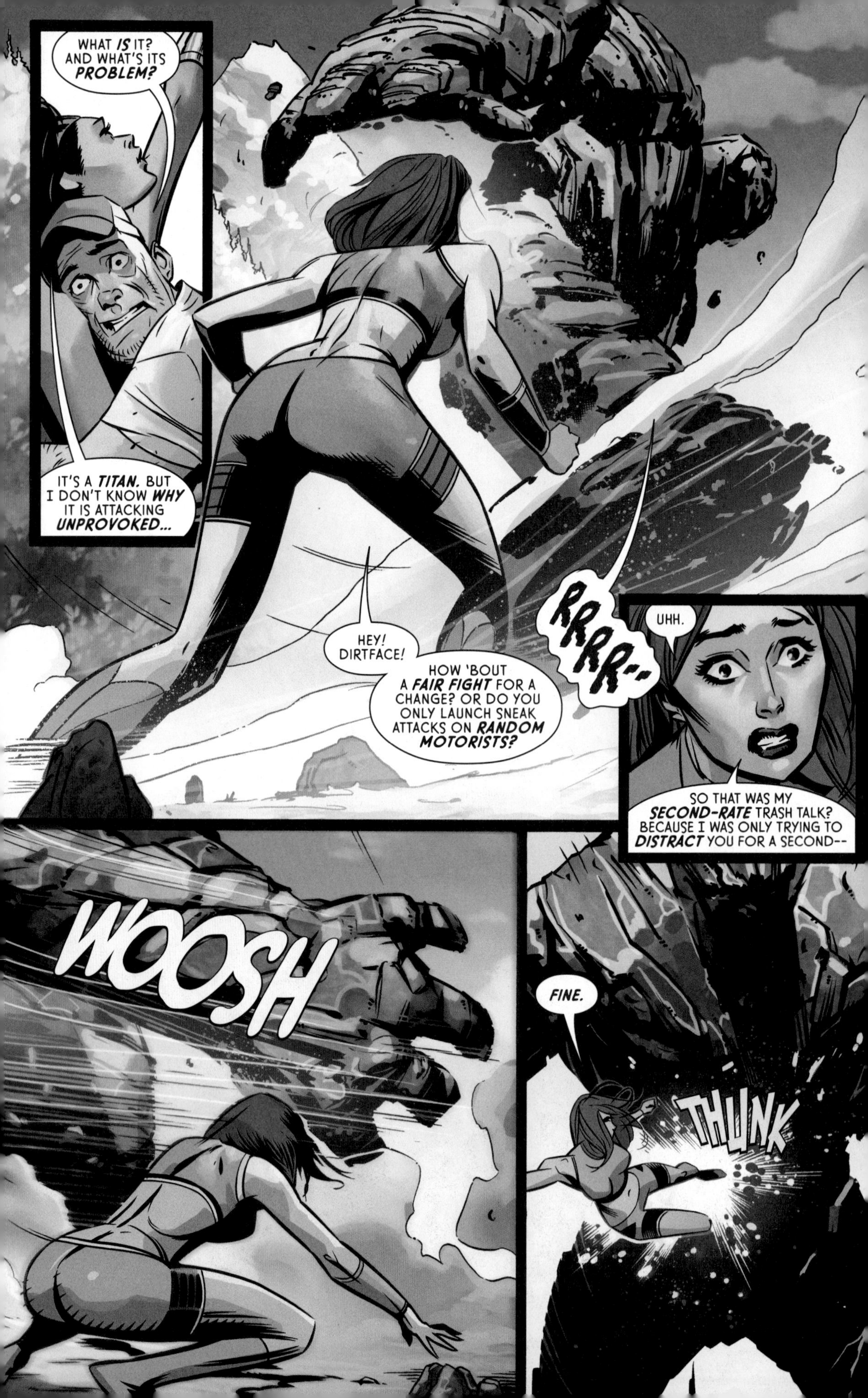
WHAT *IS* IT? AND WHAT'S ITS *PROBLEM?*
IT'S A *TITAN.* BUT I DON'T KNOW *WHY* IT IS ATTACKING *UNPROVOKED...*
HEY! DIRTFACE!
HOW 'BOUT A *FAIR FIGHT* FOR A CHANGE? OR DO YOU ONLY LAUNCH SNEAK ATTACKS ON *RANDOM MOTORISTS?*
RRRRR--
UHH.
SO THAT WAS MY *SECOND-RATE* TRASH TALK? BECAUSE I WAS ONLY TRYING TO *DISTRACT* YOU FOR A SECOND--
WOOSH
FINE.
THUNK

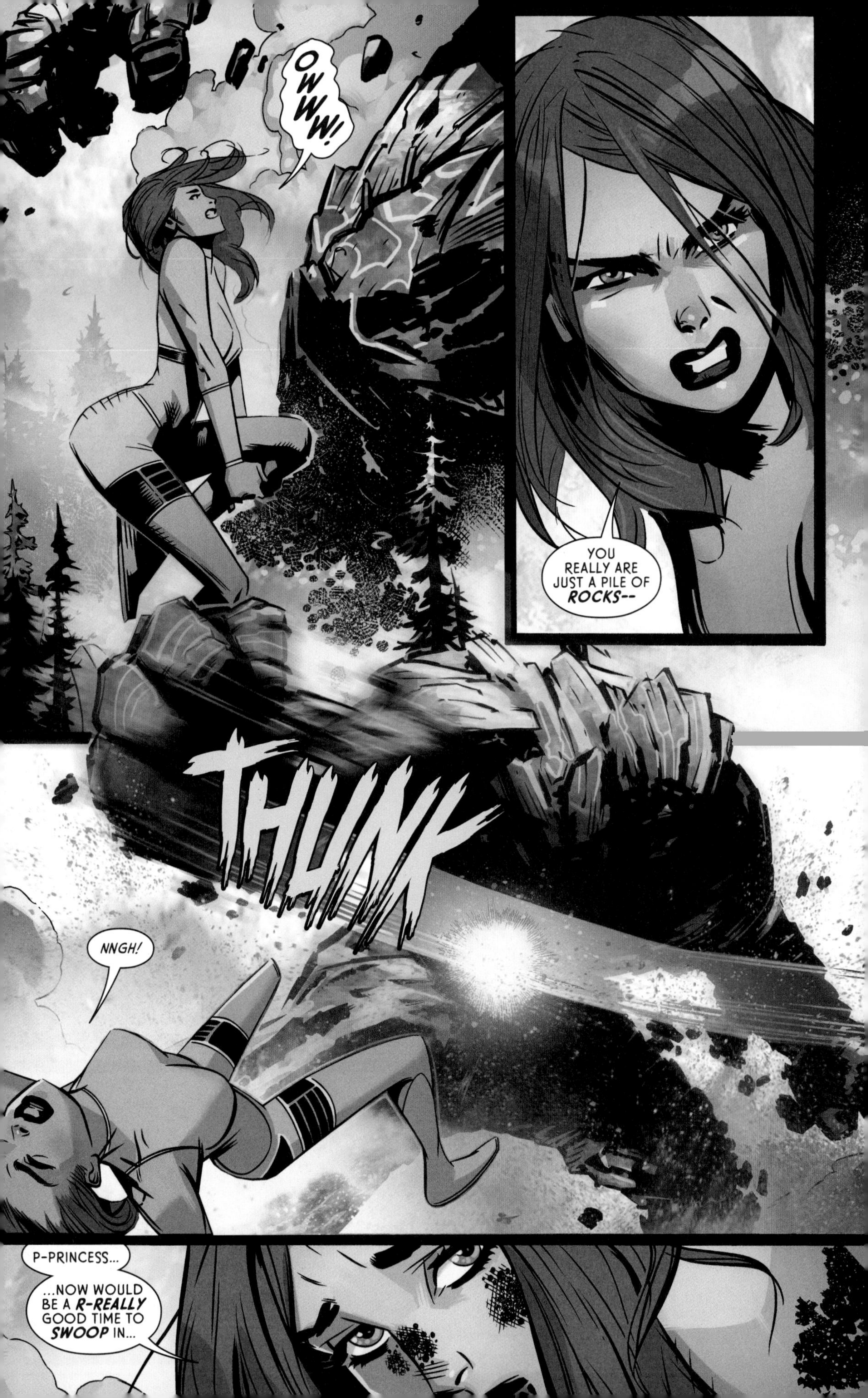
OWWW!
YOU REALLY ARE JUST A PILE OF ROCKS--
THUNK
NNGH!
P-PRINCESS...
...NOW WOULD BE A R-REALLY GOOD TIME TO SWOOP IN...

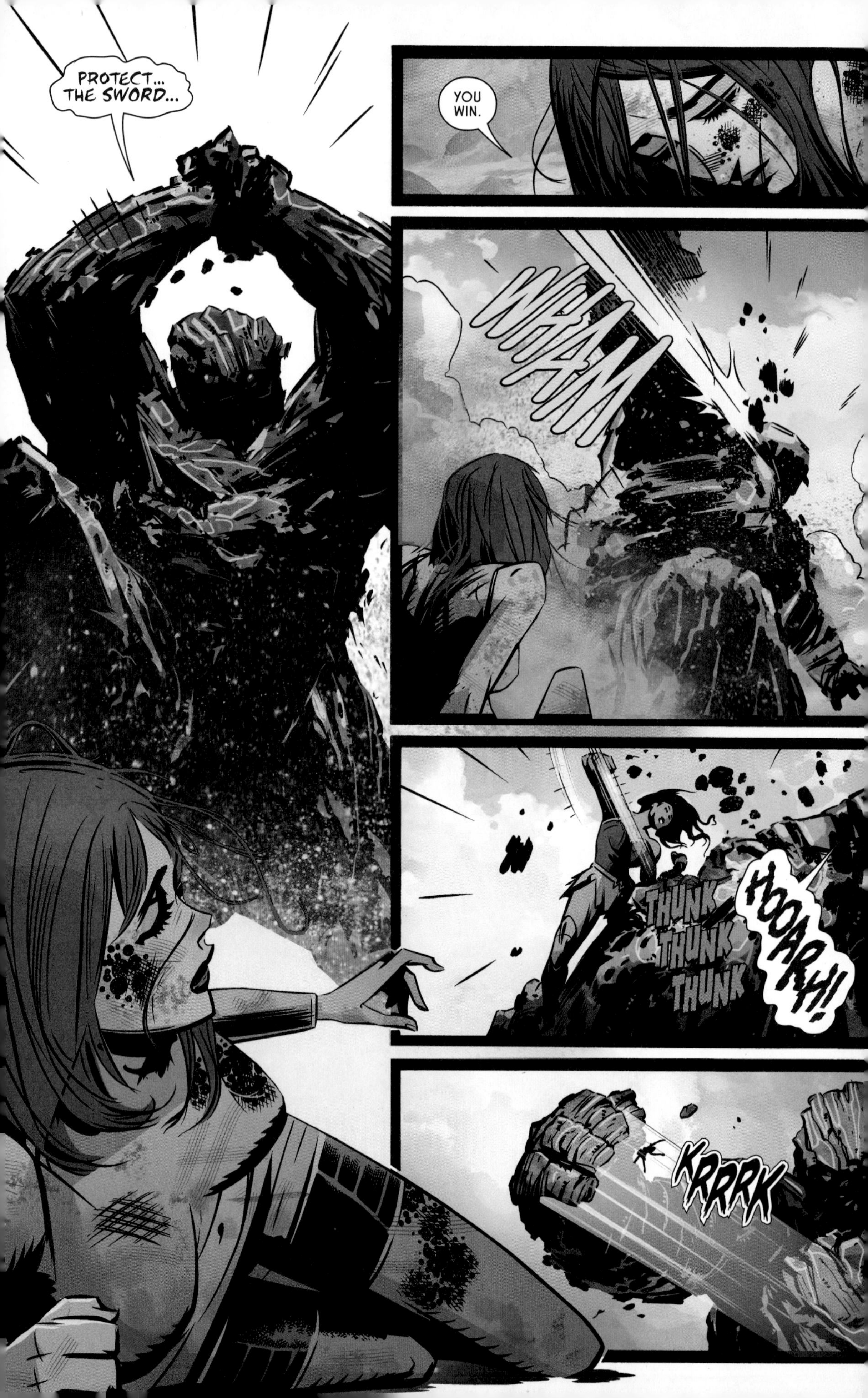
PROTECT... THE SWORD...
YOU WIN.
WHAM
THUNK THUNK THUNK
HOOARH!
KRRRK

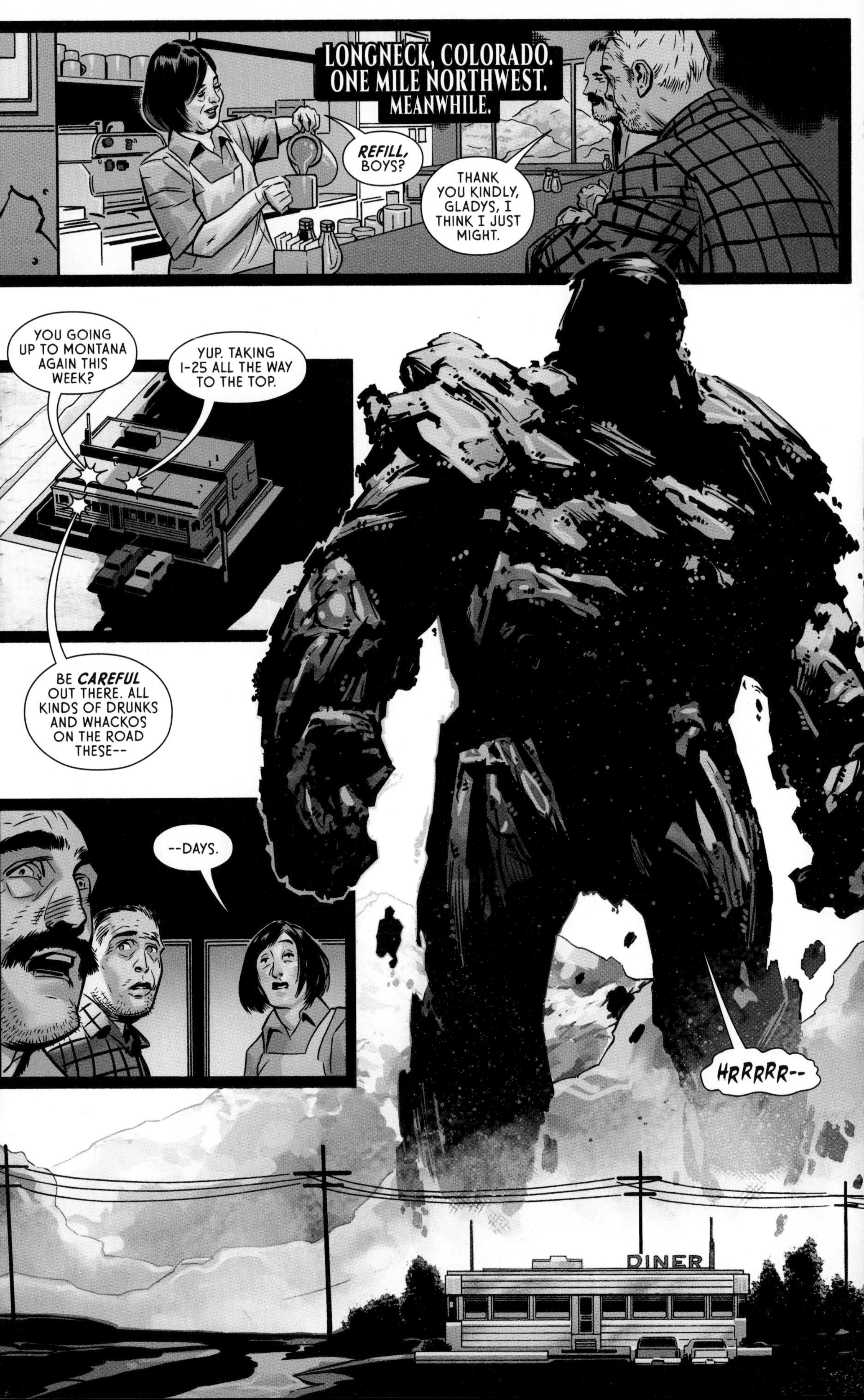
LONGNECK, COLORADO. ONE MILE NORTHWEST. MEANWHILE.
REFILL, BOYS?
THANK YOU KINDLY, GLADYS, I THINK I JUST MIGHT.
YOU GOING UP TO MONTANA AGAIN THIS WEEK?
YUP. TAKING I-25 ALL THE WAY TO THE TOP.
BE CAREFUL OUT THERE. ALL KINDS OF DRUNKS AND WHACKOS ON THE ROAD THESE--
--DAYS.
HRRRRR--
DINER

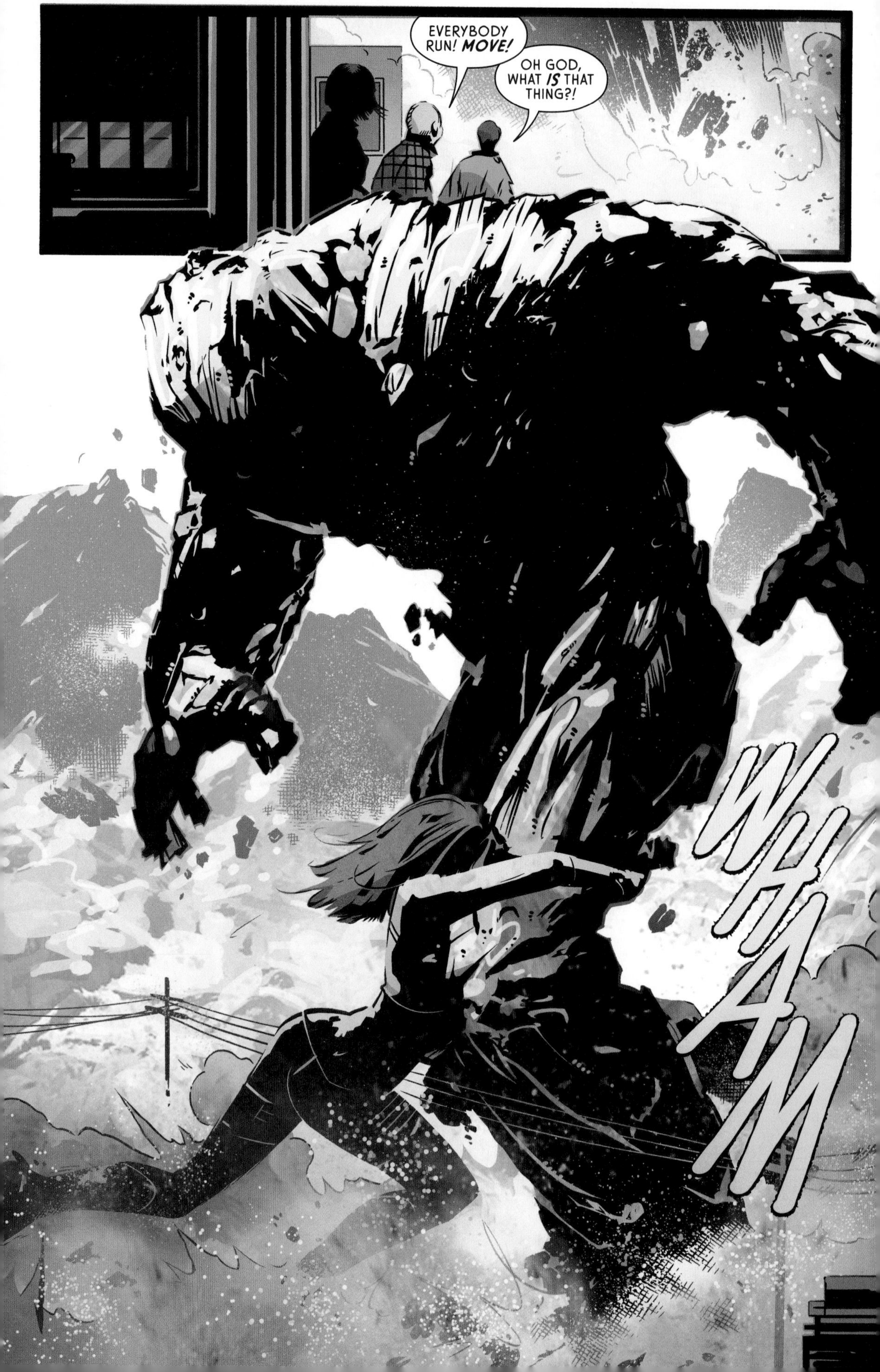
EVERYBODY RUN! MOVE!
OH GOD, WHAT IS THAT THING?!
WHAM

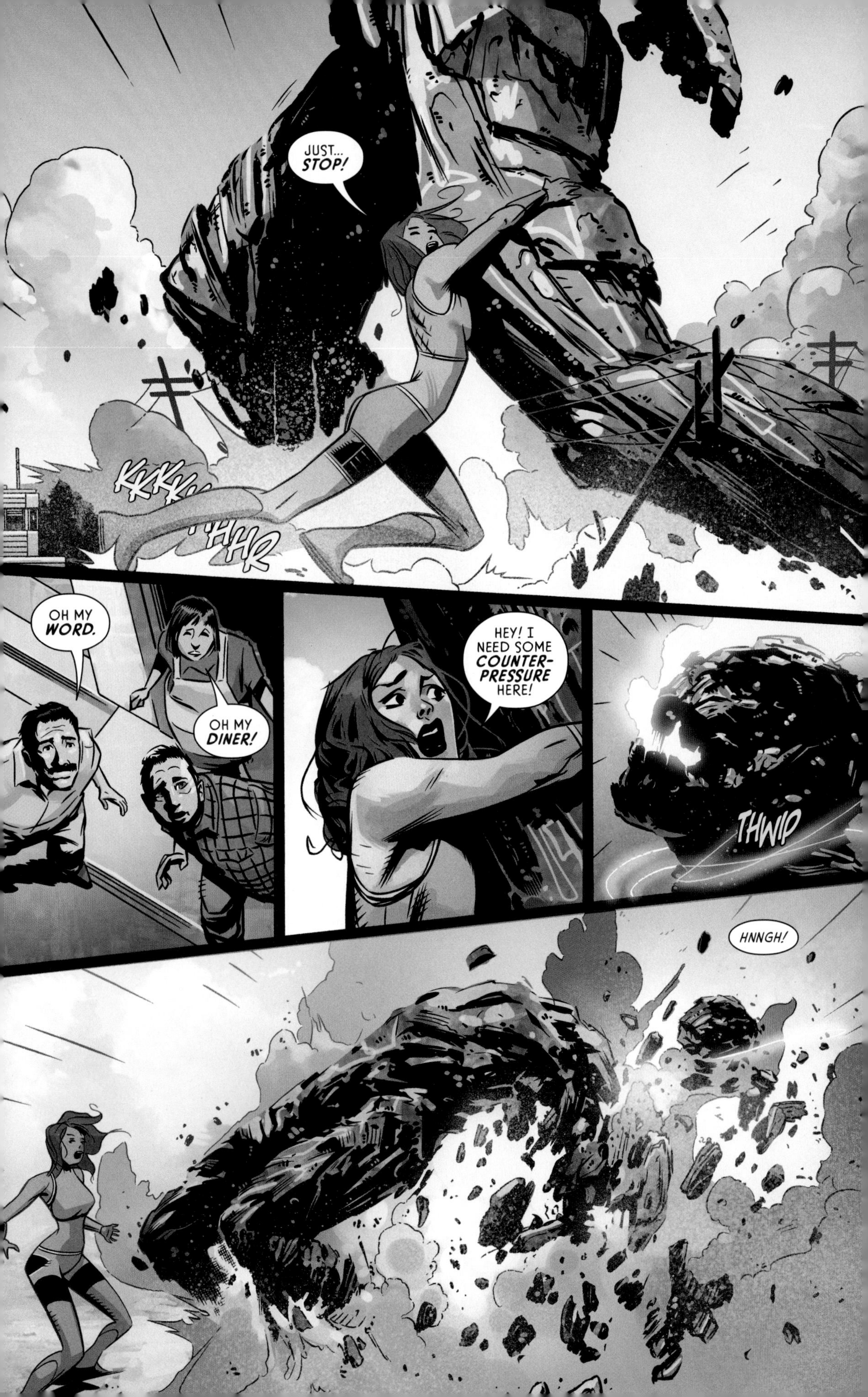
JUST... STOP!
KKKKKHHHR
OH MY WORD.
OH MY DINER!
HEY! I NEED SOME COUNTER-PRESSURE HERE!
THWIP
HNNGH!

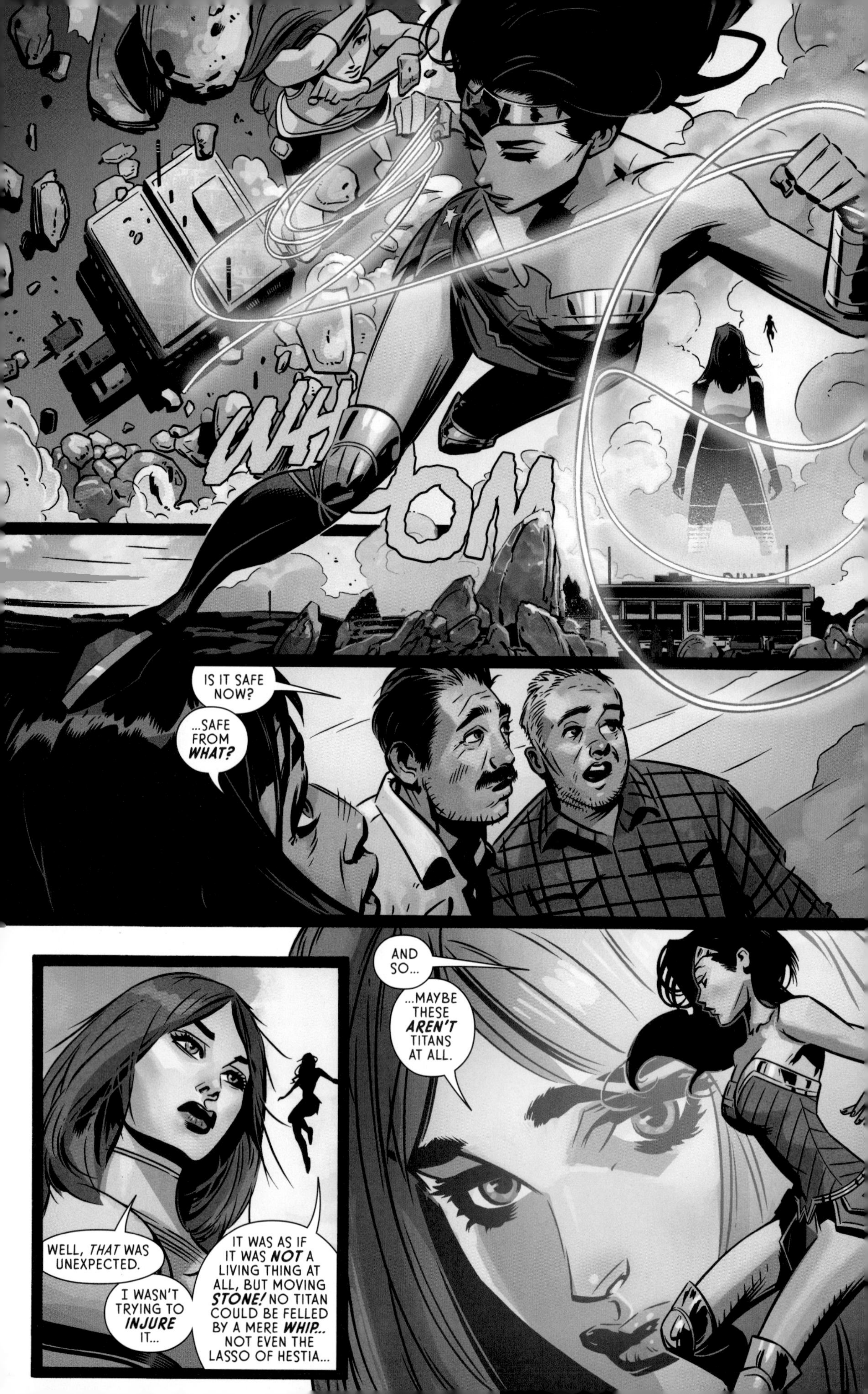
WHHOOM
IS IT SAFE NOW?
...SAFE FROM WHAT?
AND SO...
...MAYBE THESE AREN'T TITANS AT ALL.
WELL, THAT WAS UNEXPECTED.
I WASN'T TRYING TO INJURE IT...
IT WAS AS IF IT WAS NOT A LIVING THING AT ALL, BUT MOVING STONE! NO TITAN COULD BE FELLED BY A MERE WHIP... NOT EVEN THE LASSO OF HESTIA...

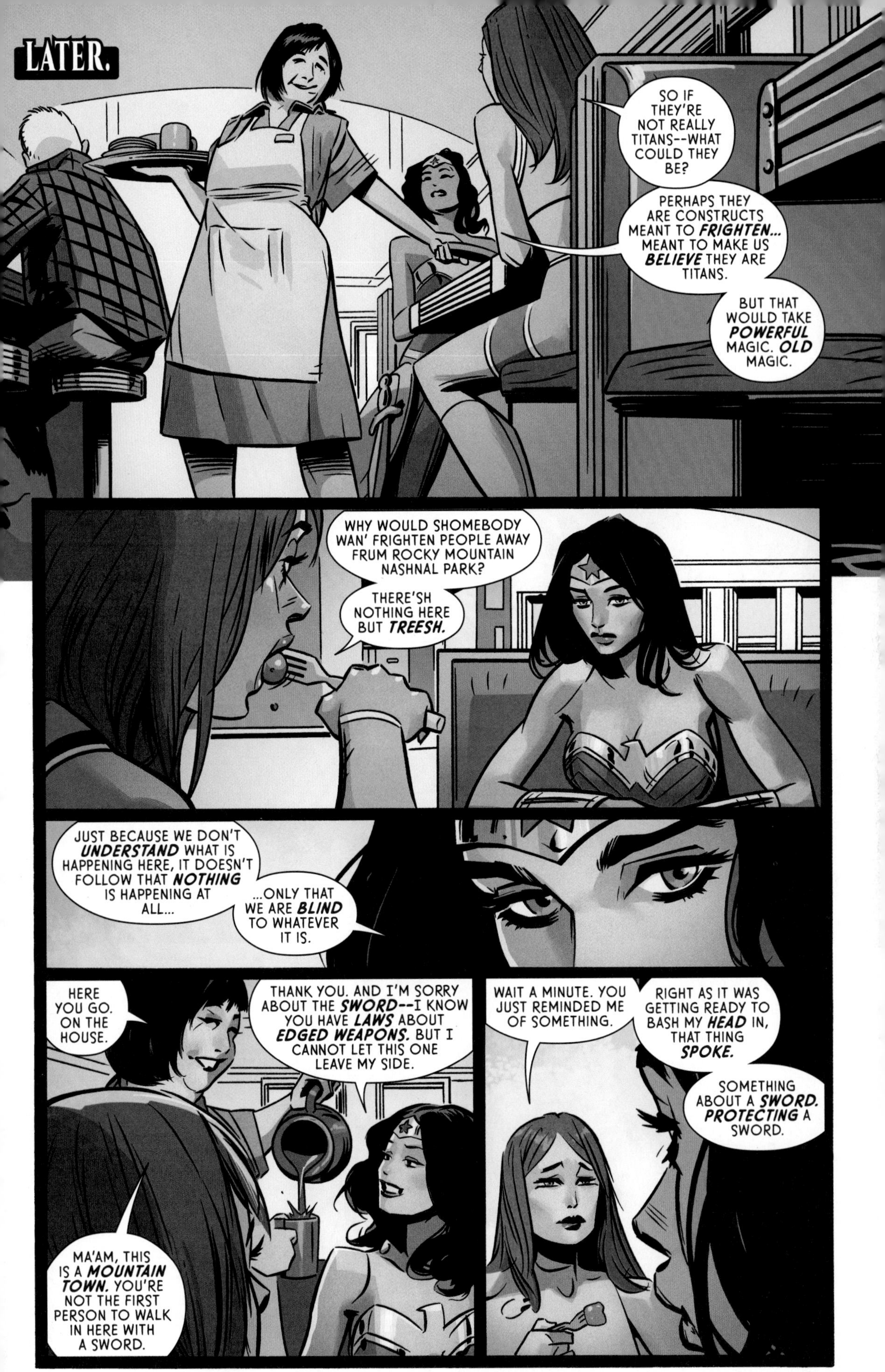
LATER.
SO IF THEY'RE NOT REALLY TITANS--WHAT COULD THEY BE?
PERHAPS THEY ARE CONSTRUCTS MEANT TO FRIGHTEN... MEANT TO MAKE US BELIEVE THEY ARE TITANS.
BUT THAT WOULD TAKE POWERFUL MAGIC. OLD MAGIC.
WHY WOULD SHOMEBODY WAN' FRIGHTEN PEOPLE AWAY FRUM ROCKY MOUNTAIN NASHNAL PARK?
THERE'SH NOTHING HERE BUT TREESH.
JUST BECAUSE WE DON'T UNDERSTAND WHAT IS HAPPENING HERE, IT DOESN'T FOLLOW THAT NOTHING IS HAPPENING AT ALL...
...ONLY THAT WE ARE BLIND TO WHATEVER IT IS.
HERE YOU GO. ON THE HOUSE.
THANK YOU. AND I'M SORRY ABOUT THE SWORD--I KNOW YOU HAVE LAWS ABOUT EDGED WEAPONS. BUT I CANNOT LET THIS ONE LEAVE MY SIDE.
MA'AM, THIS IS A MOUNTAIN TOWN. YOU'RE NOT THE FIRST PERSON TO WALK IN HERE WITH A SWORD.
WAIT A MINUTE. YOU JUST REMINDED ME OF SOMETHING.
RIGHT AS IT WAS GETTING READY TO BASH MY HEAD IN, THAT THING SPOKE.
SOMETHING ABOUT A SWORD. PROTECTING A SWORD.

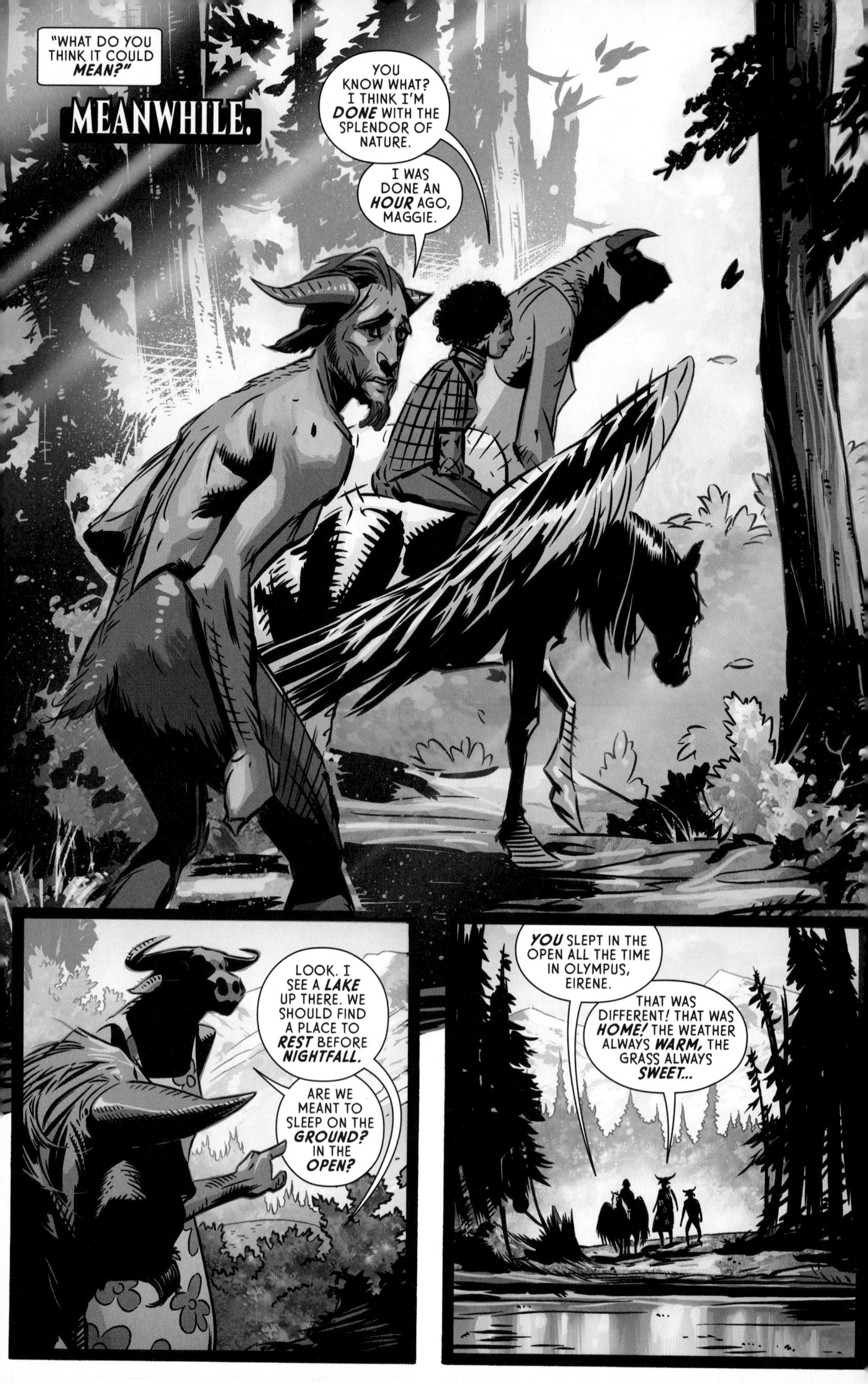
"WHAT DO YOU THINK IT COULD MEAN?"
MEANWHILE.
YOU KNOW WHAT? I THINK I'M DONE WITH THE SPLENDOR OF NATURE.
I WAS DONE AN HOUR AGO, MAGGIE.
LOOK. I SEE A LAKE UP THERE. WE SHOULD FIND A PLACE TO REST BEFORE NIGHTFALL.
ARE WE MEANT TO SLEEP ON THE GROUND? IN THE OPEN?
YOU SLEPT IN THE OPEN ALL THE TIME IN OLYMPUS, EIRENE.
THAT WAS DIFFERENT! THAT WAS HOME! THE WEATHER ALWAYS WARM, THE GRASS ALWAYS SWEET...

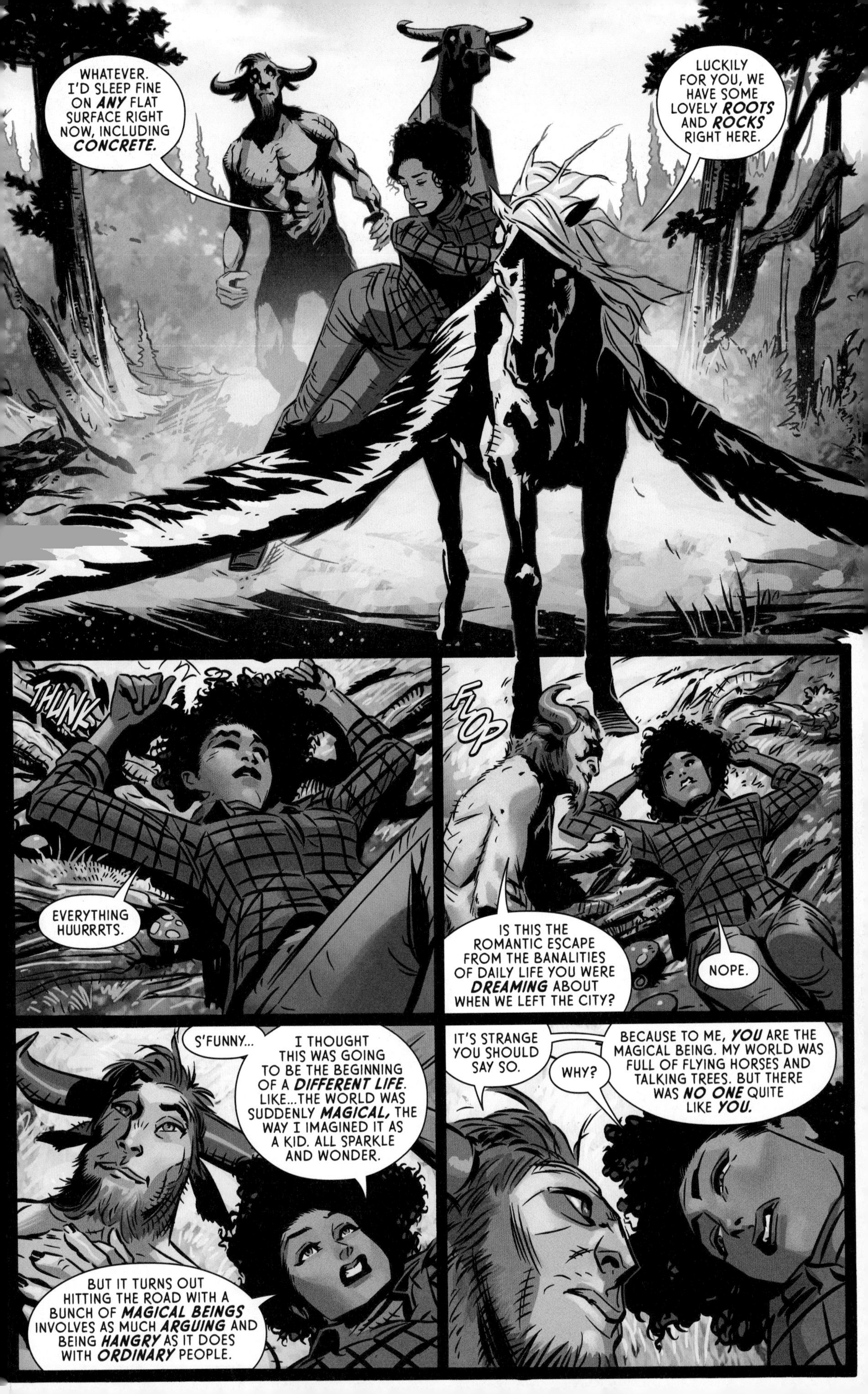
WHATEVER. I'D SLEEP FINE ON ANY FLAT SURFACE RIGHT NOW, INCLUDING CONCRETE.
LUCKILY FOR YOU, WE HAVE SOME LOVELY ROOTS AND ROCKS RIGHT HERE.
THUNK
EVERYTHING HUURRRTS.
FLOP
IS THIS THE ROMANTIC ESCAPE FROM THE BANALITIES OF DAILY LIFE YOU WERE DREAMING ABOUT WHEN WE LEFT THE CITY?
NOPE.
S'FUNNY...
I THOUGHT THIS WAS GOING TO BE THE BEGINNING OF A DIFFERENT LIFE. LIKE...THE WORLD WAS SUDDENLY MAGICAL, THE WAY I IMAGINED IT AS A KID. ALL SPARKLE AND WONDER.
BUT IT TURNS OUT HITTING THE ROAD WITH A BUNCH OF MAGICAL BEINGS INVOLVES AS MUCH ARGUING AND BEING HANGRY AS IT DOES WITH ORDINARY PEOPLE.
IT'S STRANGE YOU SHOULD SAY SO.
WHY?
BECAUSE TO ME, YOU ARE THE MAGICAL BEING. MY WORLD WAS FULL OF FLYING HORSES AND TALKING TREES. BUT THERE WAS NO ONE QUITE LIKE YOU.

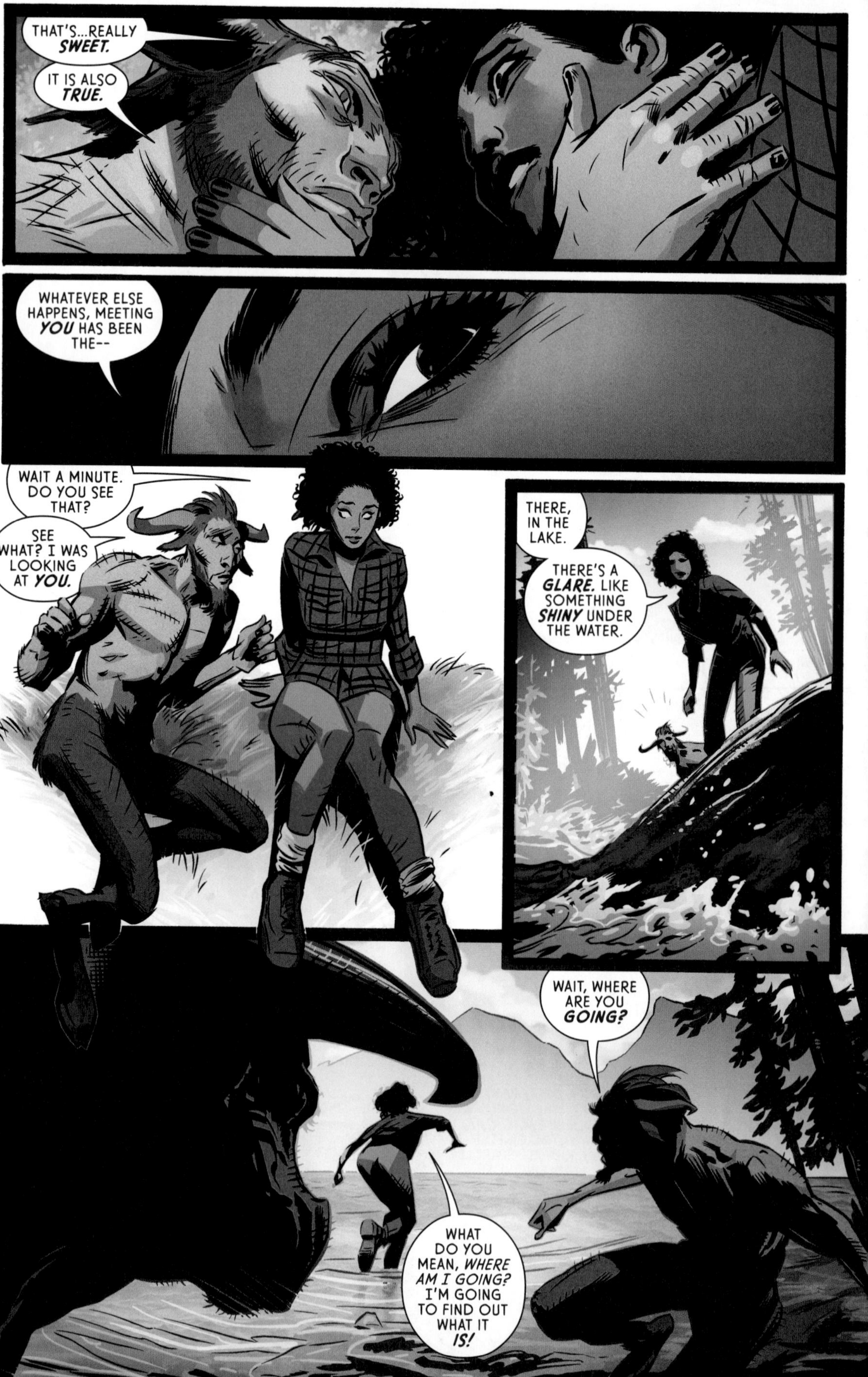
THAT'S...REALLY *SWEET.*
IT IS ALSO *TRUE.*
WHATEVER ELSE HAPPENS, MEETING *YOU* HAS BEEN THE--
WAIT A MINUTE. DO YOU SEE THAT?
SEE WHAT? I WAS LOOKING AT *YOU.*
THERE, IN THE LAKE.
THERE'S A *GLARE.* LIKE SOMETHING *SHINY* UNDER THE WATER.
WAIT, WHERE ARE YOU *GOING?*
WHAT DO YOU MEAN, *WHERE AM I GOING?* I'M GOING TO FIND OUT WHAT IT *IS!*

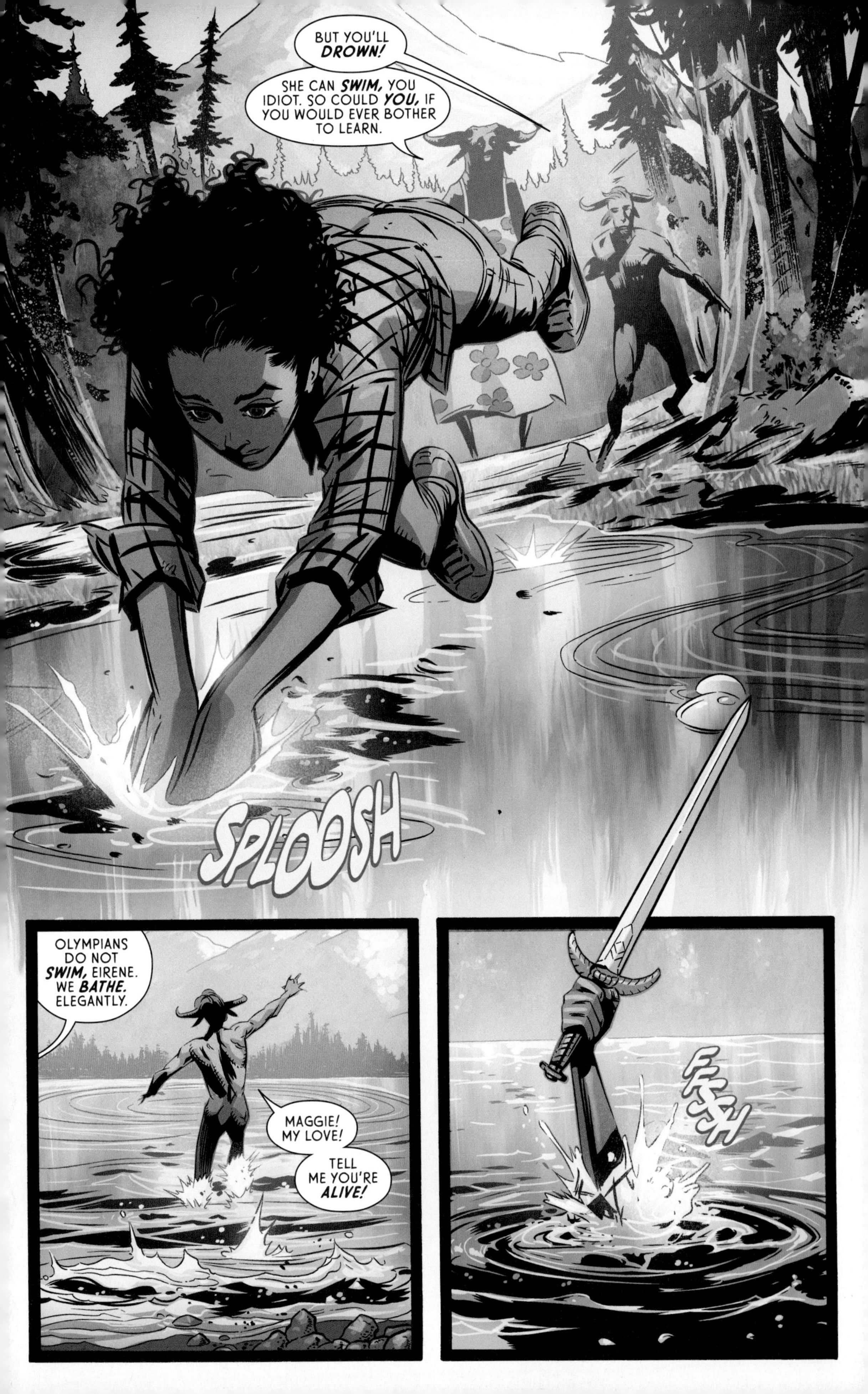
BUT YOU'LL DROWN!
SHE CAN SWIM, YOU IDIOT. SO COULD YOU, IF YOU WOULD EVER BOTHER TO LEARN.
SPLOOSH
OLYMPIANS DO NOT SWIM, EIRENE. WE BATHE. ELEGANTLY.
MAGGIE! MY LOVE!
TELL ME YOU'RE ALIVE!
FSSH

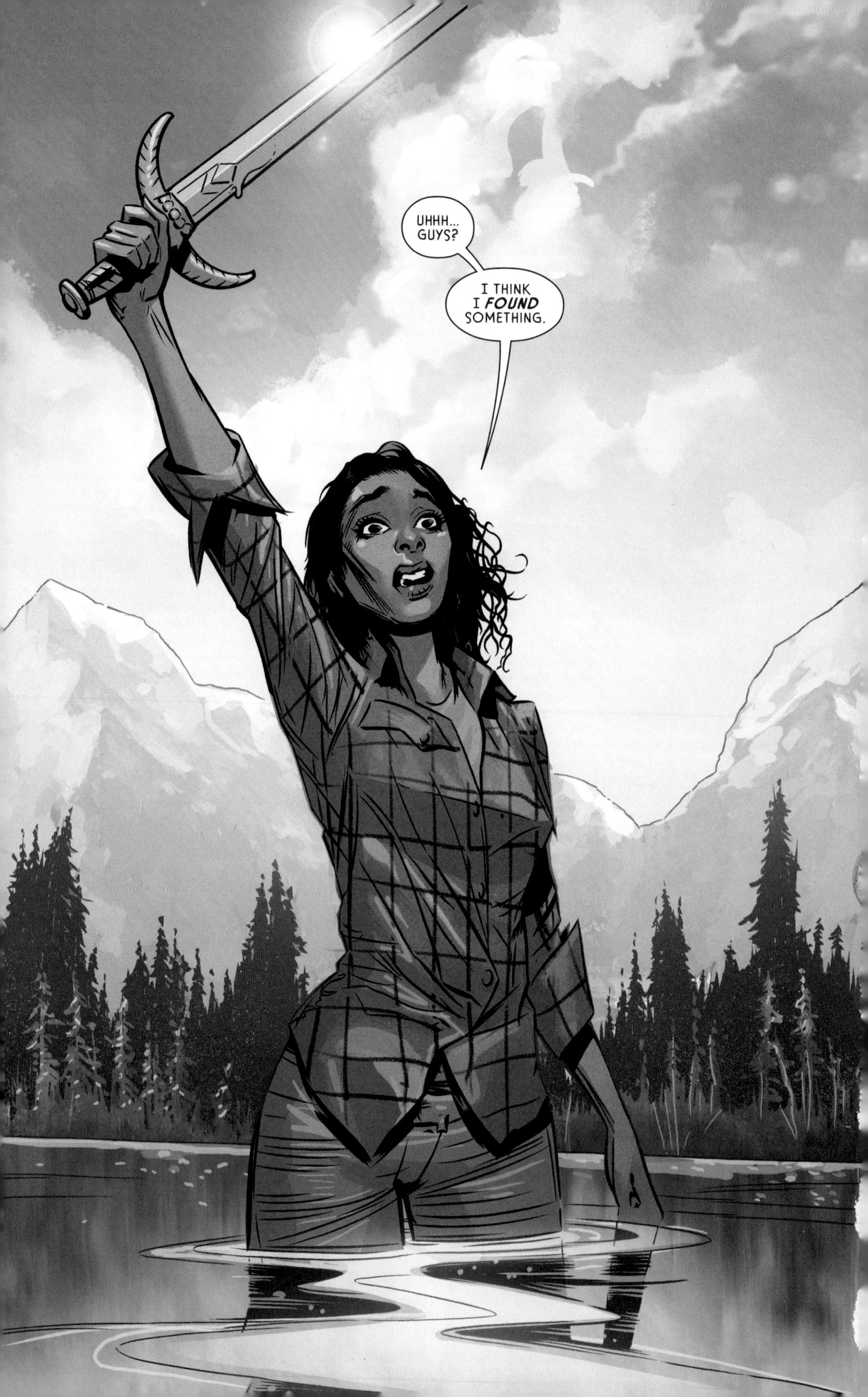
UHHH... GUYS?
I THINK I *FOUND* SOMETHING.

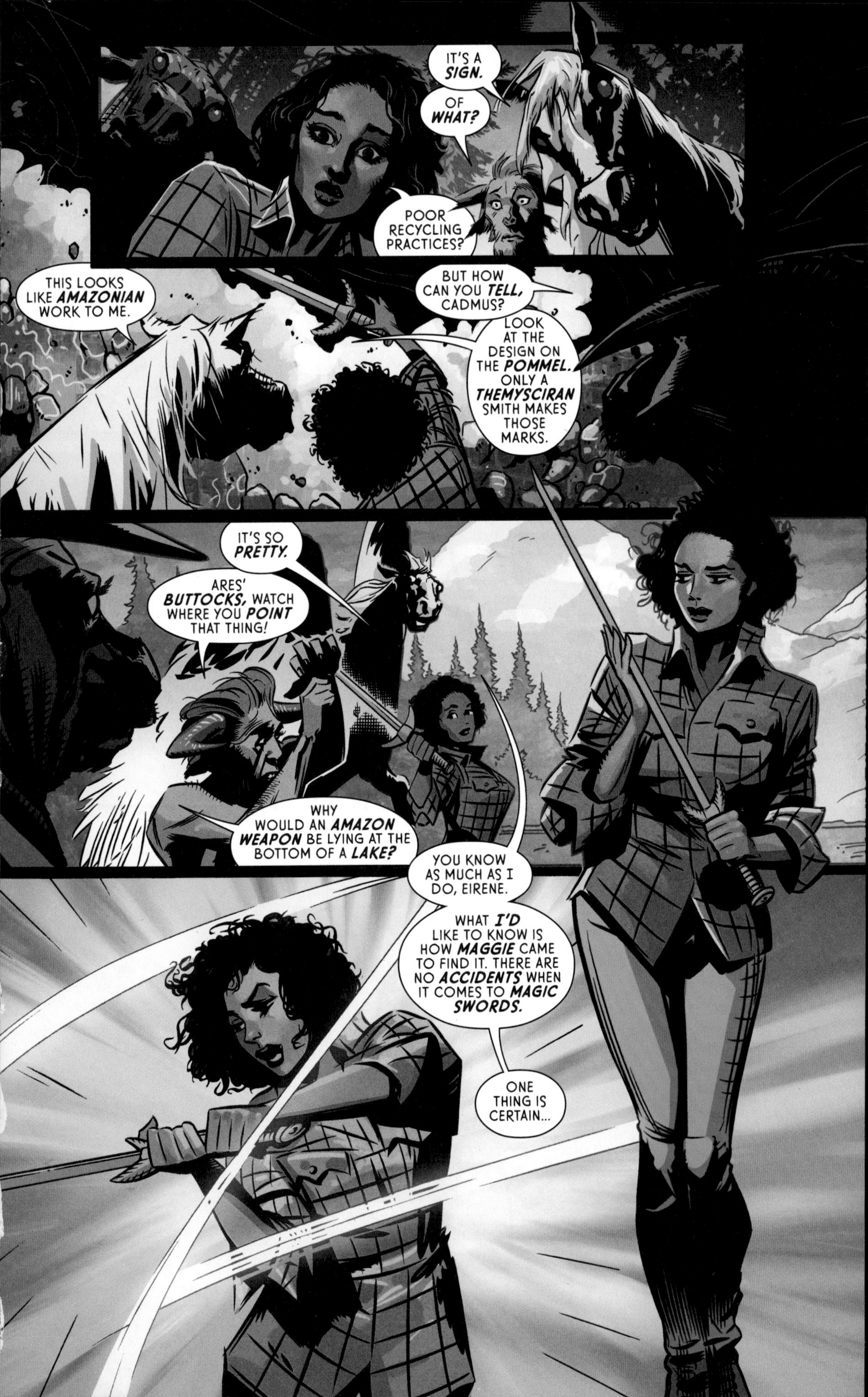

IT'S A SIGN.
OF WHAT?
POOR RECYCLING PRACTICES?
THIS LOOKS LIKE AMAZONIAN WORK TO ME.
BUT HOW CAN YOU TELL, CADMUS?
LOOK AT THE DESIGN ON THE POMMEL. ONLY A THEMYSCIRAN SMITH MAKES THOSE MARKS.
IT'S SO PRETTY.
ARES' BUTTOCKS, WATCH WHERE YOU POINT THAT THING!
WHY WOULD AN AMAZON WEAPON BE LYING AT THE BOTTOM OF A LAKE?
YOU KNOW AS MUCH AS I DO, EIRENE.
WHAT I'D LIKE TO KNOW IS HOW MAGGIE CAME TO FIND IT. THERE ARE NO ACCIDENTS WHEN IT COMES TO MAGIC SWORDS.
ONE THING IS CERTAIN...

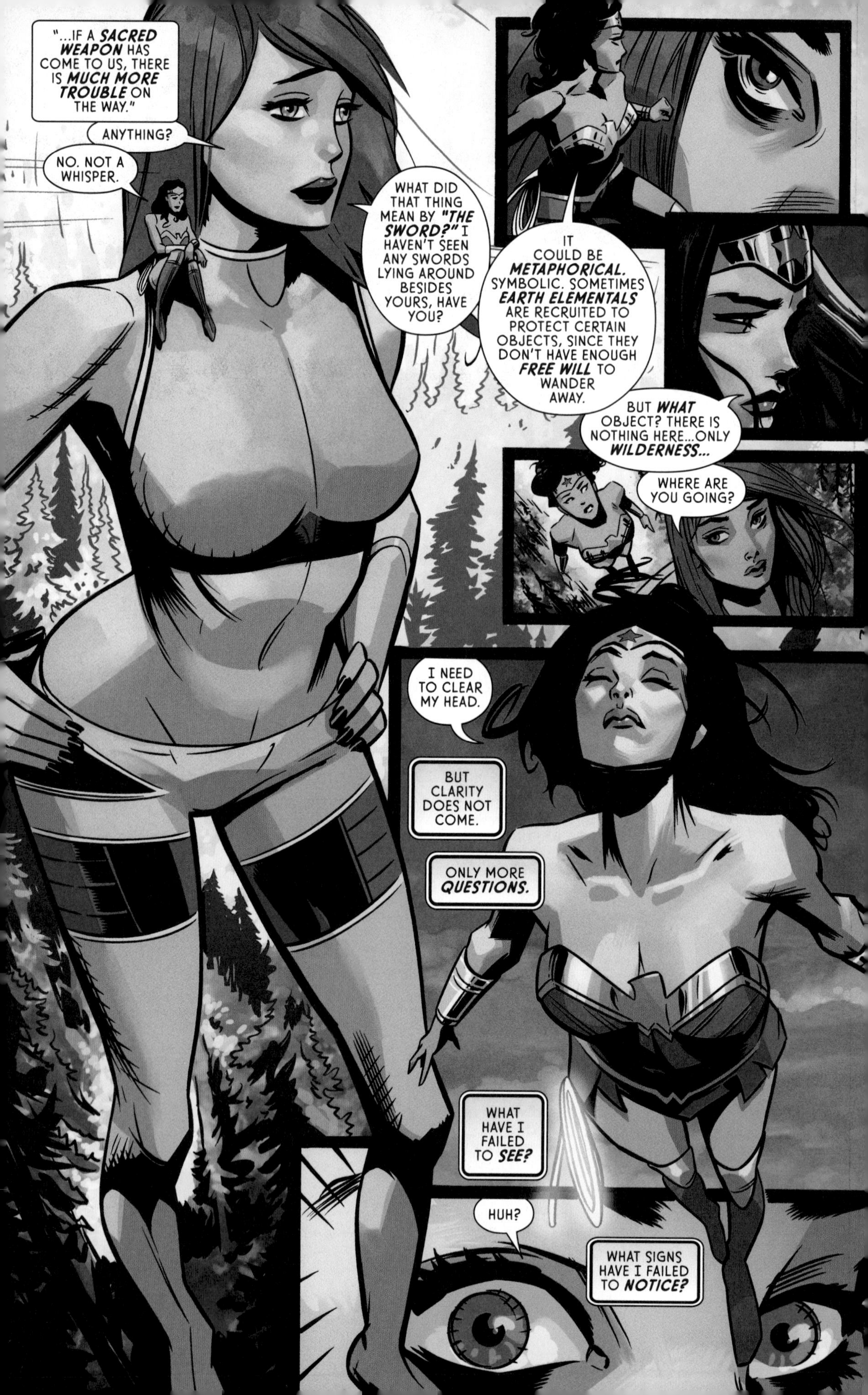
"...IF A SACRED WEAPON HAS COME TO US, THERE IS MUCH MORE TROUBLE ON THE WAY."
ANYTHING?
NO. NOT A WHISPER.
WHAT DID THAT THING MEAN BY "THE SWORD?" I HAVEN'T SEEN ANY SWORDS LYING AROUND BESIDES YOURS, HAVE YOU?
IT COULD BE METAPHORICAL. SYMBOLIC. SOMETIMES EARTH ELEMENTALS ARE RECRUITED TO PROTECT CERTAIN OBJECTS, SINCE THEY DON'T HAVE ENOUGH FREE WILL TO WANDER AWAY.
BUT WHAT OBJECT? THERE IS NOTHING HERE...ONLY WILDERNESS...
WHERE ARE YOU GOING?
I NEED TO CLEAR MY HEAD.
BUT CLARITY DOES NOT COME.
ONLY MORE QUESTIONS.
WHAT HAVE I FAILED TO SEE?
HUH?
WHAT SIGNS HAVE I FAILED TO NOTICE?

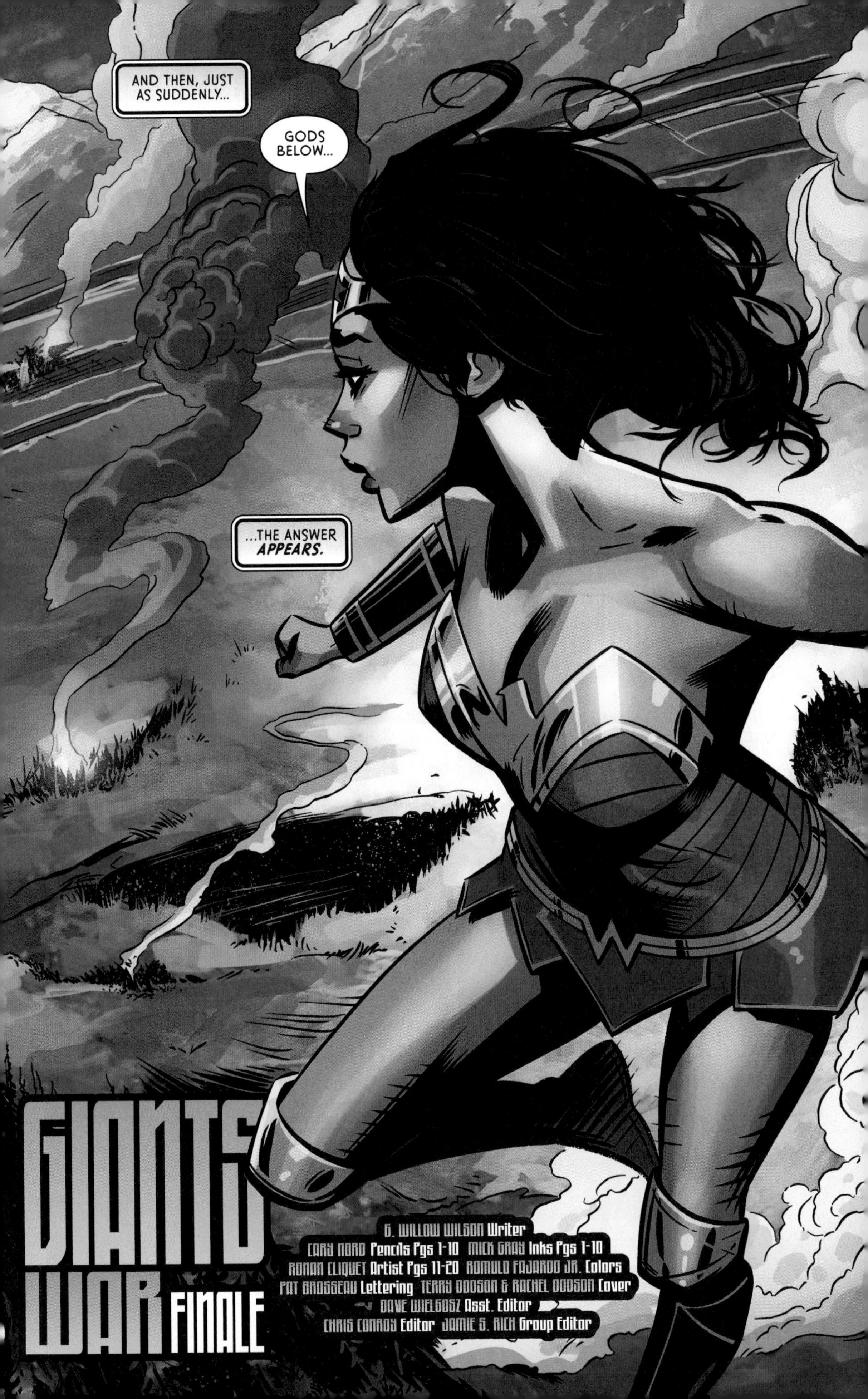
AND THEN, JUST AS SUDDENLY...
GODS BELOW...
...THE ANSWER *APPEARS.*
GIANTS WAR FINALE
G. WILLOW WILSON Writer
CARY NORD Pencils Pgs 1-10 MICK GRAY Inks Pgs 1-10
RONAN CLIQUET Artist Pgs 11-20 ROMULO FAJARDO JR. Colors
PAT BROSSEAU Lettering TERRY DODSON & RACHEL DODSON Cover
DAVE WIELGOSZ Asst. Editor
CHRIS CONROY Editor JAMIE S. RICH Group Editor

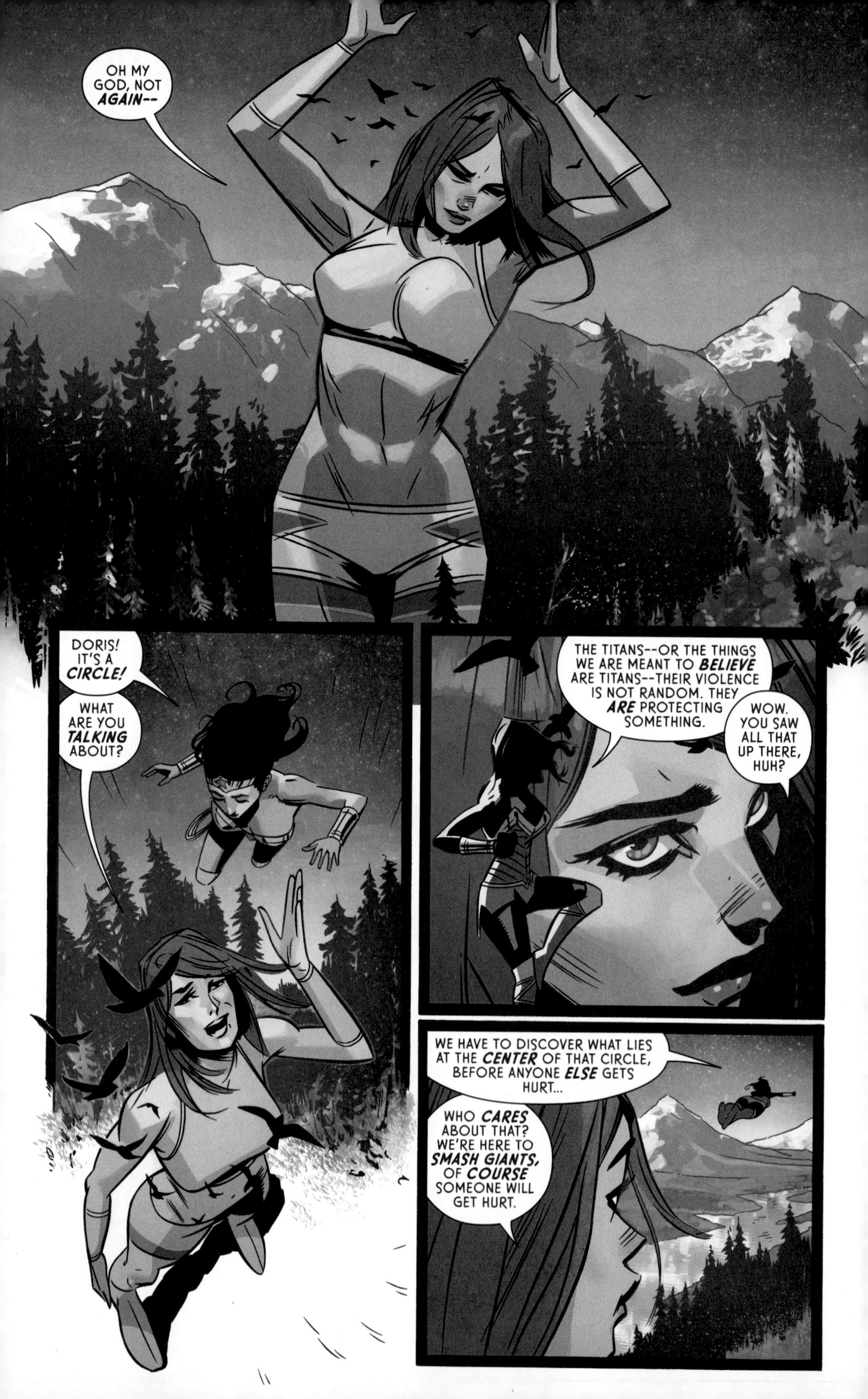
OH MY GOD, NOT *AGAIN*--
DORIS! IT'S A *CIRCLE!*
WHAT ARE YOU *TALKING* ABOUT?
THE TITANS--OR THE THINGS WE ARE MEANT TO *BELIEVE* ARE TITANS--THEIR VIOLENCE IS NOT RANDOM. THEY *ARE* PROTECTING SOMETHING.
WOW. YOU SAW ALL THAT UP THERE, HUH?
WE HAVE TO DISCOVER WHAT LIES AT THE *CENTER* OF THAT CIRCLE, BEFORE ANYONE *ELSE* GETS HURT...
WHO *CARES* ABOUT THAT? WE'RE HERE TO *SMASH GIANTS,* OF *COURSE* SOMEONE WILL GET HURT.

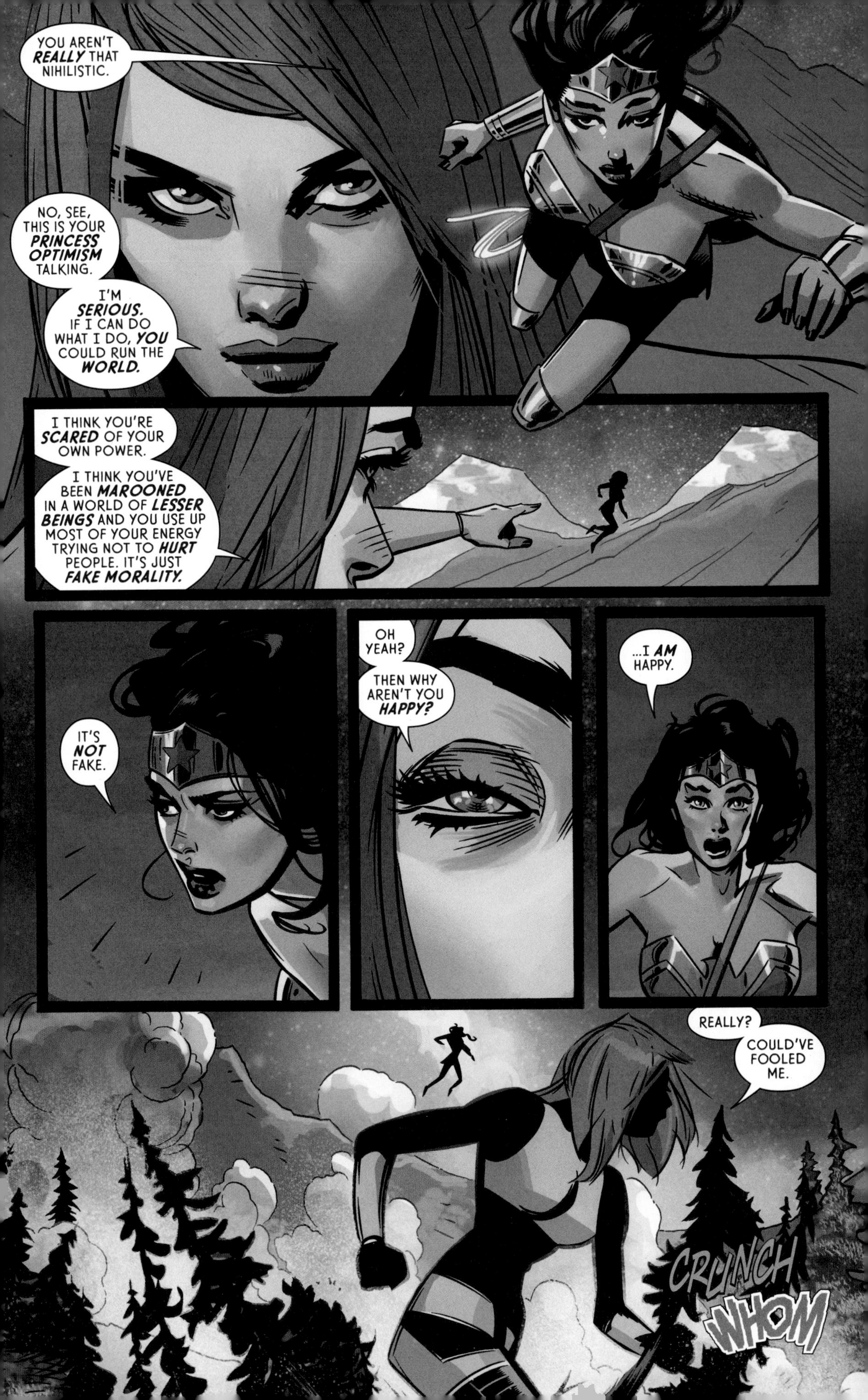
YOU AREN'T REALLY THAT NIHILISTIC.
NO, SEE, THIS IS YOUR PRINCESS OPTIMISM TALKING.
I'M SERIOUS. IF I CAN DO WHAT I DO, YOU COULD RUN THE WORLD.
I THINK YOU'RE SCARED OF YOUR OWN POWER.
I THINK YOU'VE BEEN MAROONED IN A WORLD OF LESSER BEINGS AND YOU USE UP MOST OF YOUR ENERGY TRYING NOT TO HURT PEOPLE. IT'S JUST FAKE MORALITY.
IT'S NOT FAKE.
OH YEAH?
THEN WHY AREN'T YOU HAPPY?
...I AM HAPPY.
REALLY?
COULD'VE FOOLED ME.
CRUNCH
WHOM

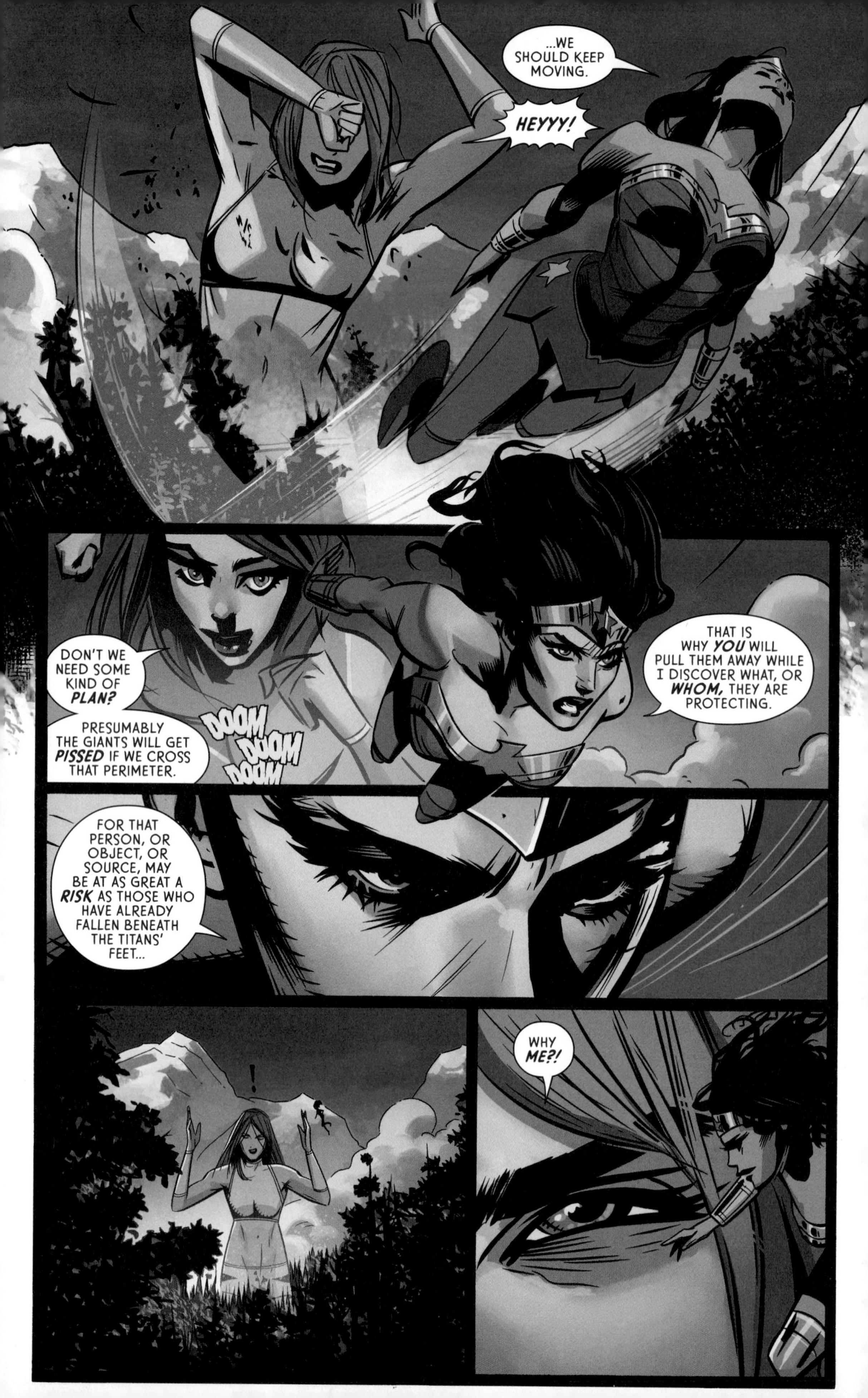
...WE SHOULD KEEP MOVING.
HEYYY!
DON'T WE NEED SOME KIND OF *PLAN?*
PRESUMABLY THE GIANTS WILL GET *PISSED* IF WE CROSS THAT PERIMETER.
DOOM DOOM DOOM
THAT IS WHY *YOU* WILL PULL THEM AWAY WHILE I DISCOVER WHAT, OR *WHOM,* THEY ARE PROTECTING.
FOR THAT PERSON, OR OBJECT, OR SOURCE, MAY BE AT AS GREAT A *RISK* AS THOSE WHO HAVE ALREADY FALLEN BENEATH THE TITANS' FEET...
!
WHY *ME?!*

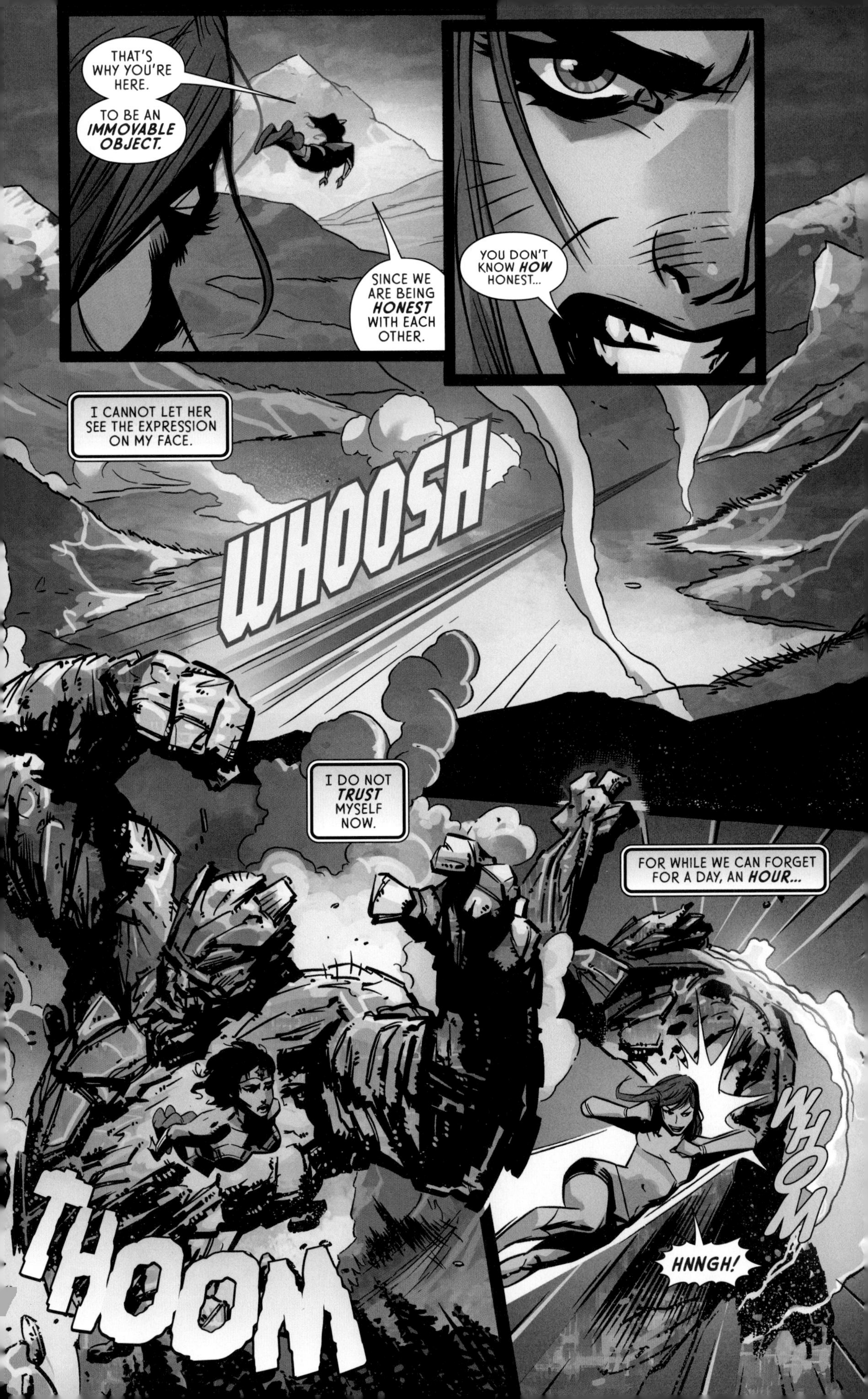
THAT'S WHY YOU'RE HERE.
TO BE AN *IMMOVABLE OBJECT.*
SINCE WE ARE BEING *HONEST* WITH EACH OTHER.
YOU DON'T KNOW *HOW* HONEST...
I CANNOT LET HER SEE THE EXPRESSION ON MY FACE.
WHOOSH
I DO NOT *TRUST* MYSELF NOW.
FOR WHILE WE CAN FORGET FOR A DAY, AN *HOUR*...
THOOM
WHOOM
HNNGH!

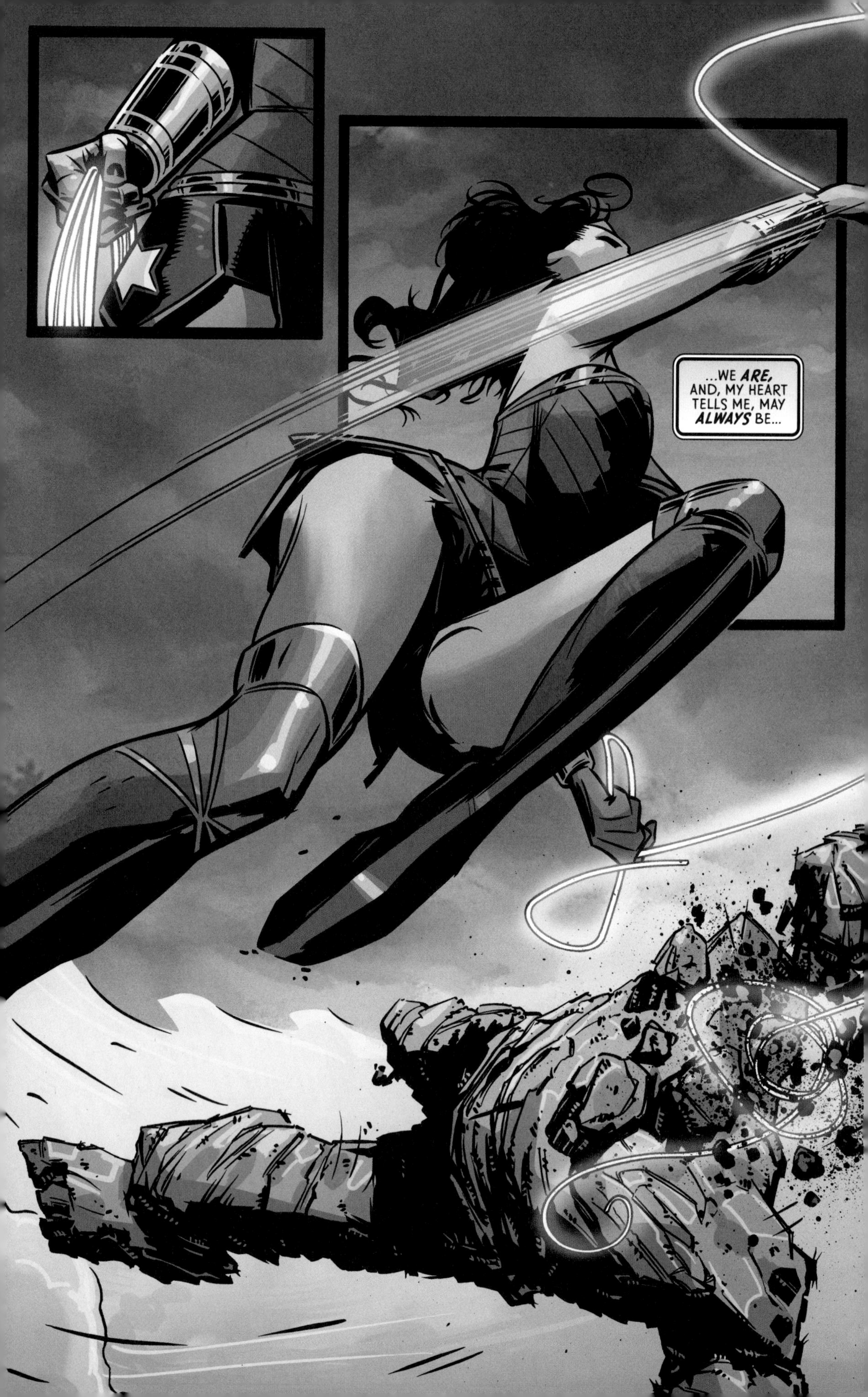
...WE ARE, AND, MY HEART TELLS ME, MAY ALWAYS BE...

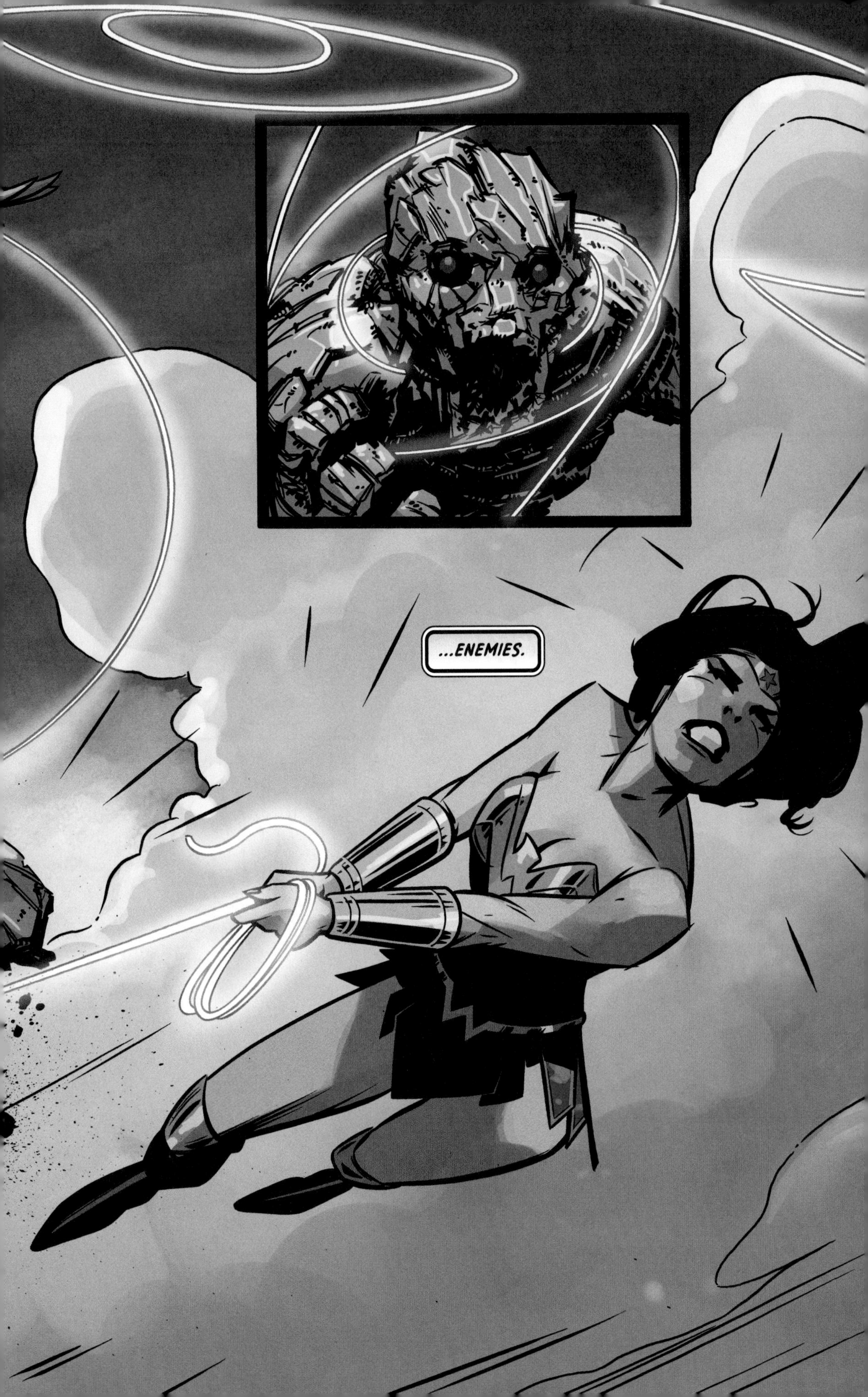
...ENEMIES.

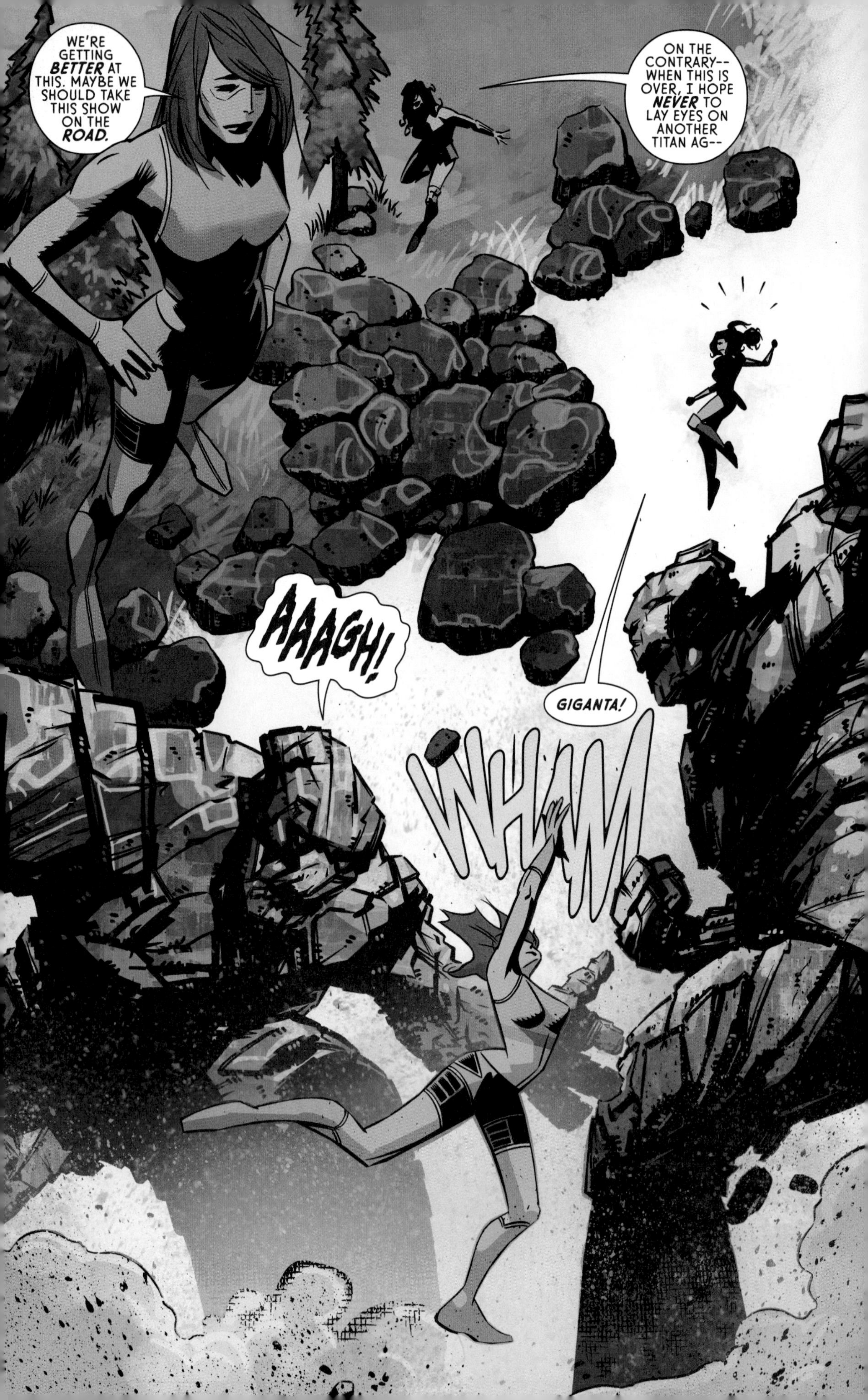
WE'RE GETTING BETTER AT THIS. MAYBE WE SHOULD TAKE THIS SHOW ON THE ROAD.
ON THE CONTRARY-- WHEN THIS IS OVER, I HOPE NEVER TO LAY EYES ON ANOTHER TITAN AG--
AAAGH!
GIGANTA!
WHAM

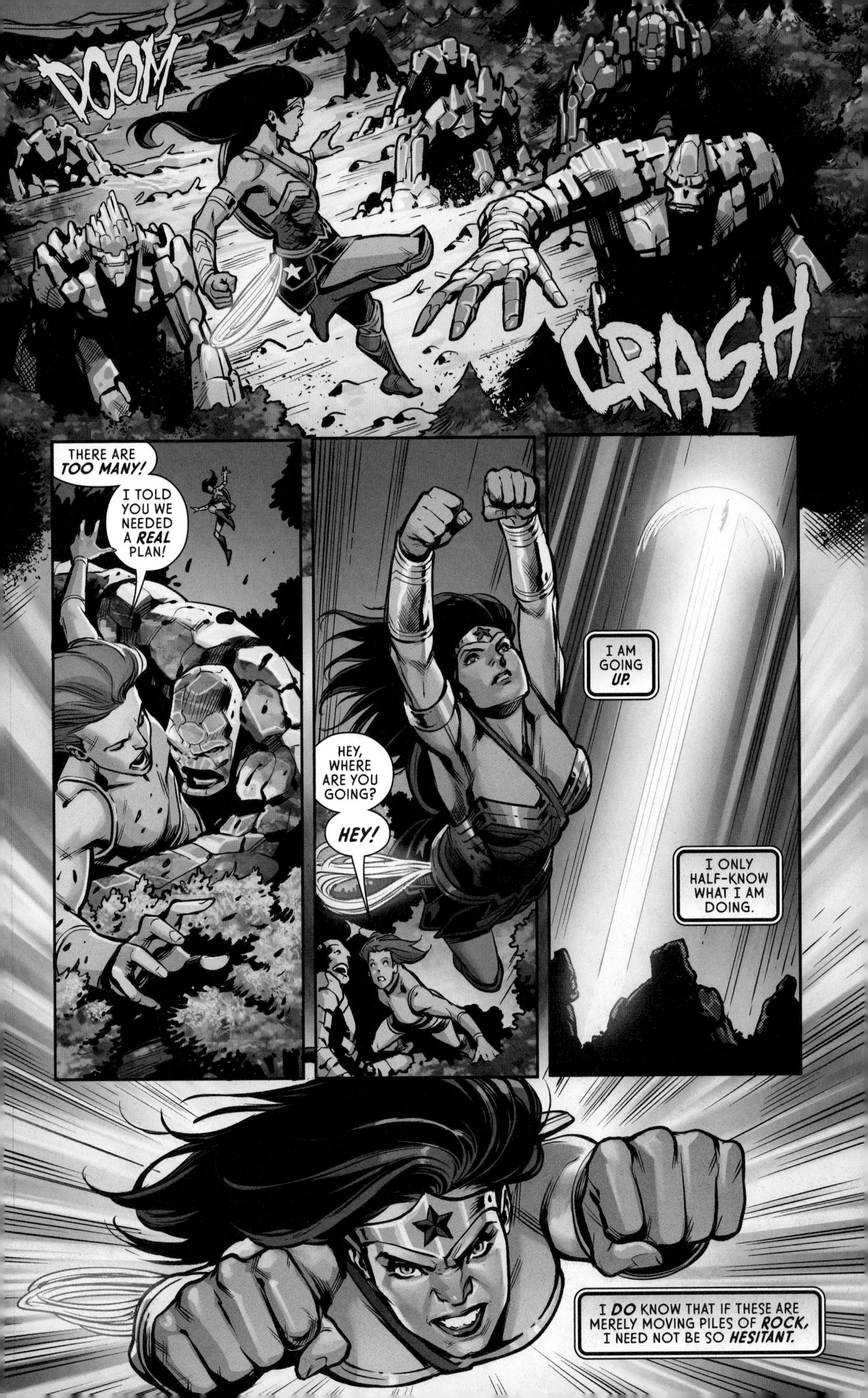
DOOM
CRASH
THERE ARE TOO MANY!
I TOLD YOU WE NEEDED A REAL PLAN!
HEY, WHERE ARE YOU GOING?
HEY!
I AM GOING UP.
I ONLY HALF-KNOW WHAT I AM DOING.
I DO KNOW THAT IF THESE ARE MERELY MOVING PILES OF ROCK, I NEED NOT BE SO HESITANT.

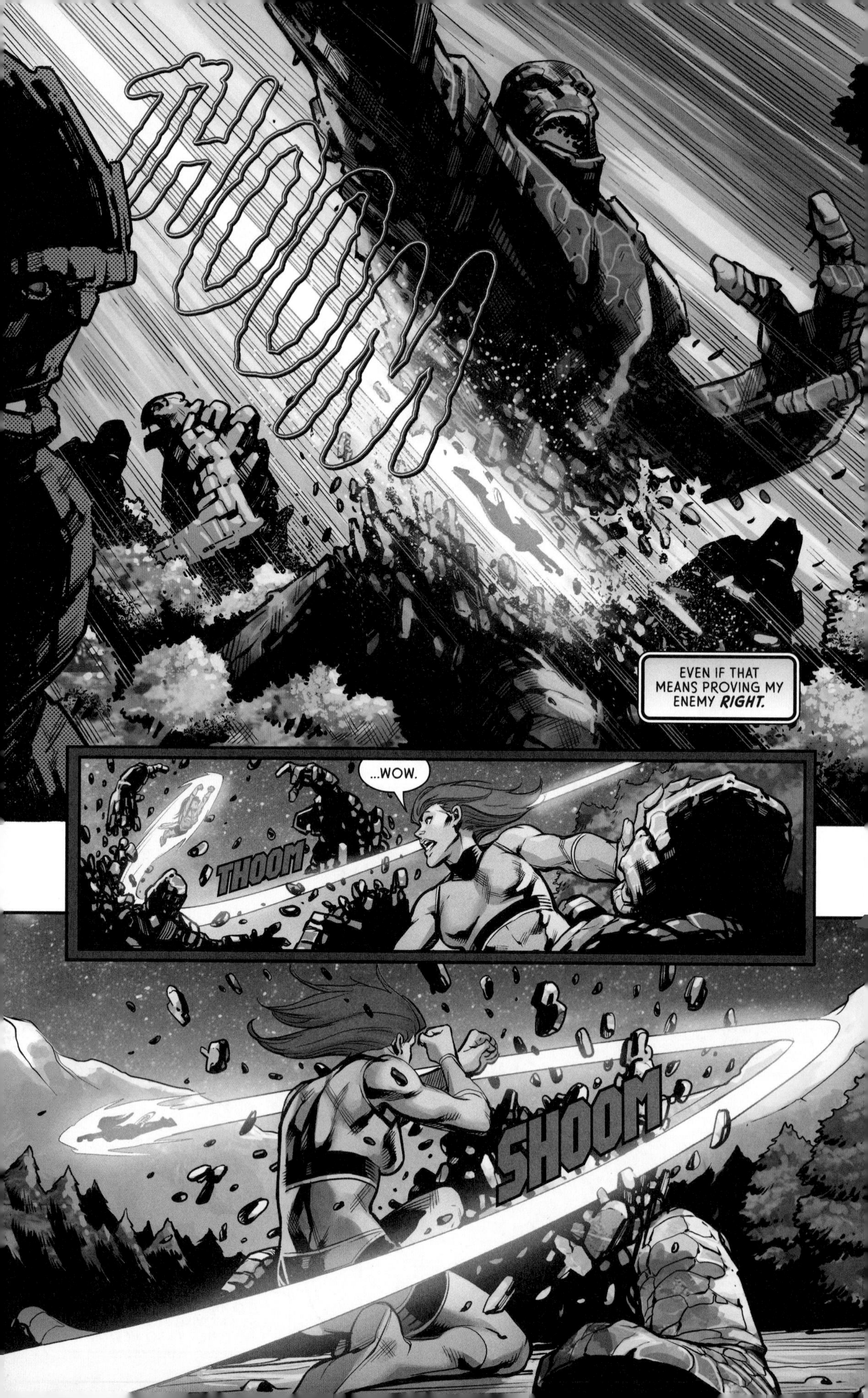
THOOM
EVEN IF THAT MEANS PROVING MY ENEMY *RIGHT.*
...WOW.
THOOM
SHOOM

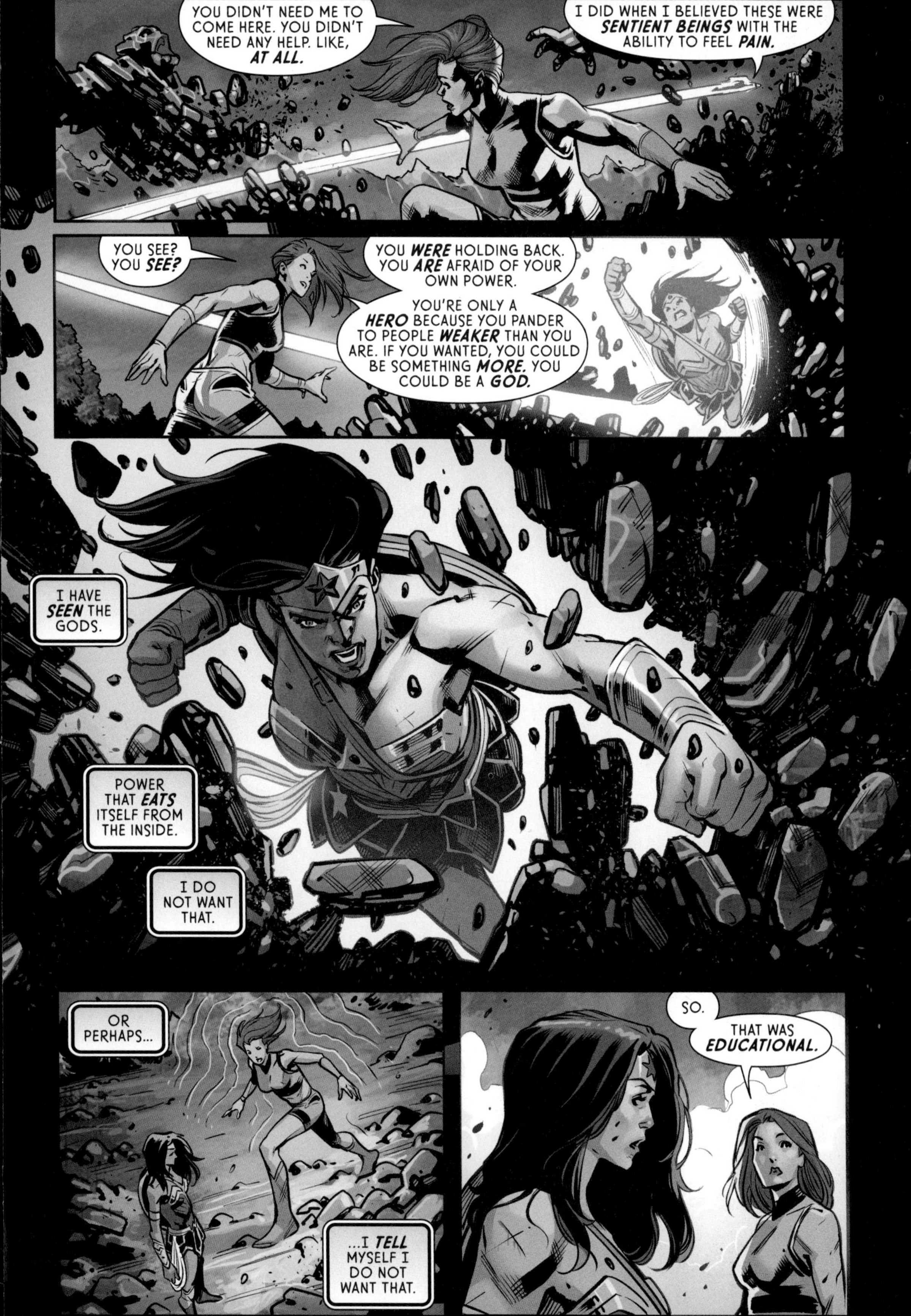
YOU DIDN'T NEED ME TO COME HERE. YOU DIDN'T NEED ANY HELP. LIKE, AT ALL.
I DID WHEN I BELIEVED THESE WERE SENTIENT BEINGS WITH THE ABILITY TO FEEL PAIN.
YOU SEE? YOU SEE?
YOU WERE HOLDING BACK. YOU ARE AFRAID OF YOUR OWN POWER.
YOU'RE ONLY A HERO BECAUSE YOU PANDER TO PEOPLE WEAKER THAN YOU ARE. IF YOU WANTED, YOU COULD BE SOMETHING MORE. YOU COULD BE A GOD.
I HAVE SEEN THE GODS.
POWER THAT EATS ITSELF FROM THE INSIDE.
I DO NOT WANT THAT.
OR PERHAPS...
...I TELL MYSELF I DO NOT WANT THAT.
SO.
THAT WAS EDUCATIONAL.

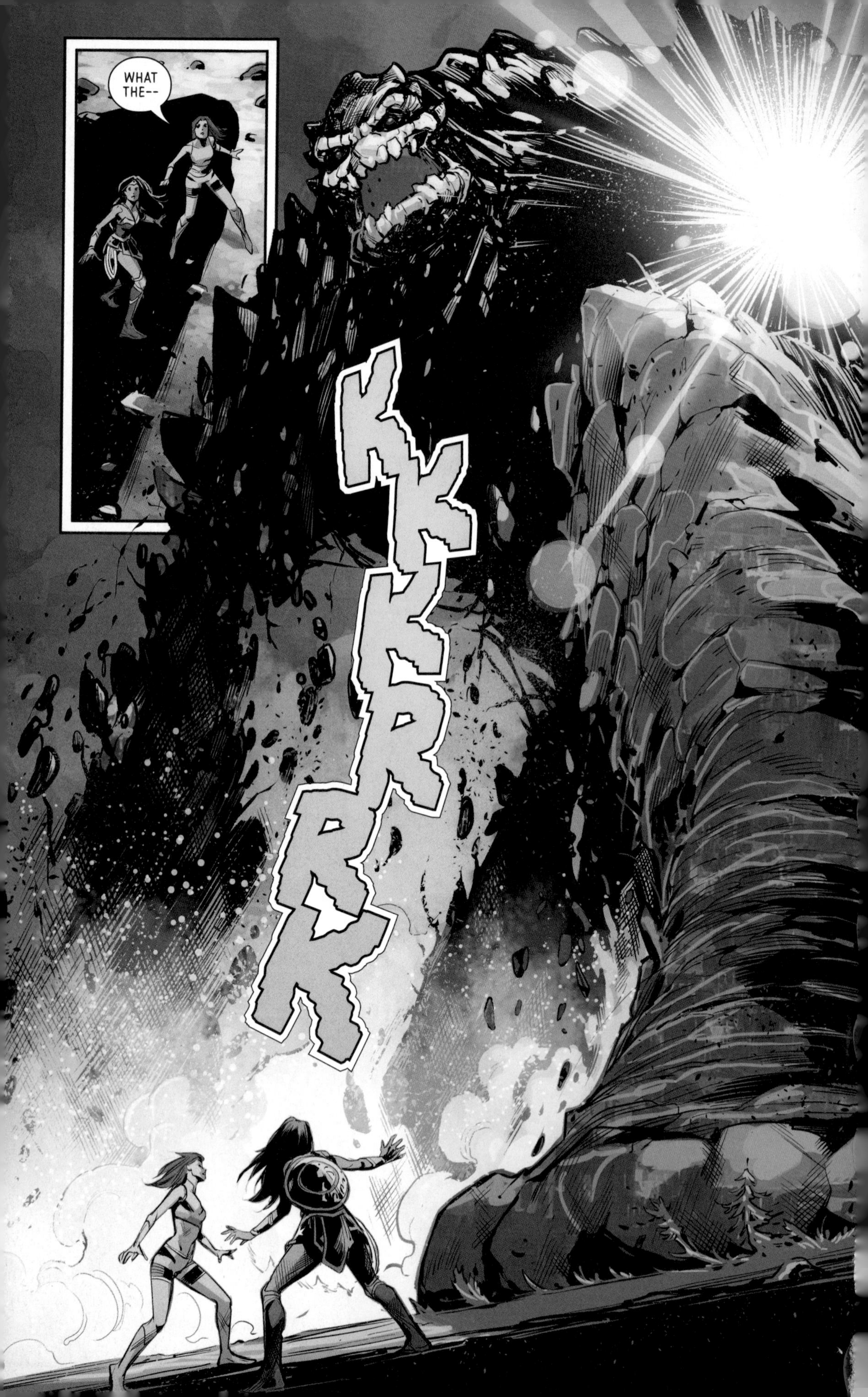
WHAT THE--
KKKRRRR

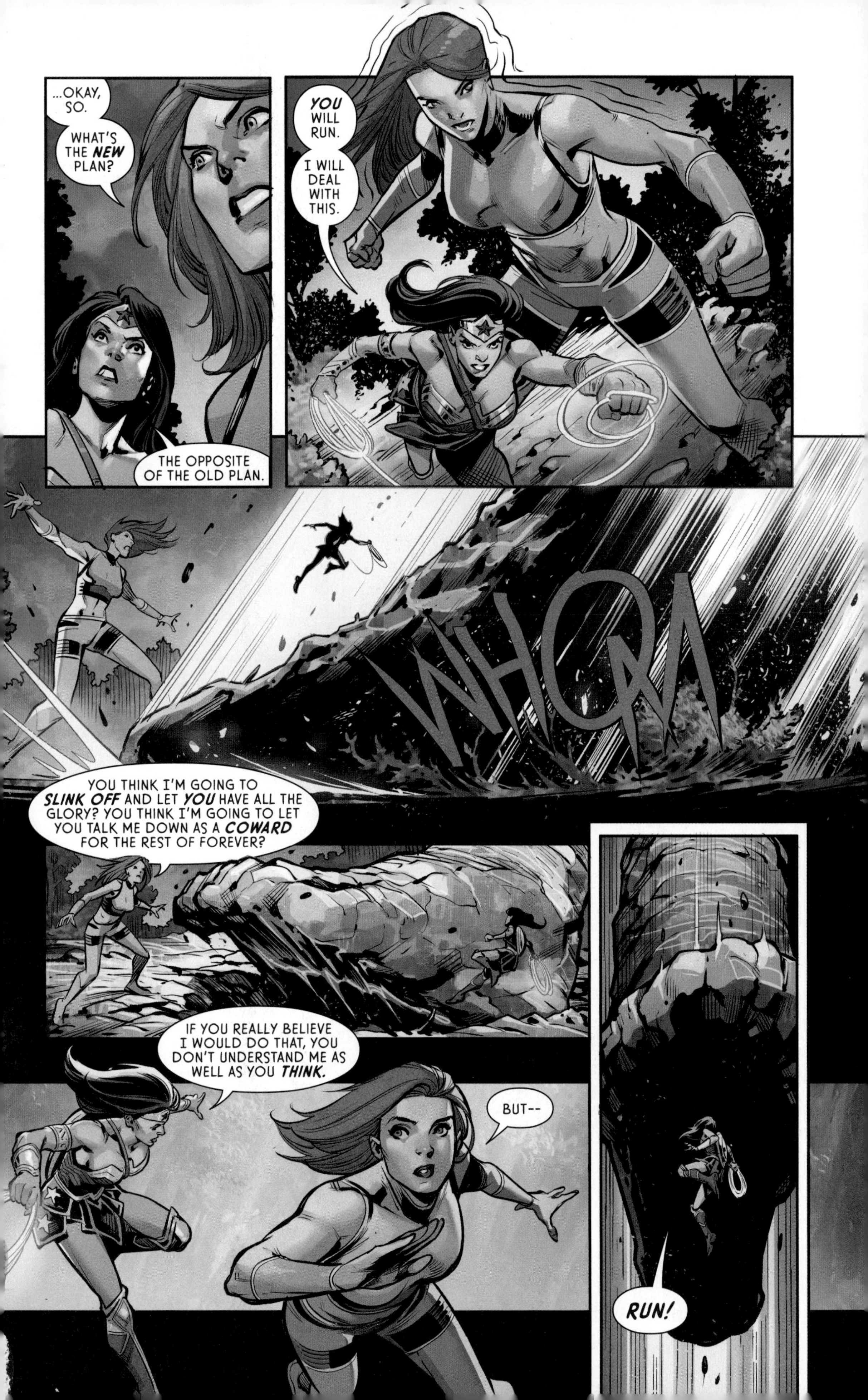
...OKAY, SO.
WHAT'S THE NEW PLAN?
THE OPPOSITE OF THE OLD PLAN.
YOU WILL RUN.
I WILL DEAL WITH THIS.
WHOA
YOU THINK I'M GOING TO SLINK OFF AND LET YOU HAVE ALL THE GLORY? YOU THINK I'M GOING TO LET YOU TALK ME DOWN AS A COWARD FOR THE REST OF FOREVER?
IF YOU REALLY BELIEVE I WOULD DO THAT, YOU DON'T UNDERSTAND ME AS WELL AS YOU THINK.
BUT--
RUN!

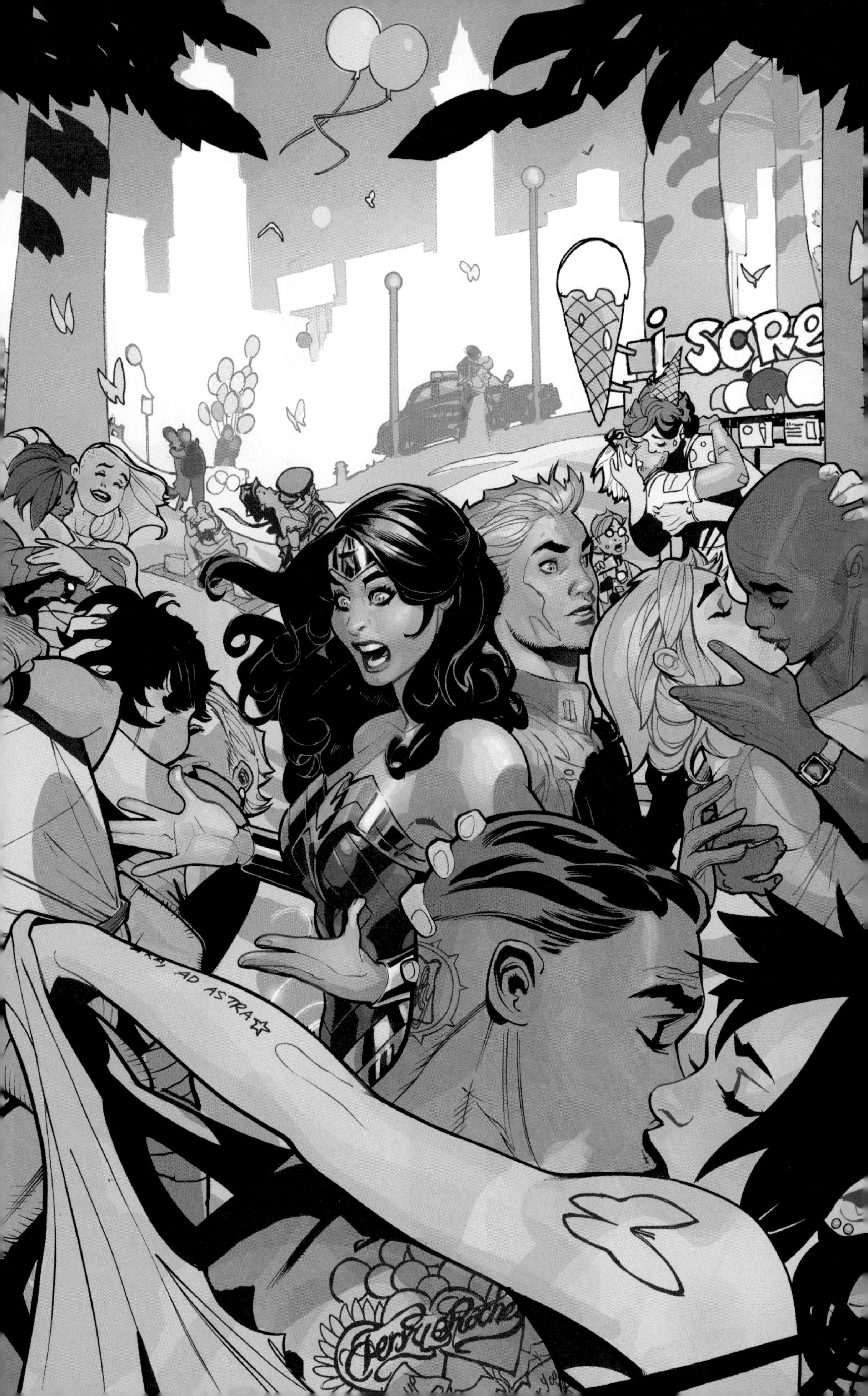

SCRE
AD ASTRA

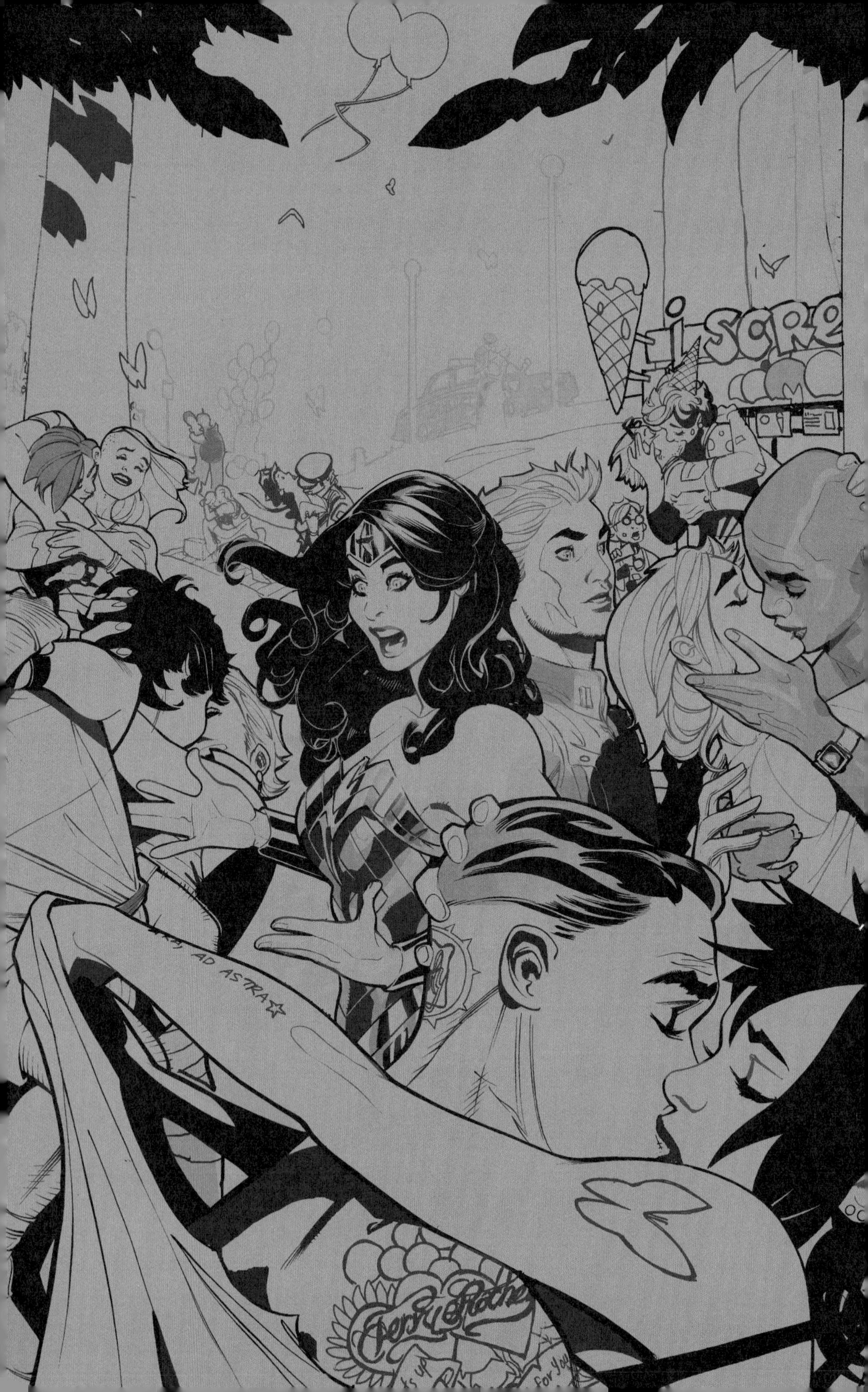
AD ASTRA

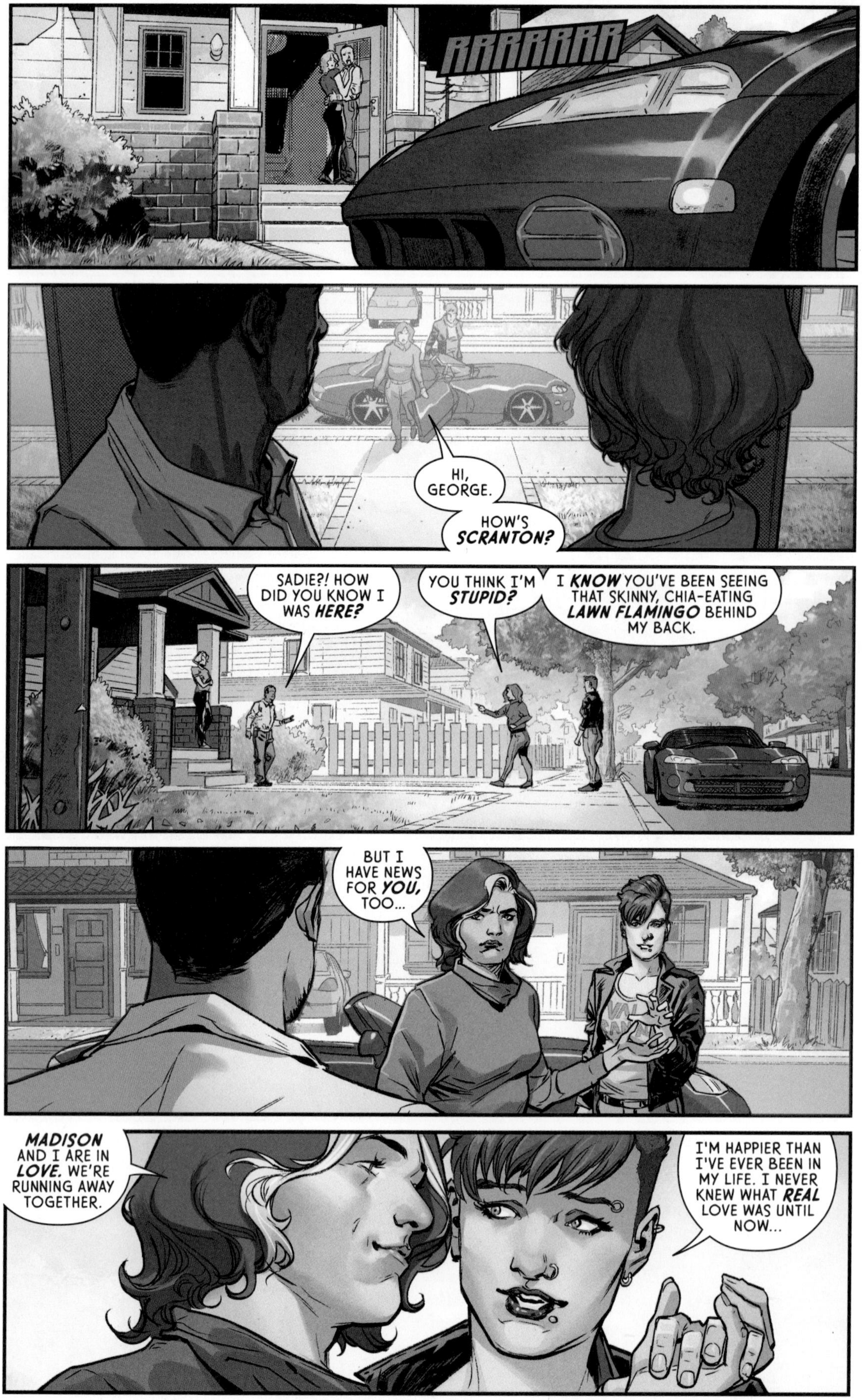

RRRRRRR
HI, GEORGE.
HOW'S SCRANTON?
SADIE?! HOW DID YOU KNOW I WAS HERE?
YOU THINK I'M STUPID?
I KNOW YOU'VE BEEN SEEING THAT SKINNY, CHIA-EATING LAWN FLAMINGO BEHIND MY BACK.
BUT I HAVE NEWS FOR YOU, TOO...
MADISON AND I ARE IN LOVE. WE'RE RUNNING AWAY TOGETHER.
I'M HAPPIER THAN I'VE EVER BEEN IN MY LIFE. I NEVER KNEW WHAT REAL LOVE WAS UNTIL NOW...

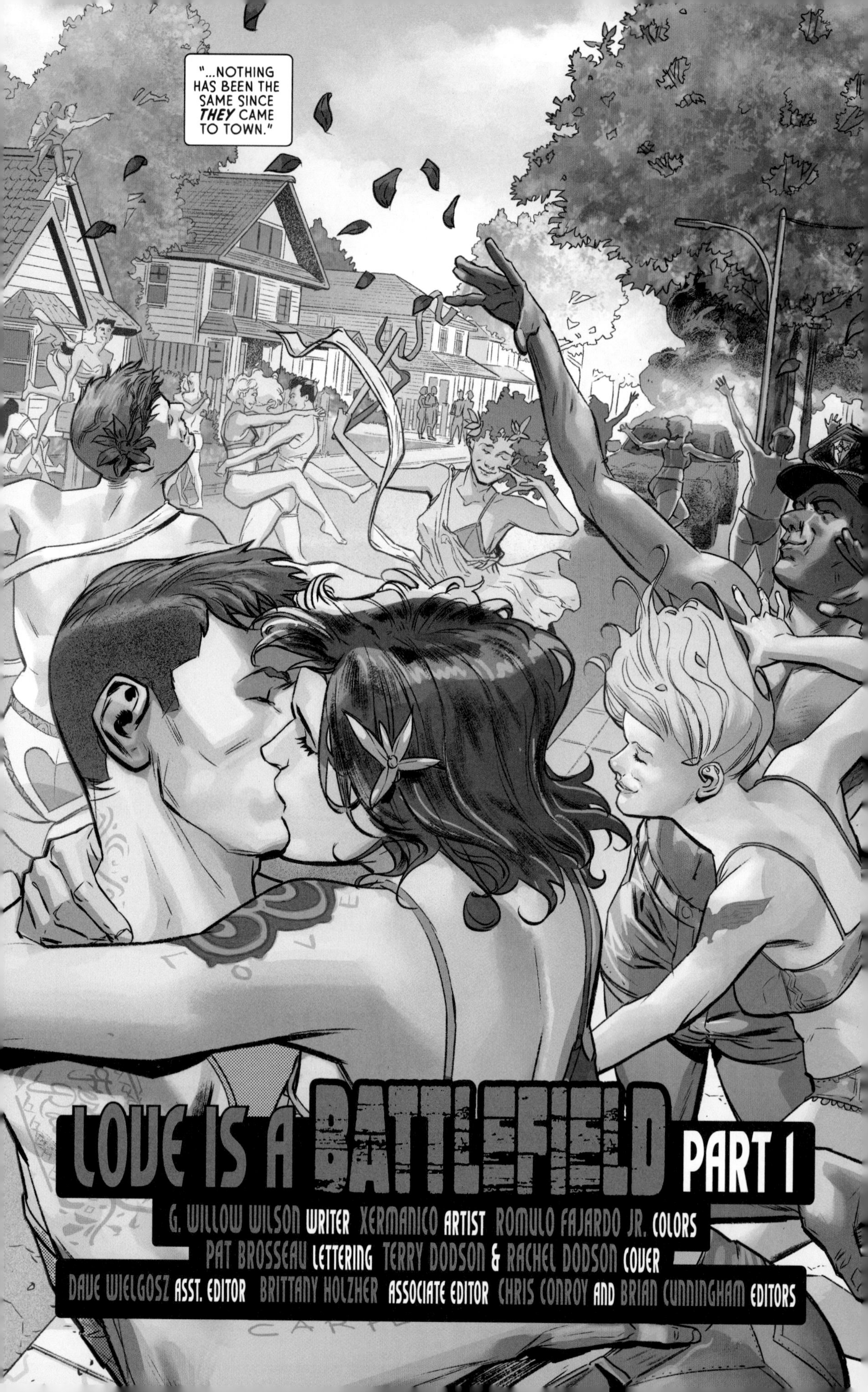
"...NOTHING HAS BEEN THE SAME SINCE *THEY* CAME TO TOWN."
LOVE IS A BATTLEFIELD PART 1
G. WILLOW WILSON WRITER XERMANICO ARTIST ROMULO FAJARDO JR. COLORS
PAT BROSSEAU LETTERING TERRY DODSON & RACHEL DODSON COVER
DAVE WIELGOSZ ASST. EDITOR BRITTANY HOLZHER ASSOCIATE EDITOR CHRIS CONROY AND BRIAN CUNNINGHAM EDITORS

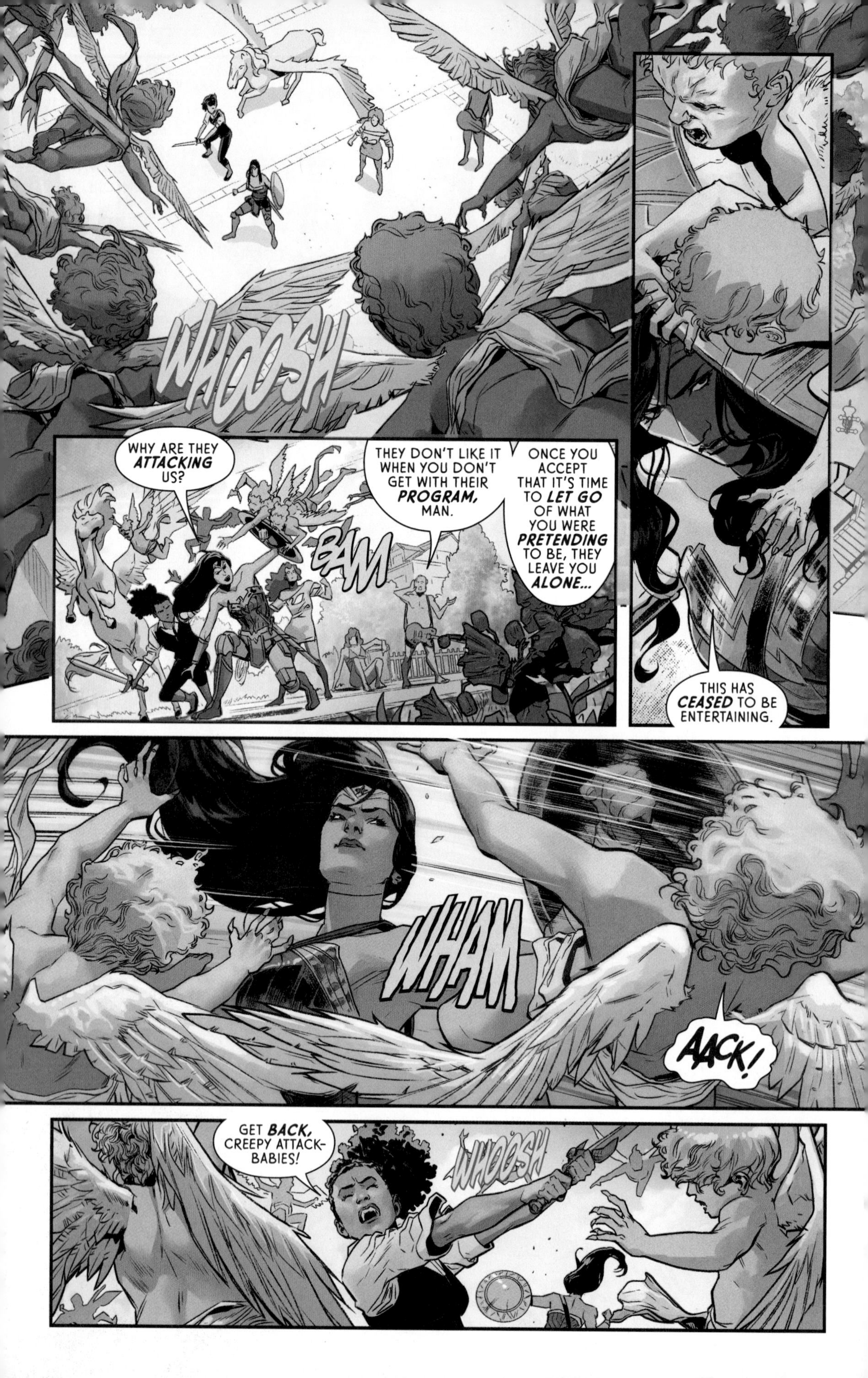
WHOOSH
WHY ARE THEY ATTACKING US?
BAM
THEY DON'T LIKE IT WHEN YOU DON'T GET WITH THEIR PROGRAM, MAN.
ONCE YOU ACCEPT THAT IT'S TIME TO LET GO OF WHAT YOU WERE PRETENDING TO BE, THEY LEAVE YOU ALONE...
THIS HAS CEASED TO BE ENTERTAINING.
WHAM
AACK!
GET BACK, CREEPY ATTACK-BABIES!
WHOOSH

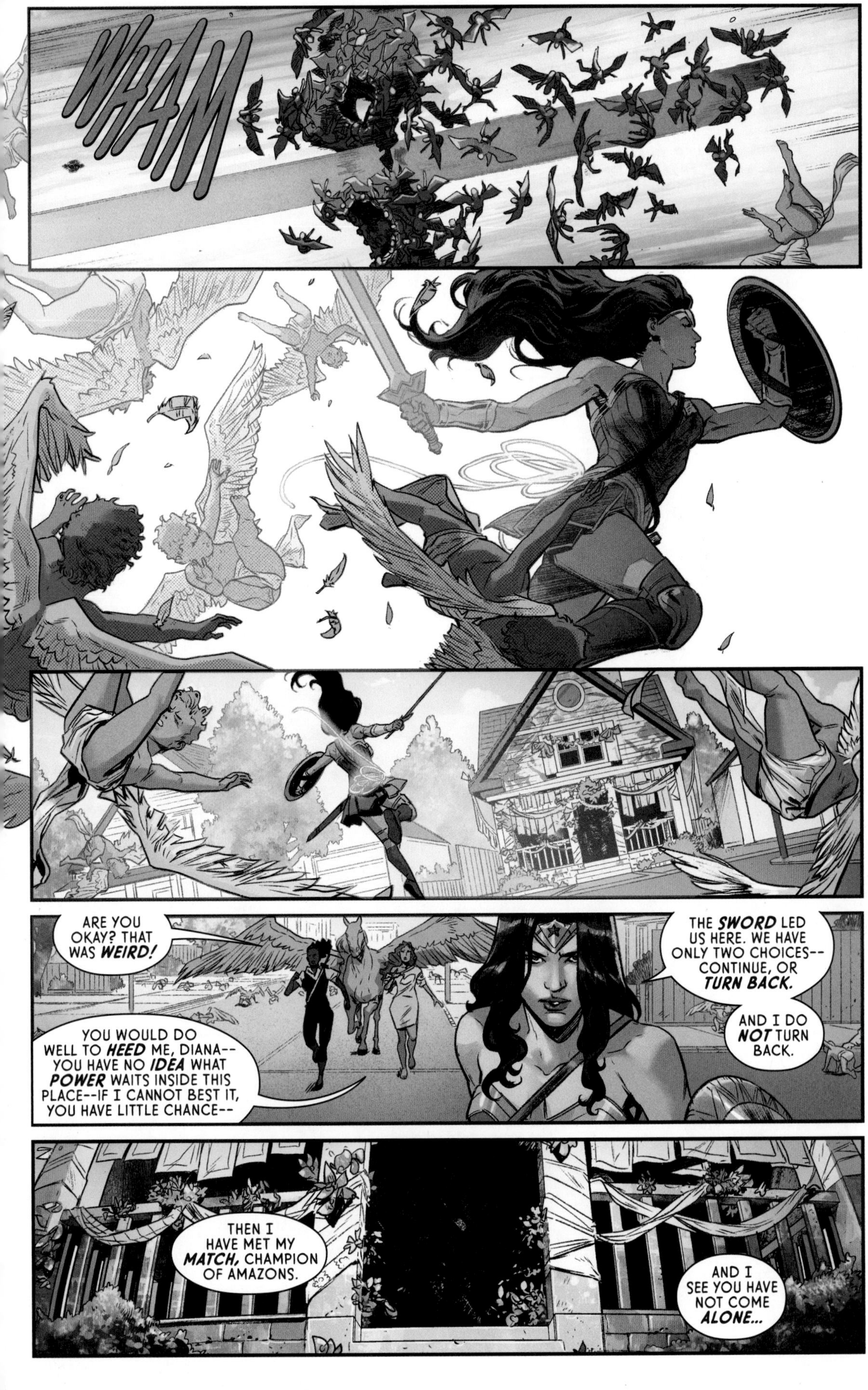
WHAM
ARE YOU OKAY? THAT WAS WEIRD!
THE SWORD LED US HERE. WE HAVE ONLY TWO CHOICES--CONTINUE, OR TURN BACK.
AND I DO NOT TURN BACK.
YOU WOULD DO WELL TO HEED ME, DIANA--YOU HAVE NO IDEA WHAT POWER WAITS INSIDE THIS PLACE--IF I CANNOT BEST IT, YOU HAVE LITTLE CHANCE--
THEN I HAVE MET MY MATCH, CHAMPION OF AMAZONS.
AND I SEE YOU HAVE NOT COME ALONE...

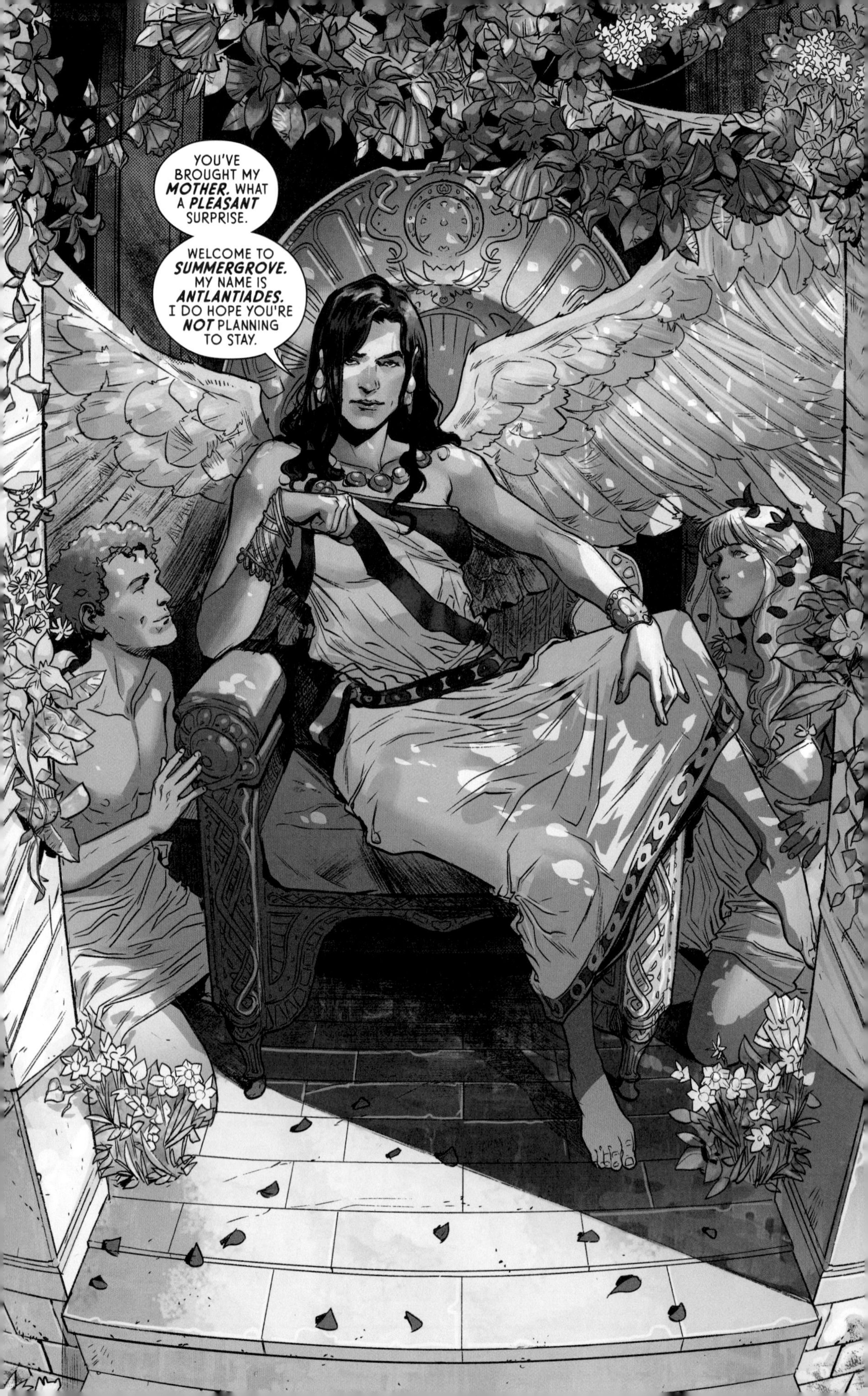

YOU'VE BROUGHT MY **MOTHER.** WHAT A **PLEASANT** SURPRISE.
WELCOME TO **SUMMERGROVE.** MY NAME IS **ANTLANTIADES.** I DO HOPE YOU'RE **NOT** PLANNING TO STAY.

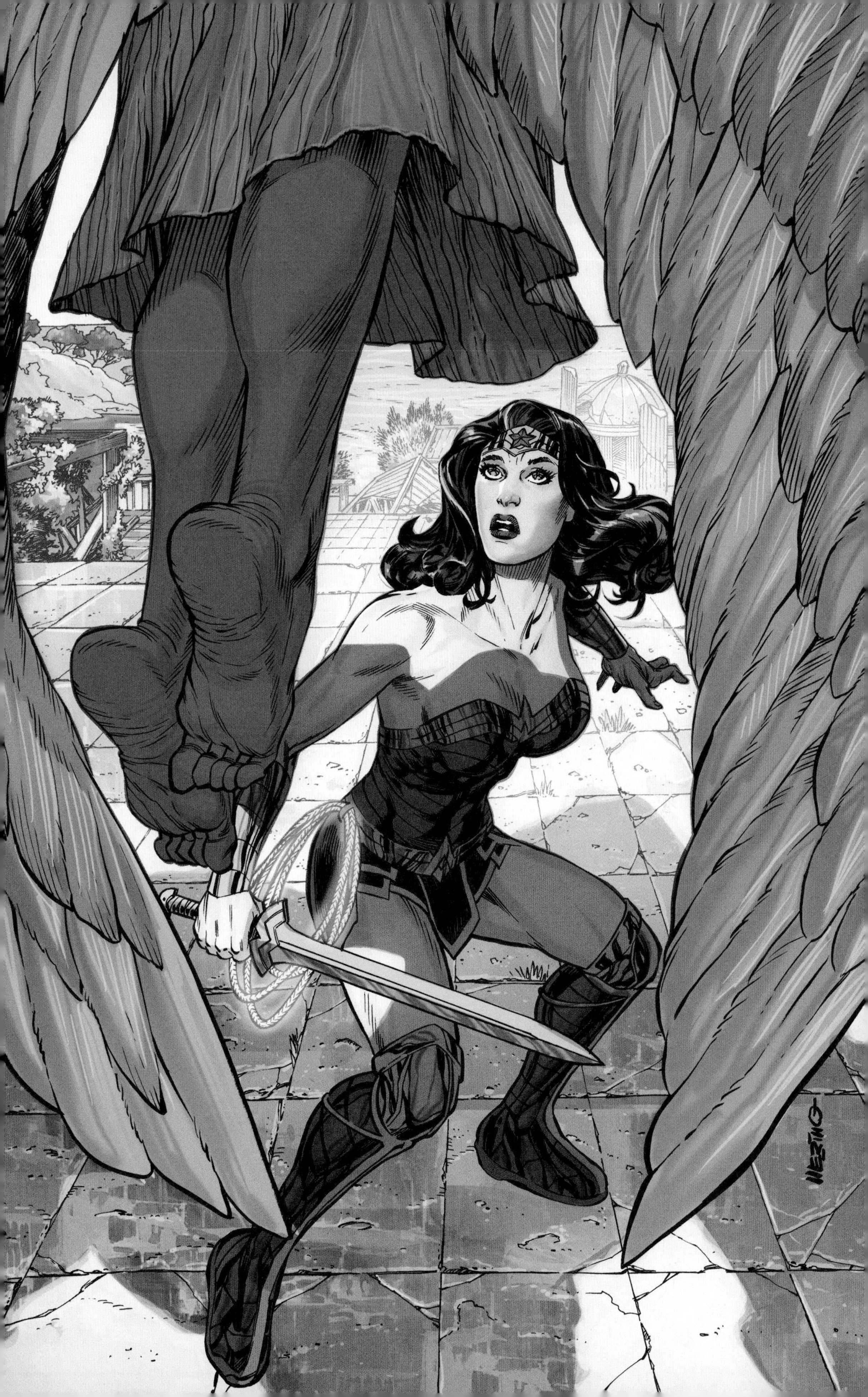

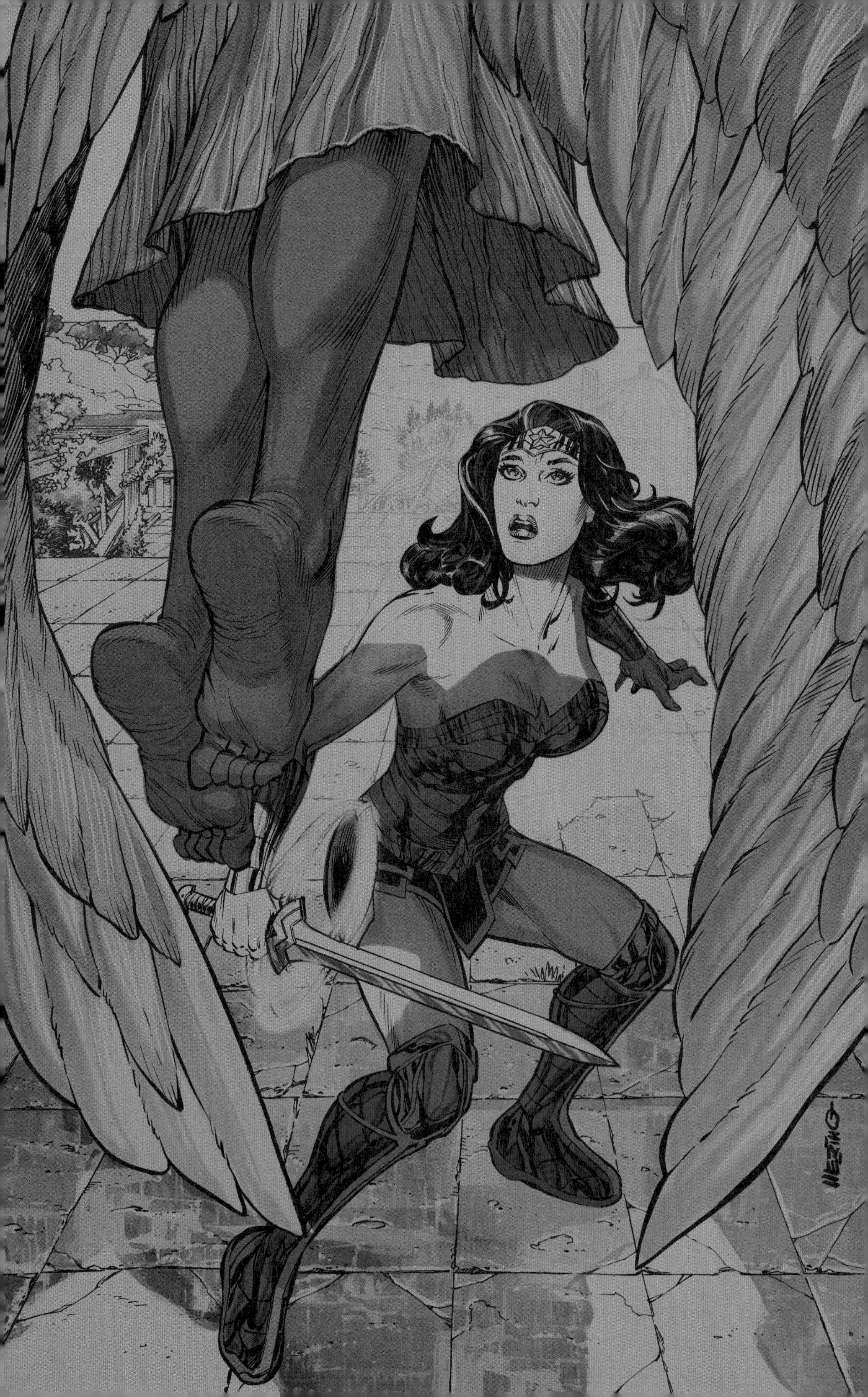

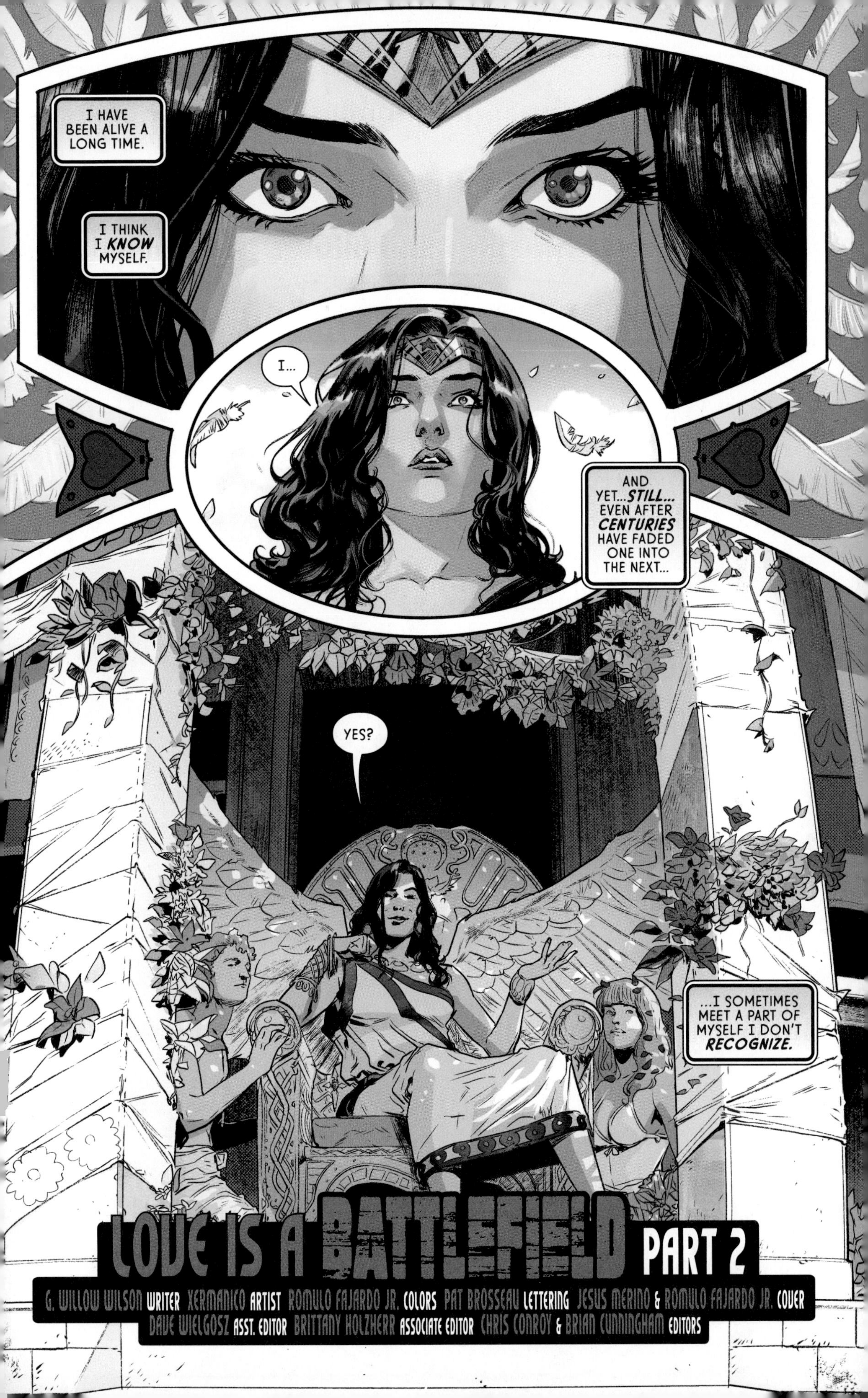

I HAVE BEEN ALIVE A LONG TIME.
I THINK I KNOW MYSELF.
I...
AND YET...STILL... EVEN AFTER CENTURIES HAVE FADED ONE INTO THE NEXT...
YES?
...I SOMETIMES MEET A PART OF MYSELF I DON'T RECOGNIZE.
LOVE IS A BATTLEFIELD PART 2
G. WILLOW WILSON WRITER XERMANICO ARTIST ROMULO FAJARDO JR. COLORS PAT BROSSEAU LETTERING JESUS MERINO & ROMULO FAJARDO JR. COVER
DAVE WIELGOSZ ASST. EDITOR BRITTANY HOLZHERR ASSOCIATE EDITOR CHRIS CONROY & BRIAN CUNNINGHAM EDITORS

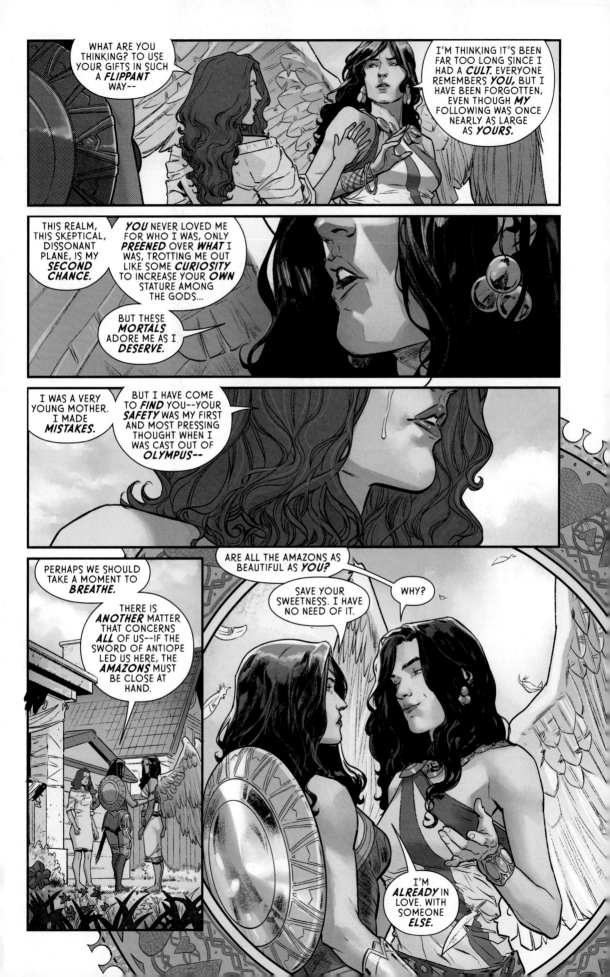

WHAT ARE YOU THINKING? TO USE YOUR GIFTS IN SUCH A *FLIPPANT* WAY--

I'M THINKING IT'S BEEN FAR TOO LONG SINCE I HAD A *CULT.* EVERYONE REMEMBERS *YOU,* BUT I HAVE BEEN FORGOTTEN, EVEN THOUGH *MY* FOLLOWING WAS ONCE NEARLY AS LARGE AS *YOURS.*

THIS REALM, THIS SKEPTICAL, DISSONANT PLANE, IS MY *SECOND CHANCE.*

YOU NEVER LOVED ME FOR WHO I WAS, ONLY *PREENED* OVER *WHAT* I WAS, TROTTING ME OUT LIKE SOME *CURIOSITY* TO INCREASE YOUR *OWN* STATURE AMONG THE GODS...

BUT THESE *MORTALS* ADORE ME AS I *DESERVE.*

I WAS A VERY YOUNG MOTHER. I MADE *MISTAKES.*

BUT I HAVE COME TO *FIND* YOU--YOUR *SAFETY* WAS MY FIRST AND MOST PRESSING THOUGHT WHEN I WAS CAST OUT OF *OLYMPUS*--

PERHAPS WE SHOULD TAKE A MOMENT TO *BREATHE.*

THERE IS *ANOTHER* MATTER THAT CONCERNS *ALL* OF US--IF THE SWORD OF ANTIOPE LED US HERE, THE *AMAZONS* MUST BE CLOSE AT HAND.

ARE ALL THE AMAZONS AS BEAUTIFUL AS *YOU?*

SAVE YOUR SWEETNESS. I HAVE NO NEED OF IT.

WHY?

I'M *ALREADY* IN LOVE. WITH SOMEONE *ELSE.*

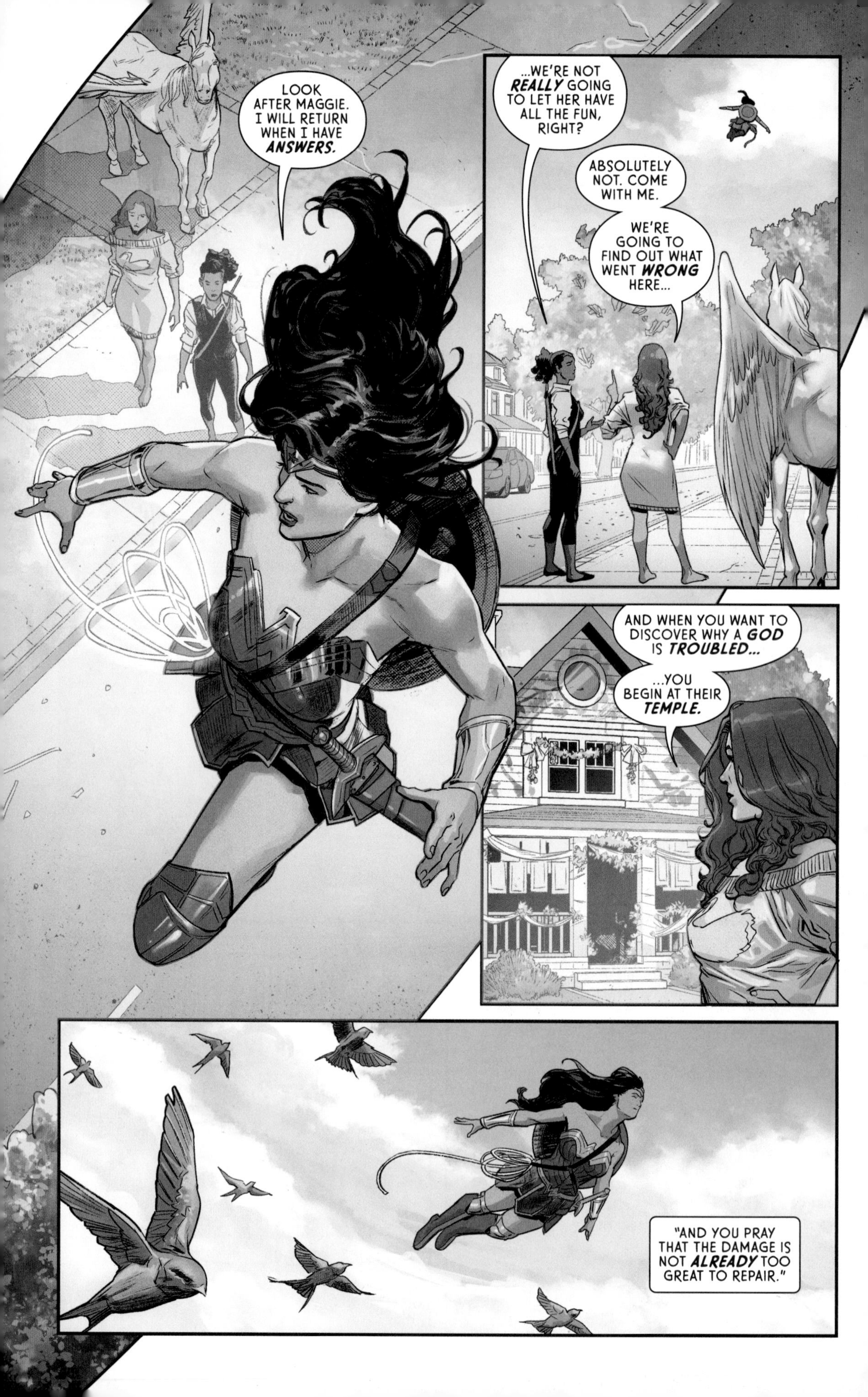
LOOK AFTER MAGGIE. I WILL RETURN WHEN I HAVE *ANSWERS.*
...WE'RE NOT *REALLY* GOING TO LET HER HAVE ALL THE FUN, RIGHT?
ABSOLUTELY NOT. COME WITH ME.
WE'RE GOING TO FIND OUT WHAT WENT *WRONG* HERE...
AND WHEN YOU WANT TO DISCOVER WHY A *GOD* IS *TROUBLED...*
...YOU BEGIN AT THEIR *TEMPLE.*
"AND YOU PRAY THAT THE DAMAGE IS NOT *ALREADY* TOO GREAT TO REPAIR."

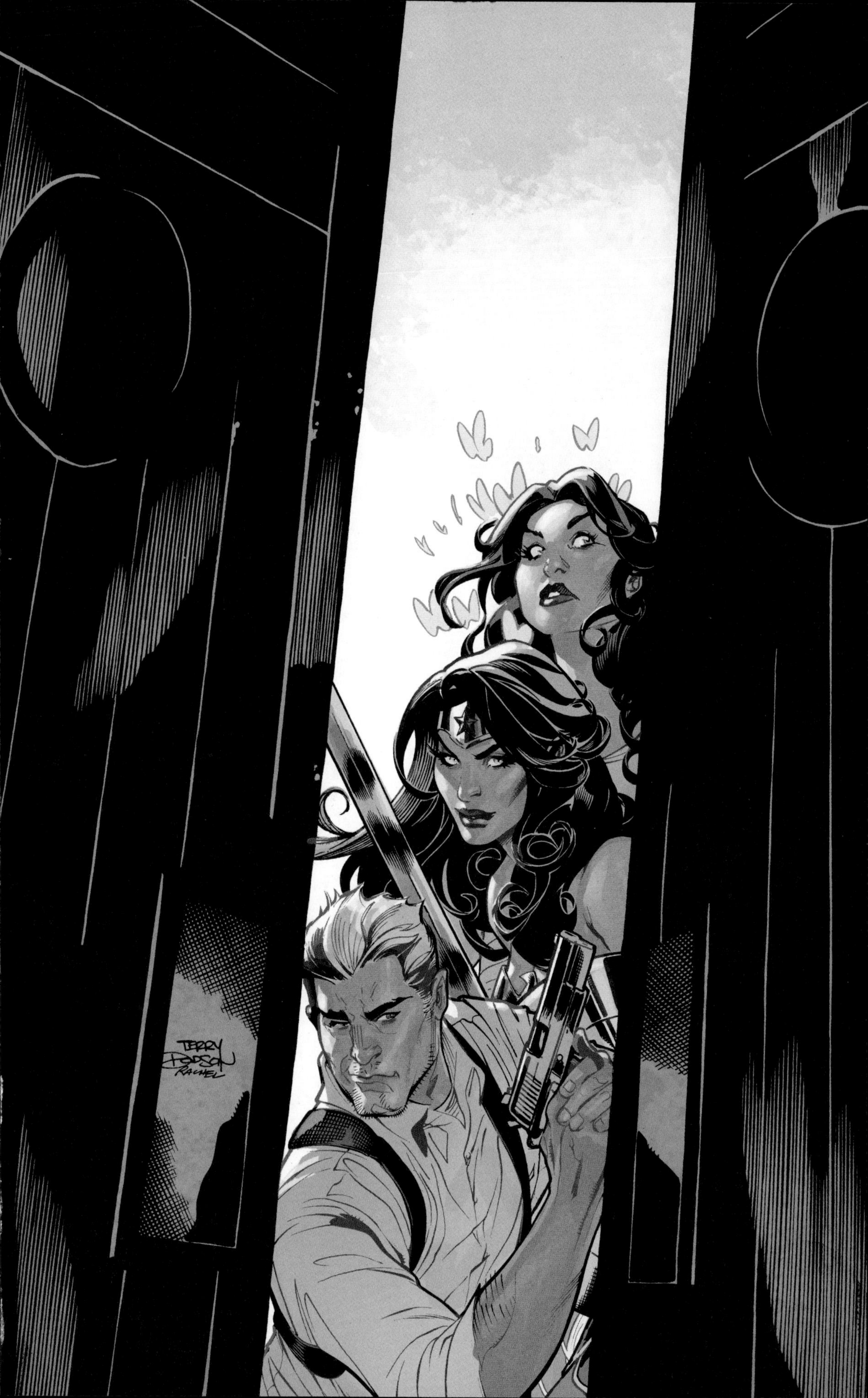
TERRY DODSON RACHEL

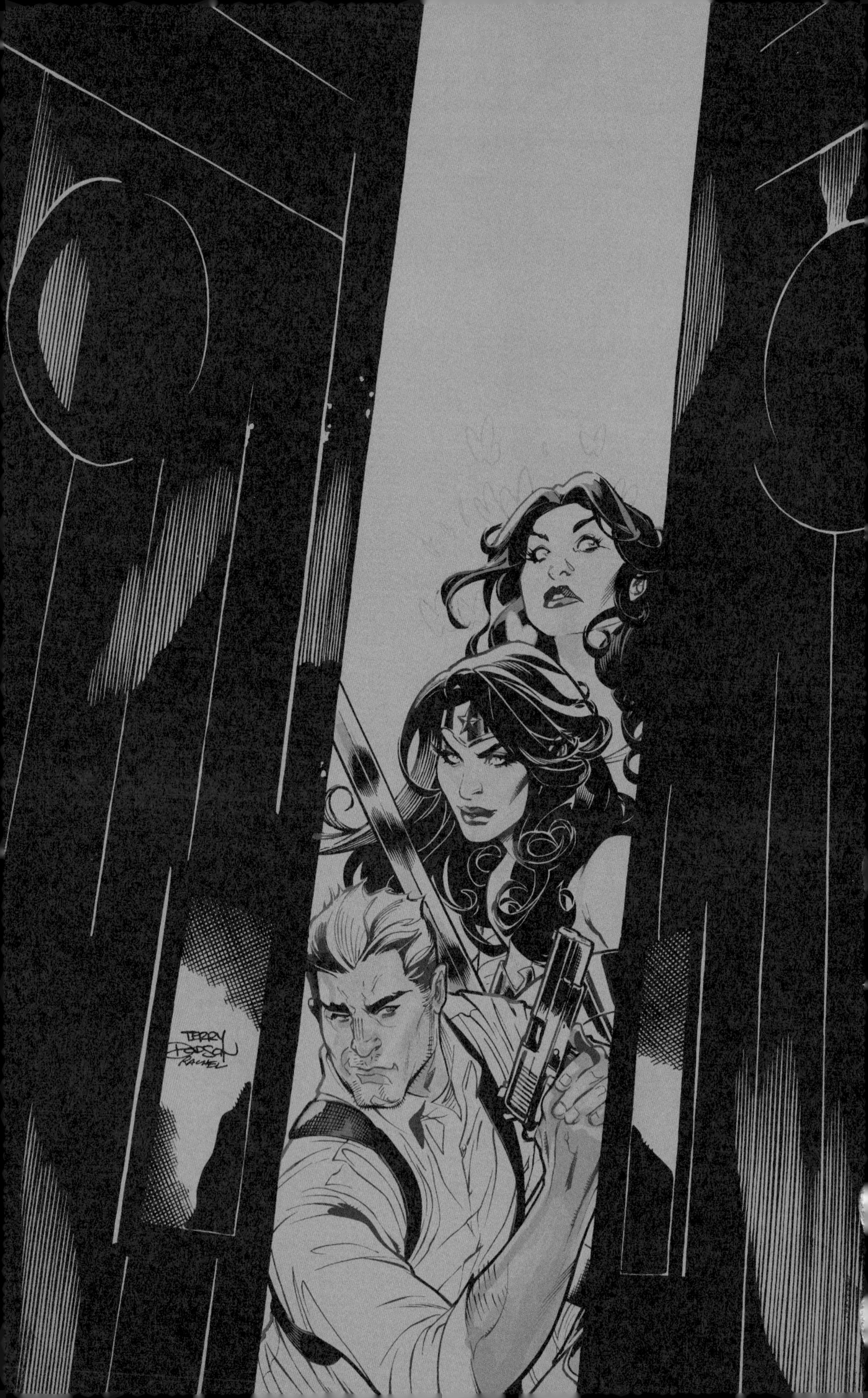
TERRY
DODSON
RACHEL

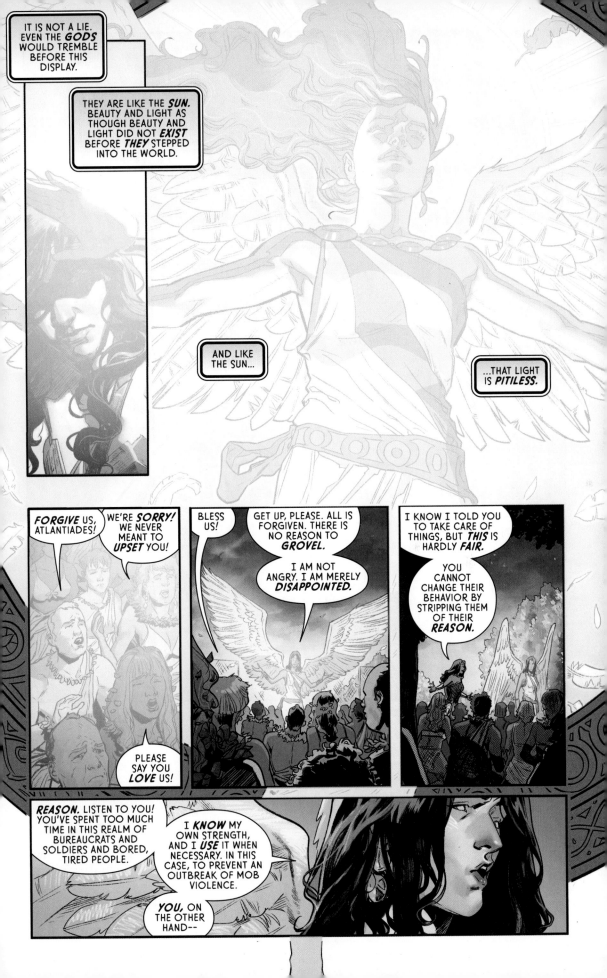

IT IS NOT A LIE. EVEN THE *GODS* WOULD TREMBLE BEFORE THIS DISPLAY.

THEY ARE LIKE THE *SUN.* BEAUTY AND LIGHT AS THOUGH BEAUTY AND LIGHT DID NOT *EXIST* BEFORE *THEY* STEPPED INTO THE WORLD.

AND LIKE THE SUN...

...THAT LIGHT IS *PITILESS.*

FORGIVE US, ATLANTIADES!

WE'RE *SORRY!* WE NEVER MEANT TO *UPSET* YOU!

PLEASE SAY YOU *LOVE* US!

BLESS US!

GET UP, PLEASE. ALL IS FORGIVEN. THERE IS NO REASON TO *GROVEL.*

I AM NOT ANGRY. I AM MERELY *DISAPPOINTED.*

I KNOW I TOLD YOU TO TAKE CARE OF THINGS, BUT *THIS* IS HARDLY *FAIR.*

YOU CANNOT CHANGE THEIR BEHAVIOR BY STRIPPING THEM OF THEIR *REASON.*

REASON. LISTEN TO YOU! YOU'VE SPENT TOO MUCH TIME IN THIS REALM OF BUREAUCRATS AND SOLDIERS AND BORED, TIRED PEOPLE.

I *KNOW* MY OWN STRENGTH, AND I *USE* IT WHEN NECESSARY. IN THIS CASE, TO PREVENT AN OUTBREAK OF MOB VIOLENCE.

YOU, ON THE OTHER HAND--

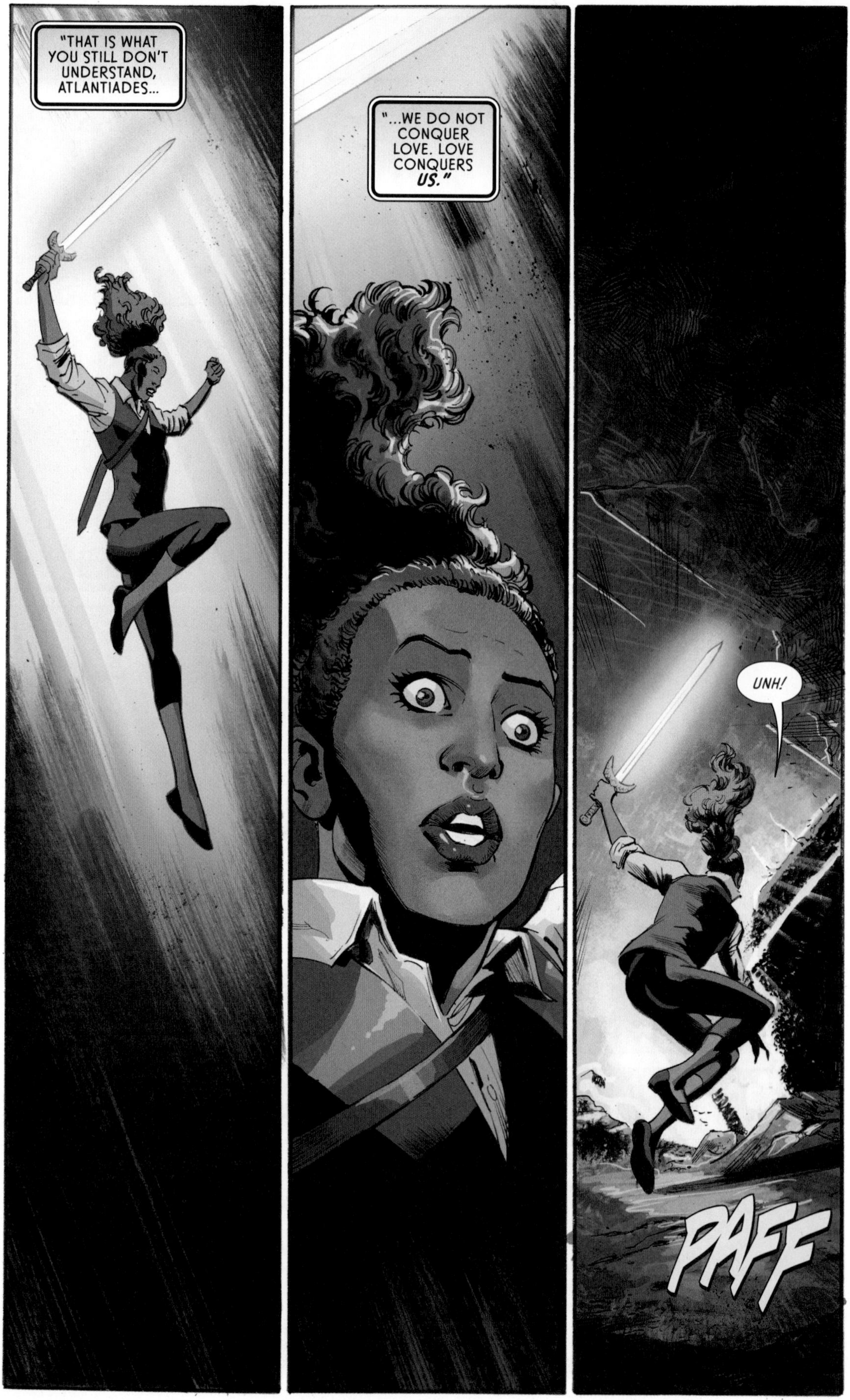
"THAT IS WHAT YOU STILL DON'T UNDERSTAND, ATLANTIADES...
"...WE DO NOT CONQUER LOVE. LOVE CONQUERS *US.*"
UNH!
PAFF

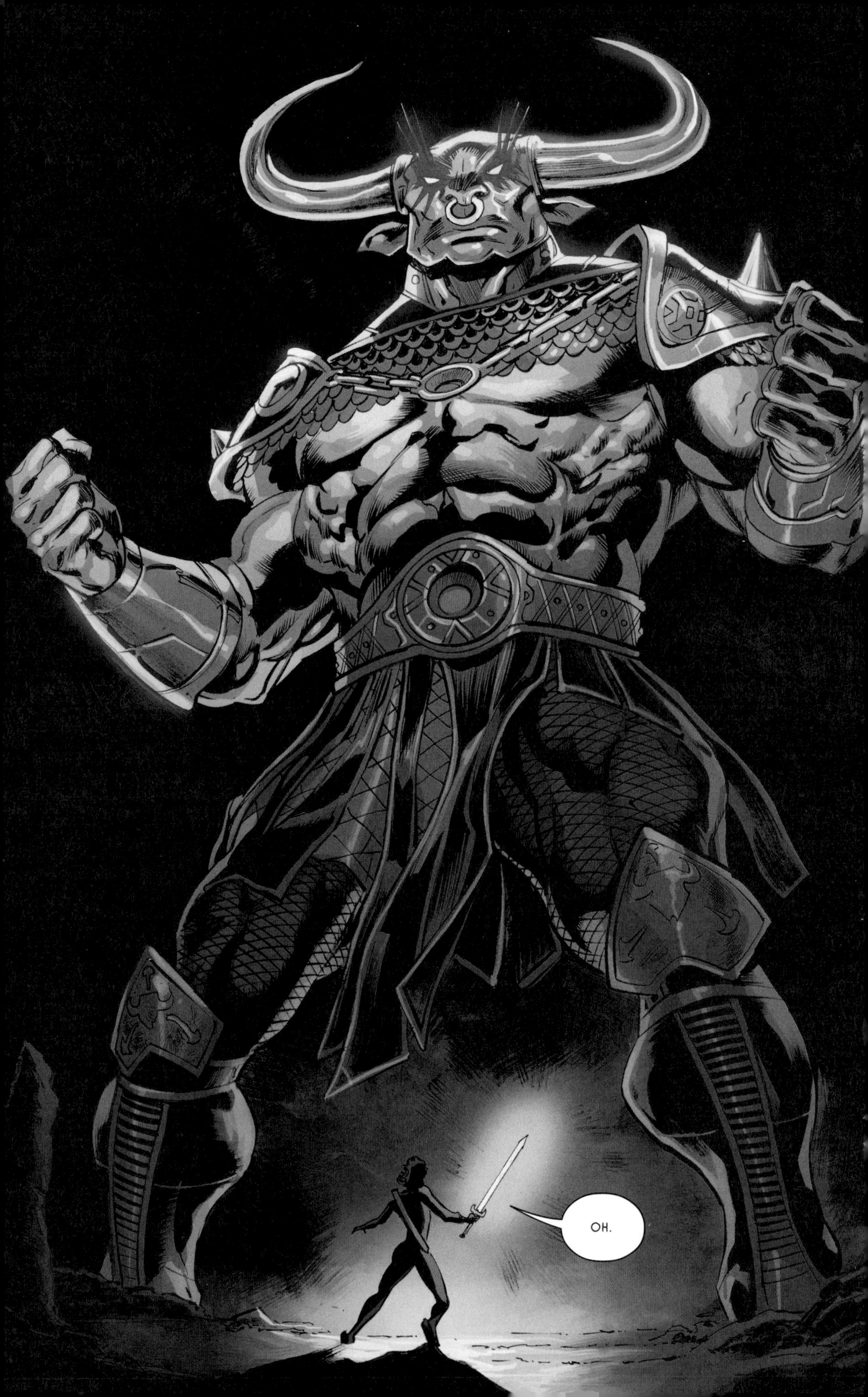
OH.

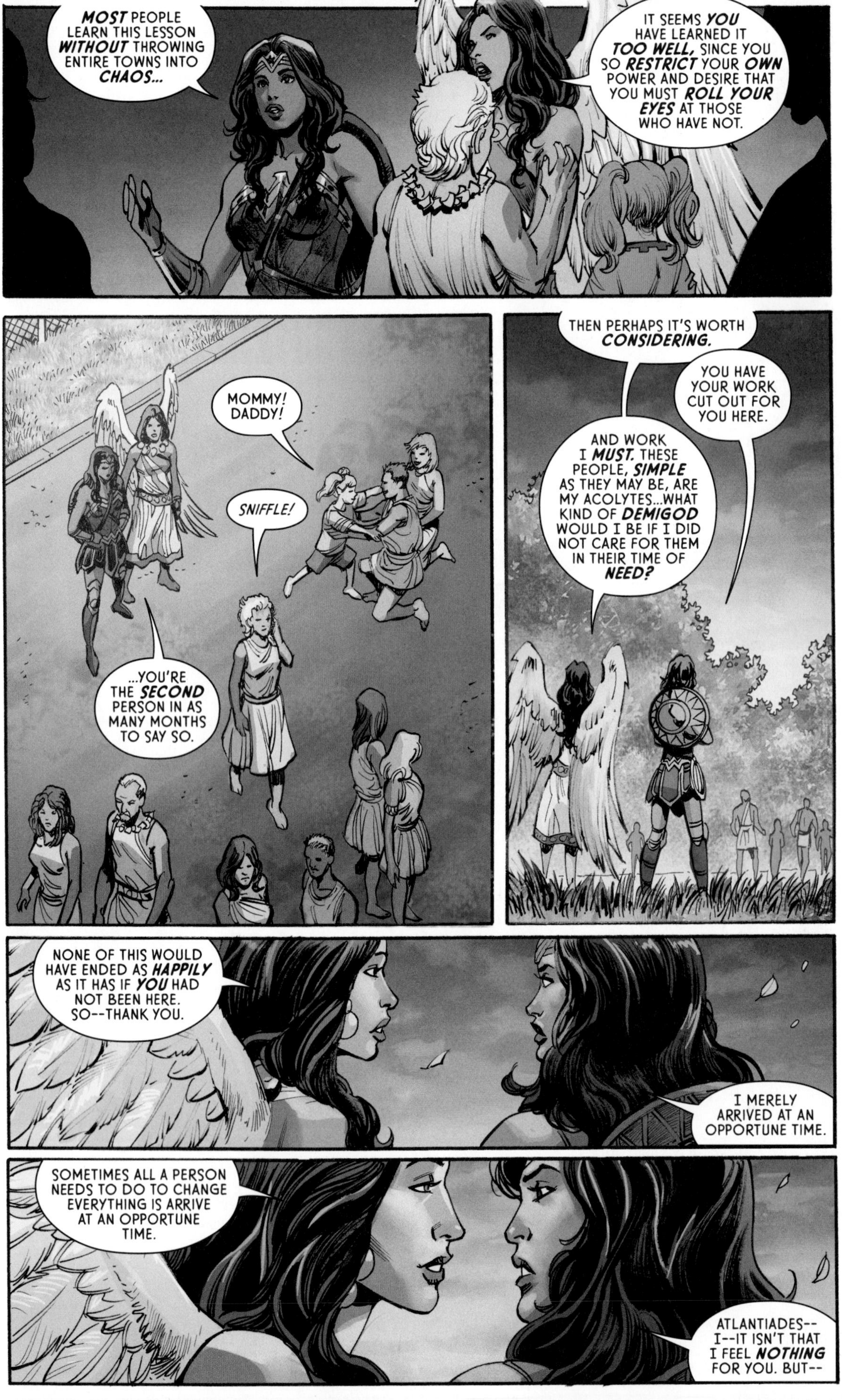
MOST PEOPLE LEARN THIS LESSON WITHOUT THROWING ENTIRE TOWNS INTO CHAOS...
IT SEEMS YOU HAVE LEARNED IT TOO WELL, SINCE YOU SO RESTRICT YOUR OWN POWER AND DESIRE THAT YOU MUST ROLL YOUR EYES AT THOSE WHO HAVE NOT.
MOMMY! DADDY!
SNIFFLE!
...YOU'RE THE SECOND PERSON IN AS MANY MONTHS TO SAY SO.
THEN PERHAPS IT'S WORTH CONSIDERING.
YOU HAVE YOUR WORK CUT OUT FOR YOU HERE.
AND WORK I MUST. THESE PEOPLE, SIMPLE AS THEY MAY BE, ARE MY ACOLYTES...WHAT KIND OF DEMIGOD WOULD I BE IF I DID NOT CARE FOR THEM IN THEIR TIME OF NEED?
NONE OF THIS WOULD HAVE ENDED AS HAPPILY AS IT HAS IF YOU HAD NOT BEEN HERE. SO--THANK YOU.
I MERELY ARRIVED AT AN OPPORTUNE TIME.
SOMETIMES ALL A PERSON NEEDS TO DO TO CHANGE EVERYTHING IS ARRIVE AT AN OPPORTUNE TIME.
ATLANTIADES-- I--IT ISN'T THAT I FEEL NOTHING FOR YOU. BUT--

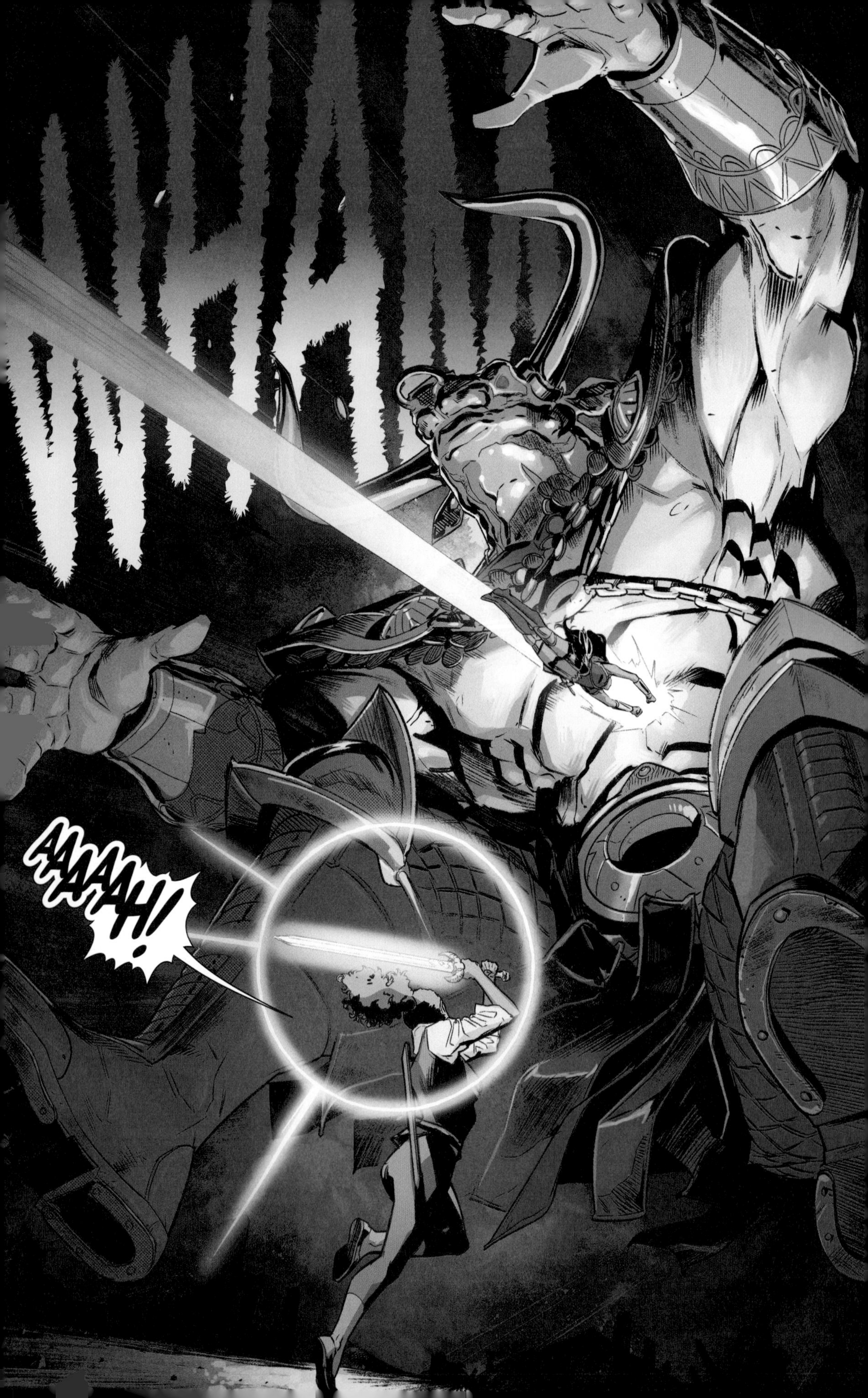
AAAAAH!

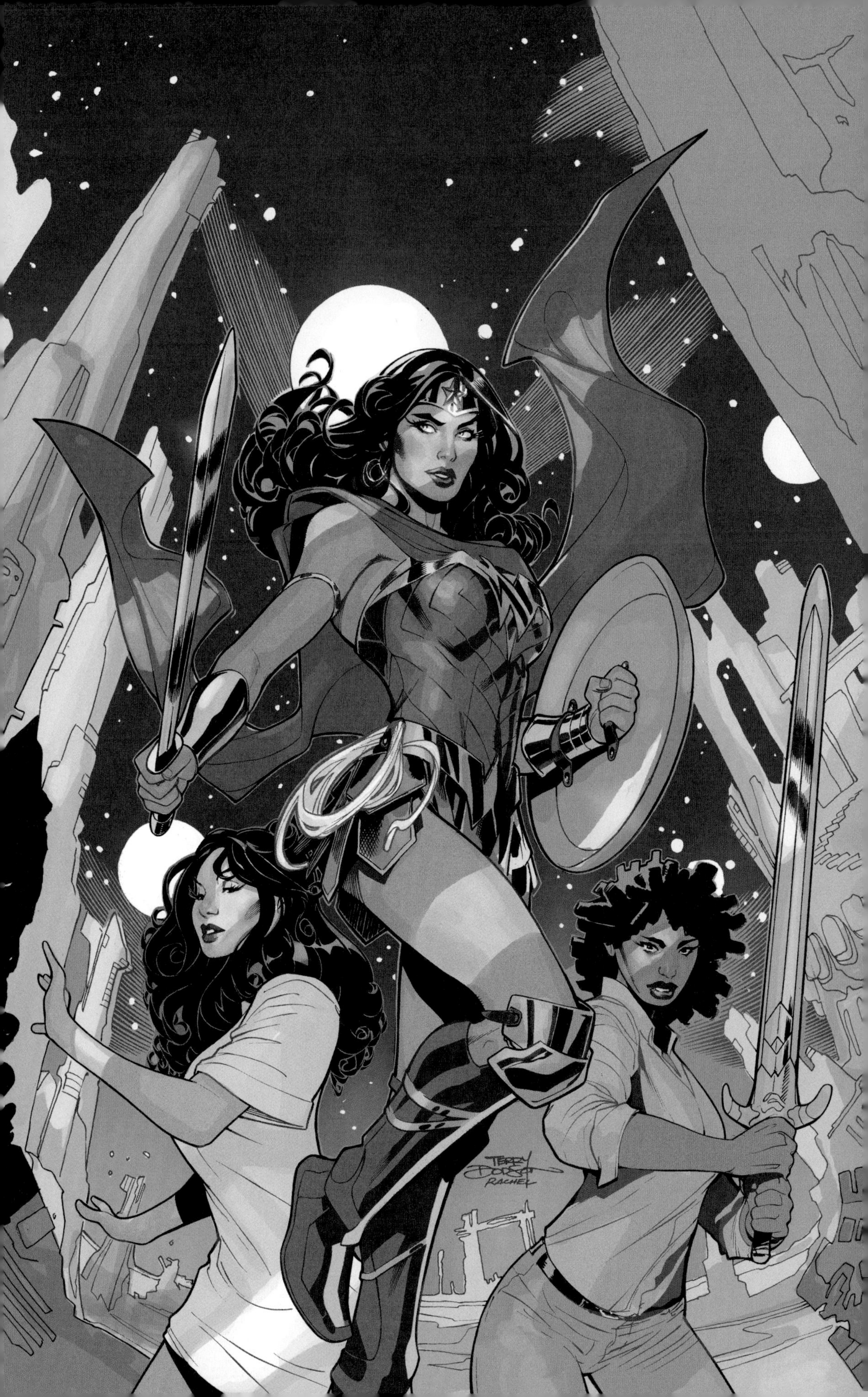
TERRY
DODSON
RACHEL

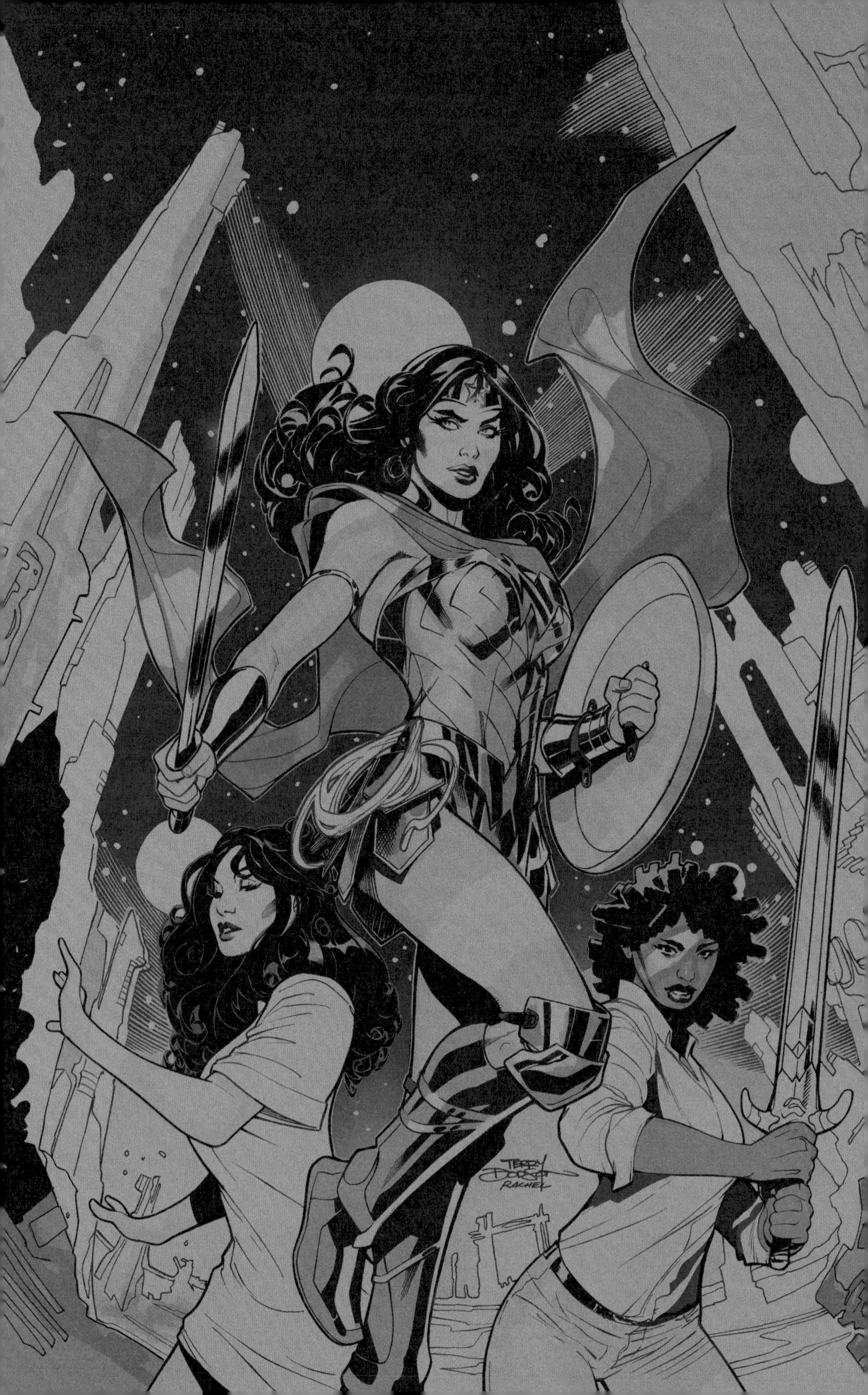

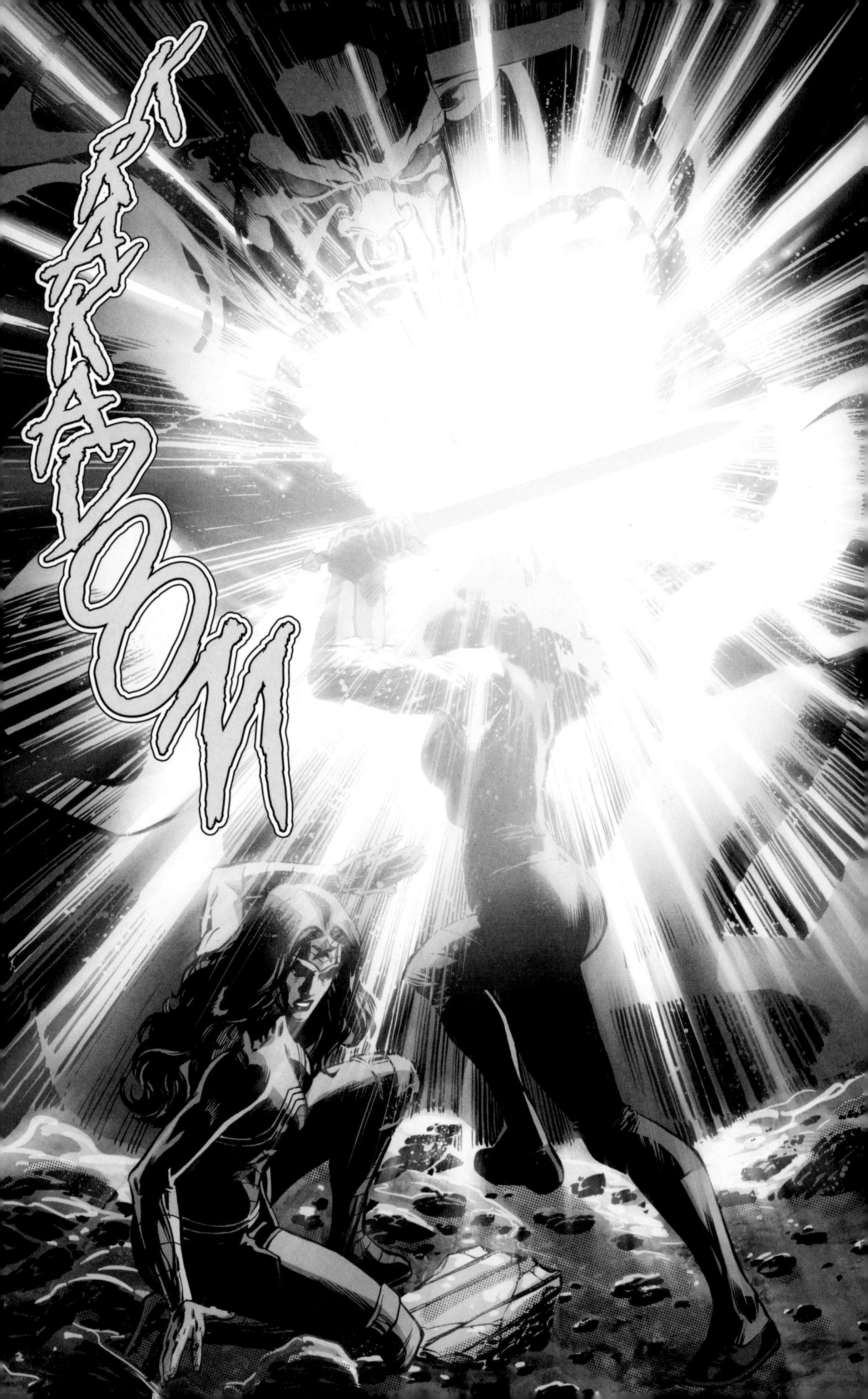
KRAKADOOM

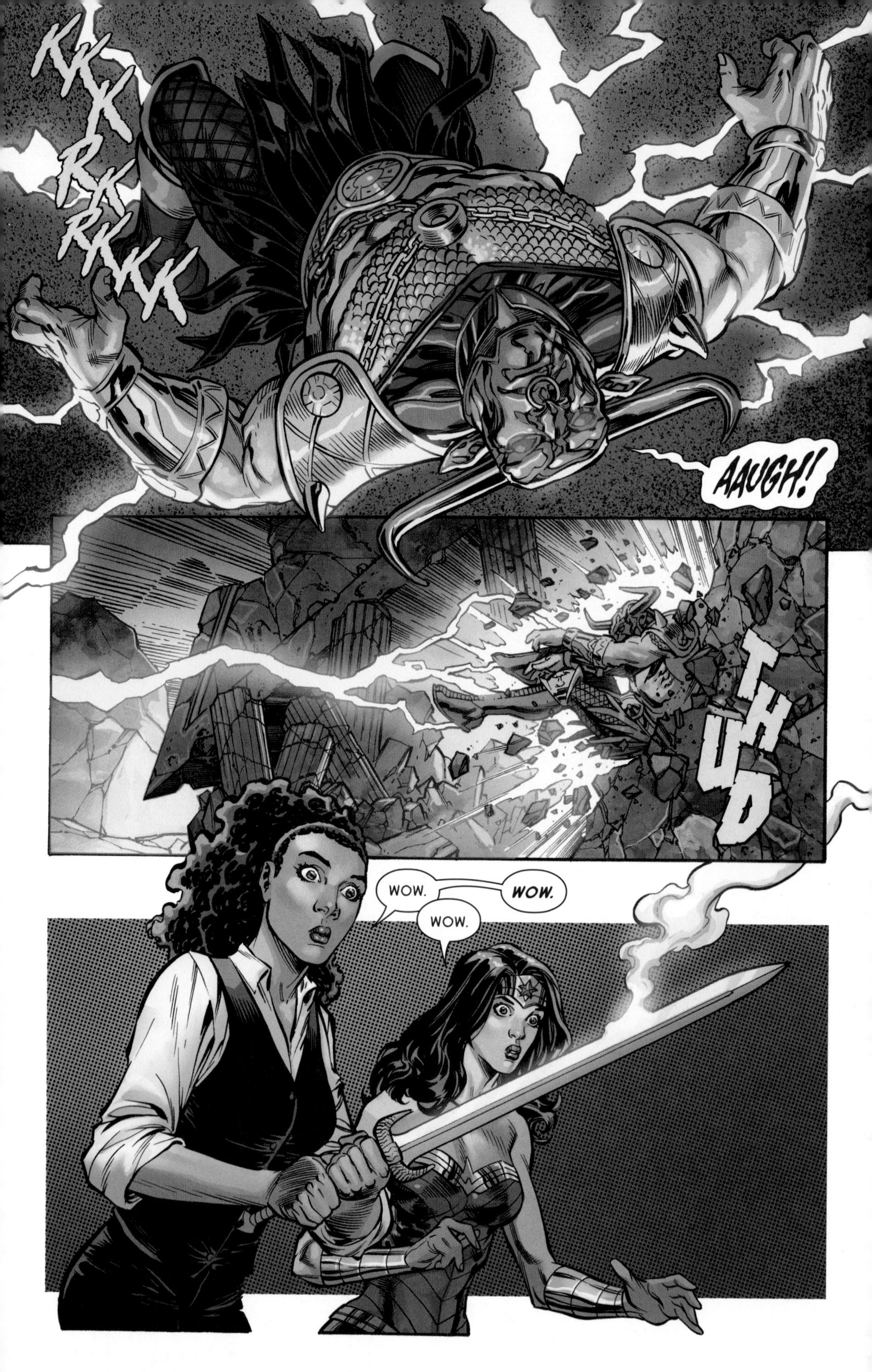
KKKRRRKKKK
AAUGH!
THUD
WOW.
WOW.
WOW.

LOVE IS A BATTLEFIELD FINALE

G. WILLOW WILSON WRITER JESUS MERINO & TOM DERENICK PENCILLERS

J. MERINO & SCOTT HANNA INKERS ROMULO FAJARDO JR. COLORS PAT BROSSEAU LETTERING

TERRY & RACHEL DODSON COVER BRITTANY HOLZHERR ASSOCIATE EDITOR

BRIAN CUNNINGHAM EDITOR

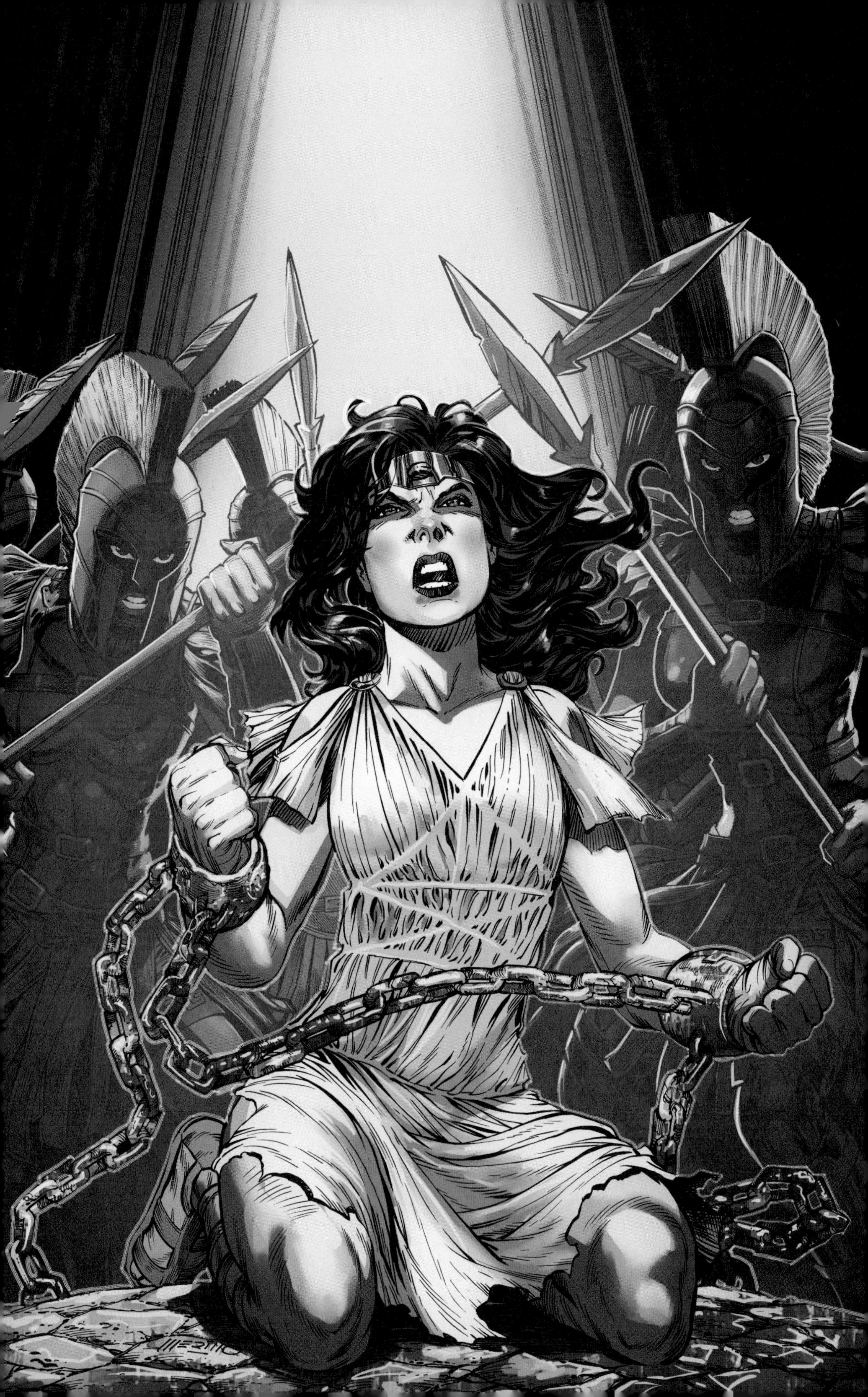

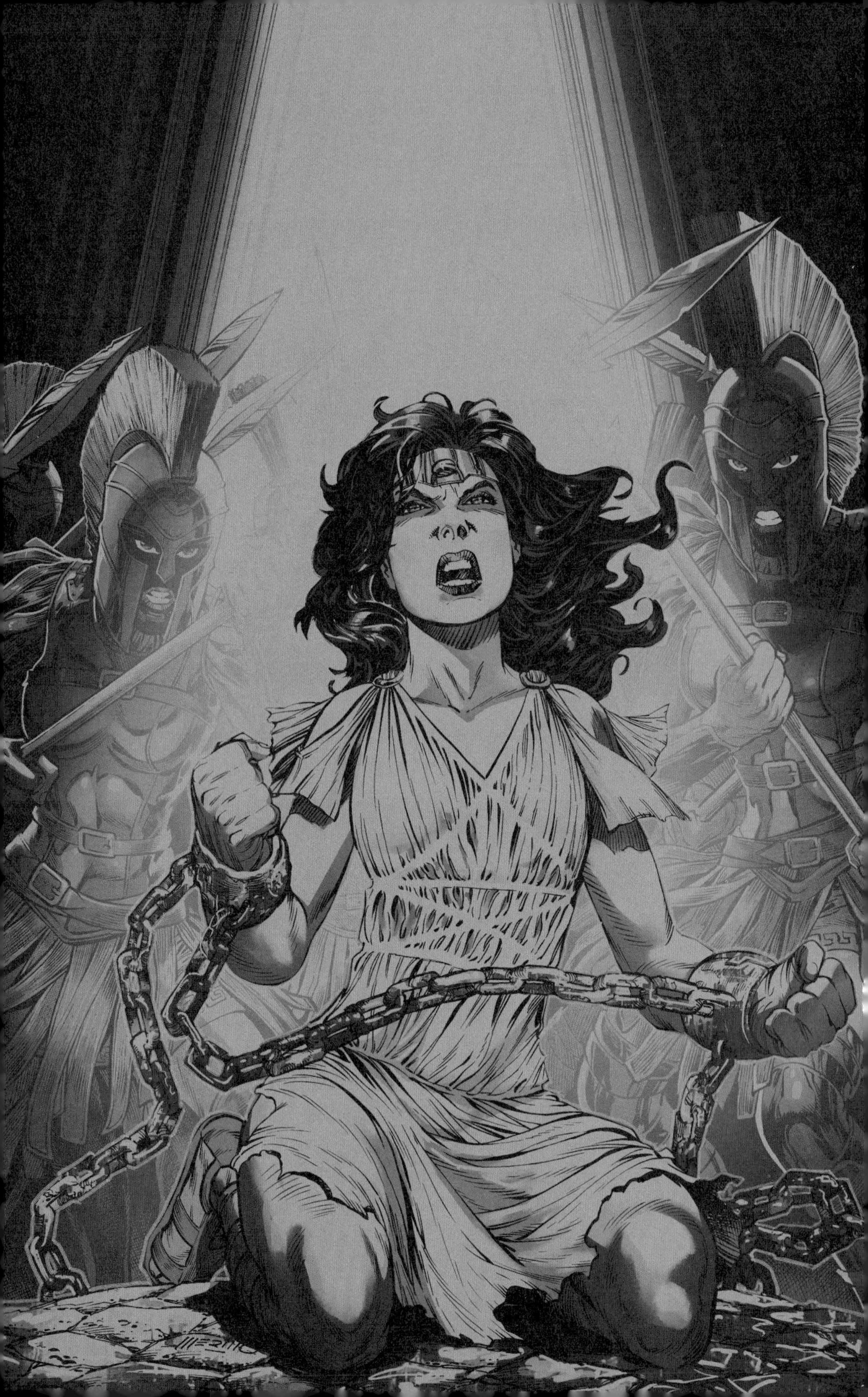

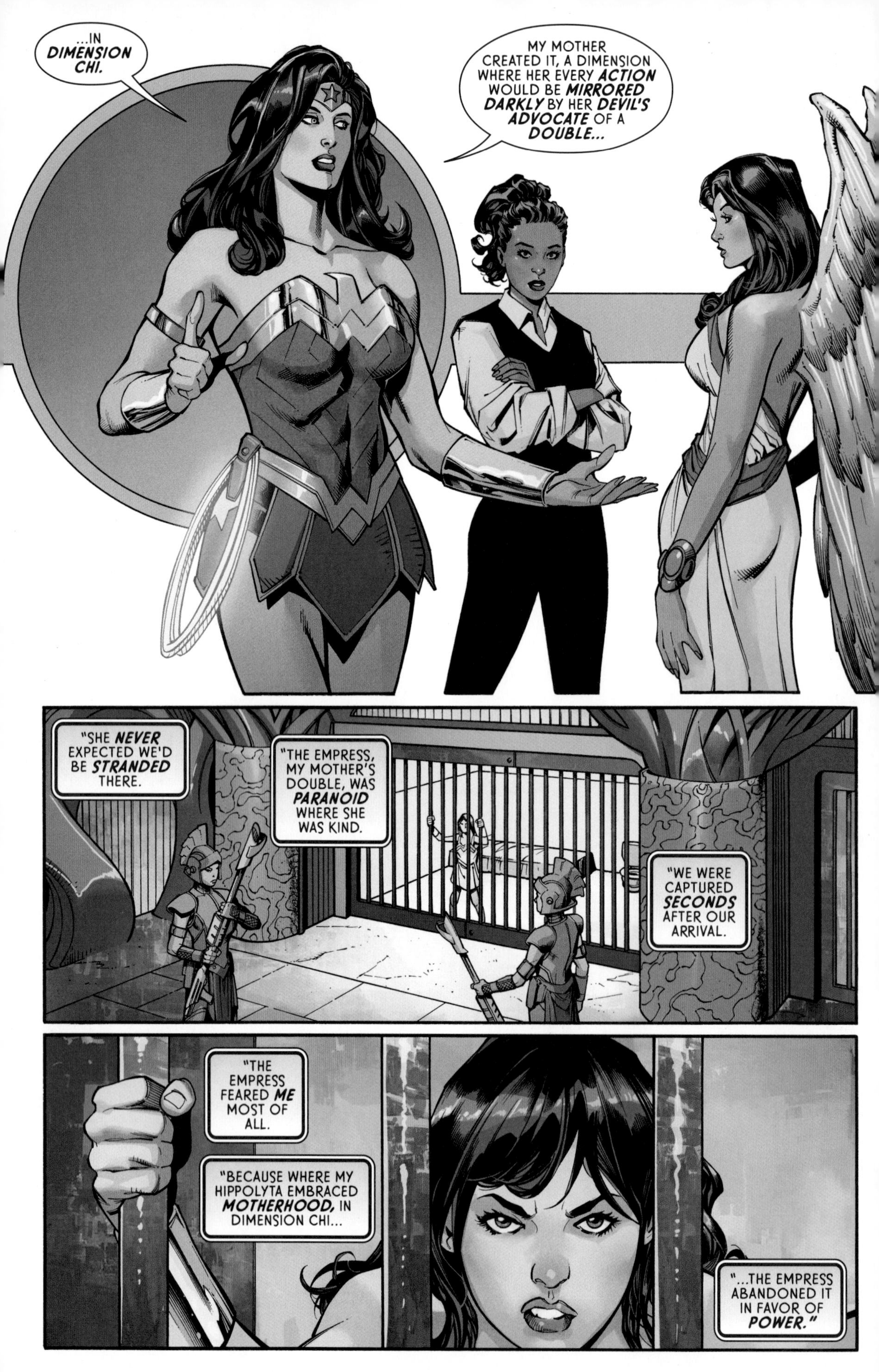
...IN DIMENSION CHI.
MY MOTHER CREATED IT, A DIMENSION WHERE HER EVERY ACTION WOULD BE MIRRORED DARKLY BY HER DEVIL'S ADVOCATE OF A DOUBLE...
"SHE NEVER EXPECTED WE'D BE STRANDED THERE.
"THE EMPRESS, MY MOTHER'S DOUBLE, WAS PARANOID WHERE SHE WAS KIND.
"WE WERE CAPTURED SECONDS AFTER OUR ARRIVAL.
"THE EMPRESS FEARED ME MOST OF ALL.
"BECAUSE WHERE MY HIPPOLYTA EMBRACED MOTHERHOOD, IN DIMENSION CHI...
"...THE EMPRESS ABANDONED IT IN FAVOR OF POWER."

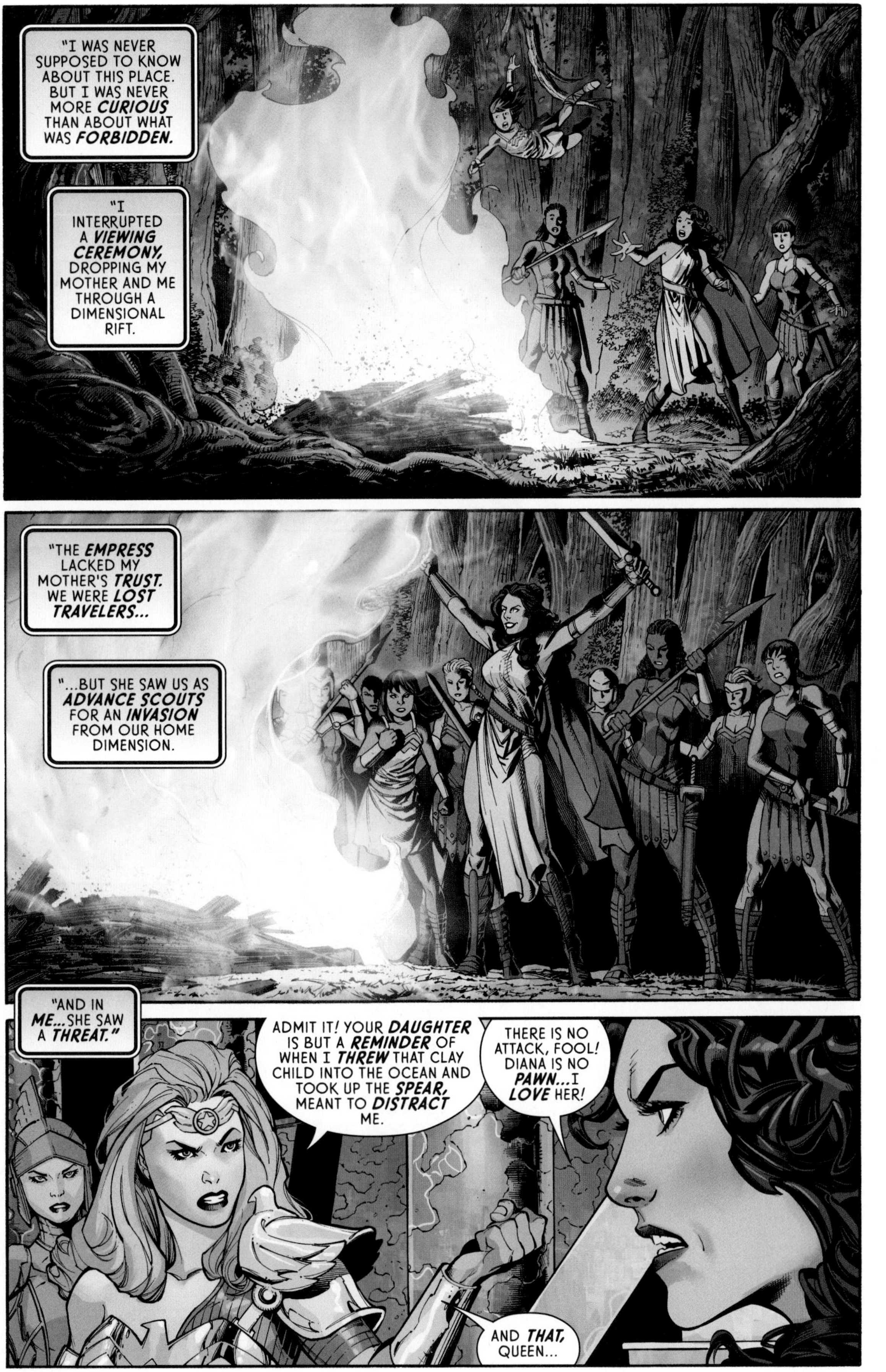
"I WAS NEVER SUPPOSED TO KNOW ABOUT THIS PLACE. BUT I WAS NEVER MORE CURIOUS THAN ABOUT WHAT WAS FORBIDDEN.
"I INTERRUPTED A VIEWING CEREMONY, DROPPING MY MOTHER AND ME THROUGH A DIMENSIONAL RIFT.
"THE EMPRESS LACKED MY MOTHER'S TRUST. WE WERE LOST TRAVELERS...
"...BUT SHE SAW US AS ADVANCE SCOUTS FOR AN INVASION FROM OUR HOME DIMENSION.
"AND IN ME...SHE SAW A THREAT."
ADMIT IT! YOUR DAUGHTER IS BUT A REMINDER OF WHEN I THREW THAT CLAY CHILD INTO THE OCEAN AND TOOK UP THE SPEAR, MEANT TO DISTRACT ME.
THERE IS NO ATTACK, FOOL! DIANA IS NO PAWN...I LOVE HER!
AND THAT, QUEEN...

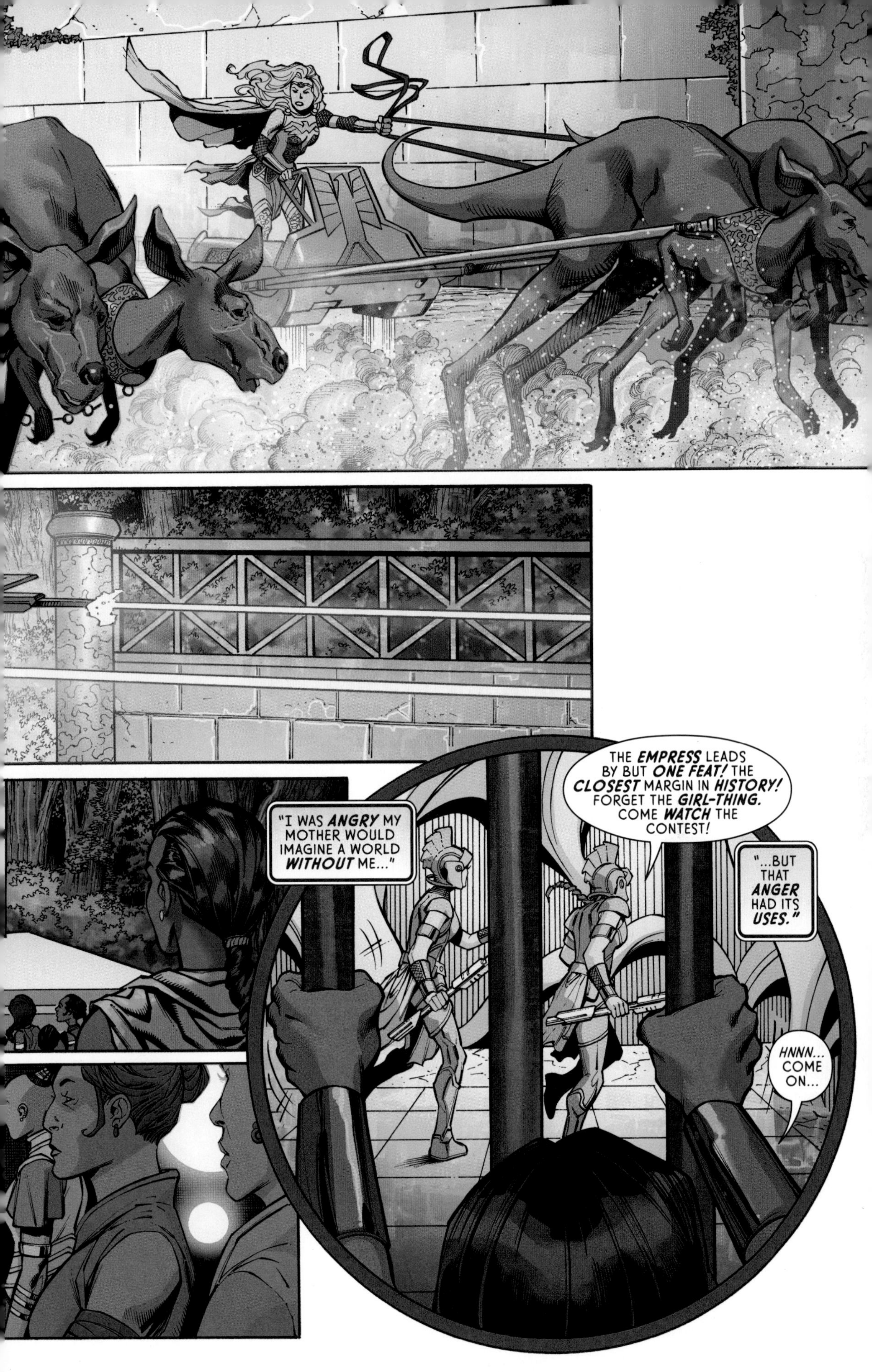
"I WAS ANGRY MY MOTHER WOULD IMAGINE A WORLD WITHOUT ME..."
THE EMPRESS LEADS BY BUT ONE FEAT! THE CLOSEST MARGIN IN HISTORY! FORGET THE GIRL-THING. COME WATCH THE CONTEST!
"...BUT THAT ANGER HAD ITS USES."
HNNN... COME ON...

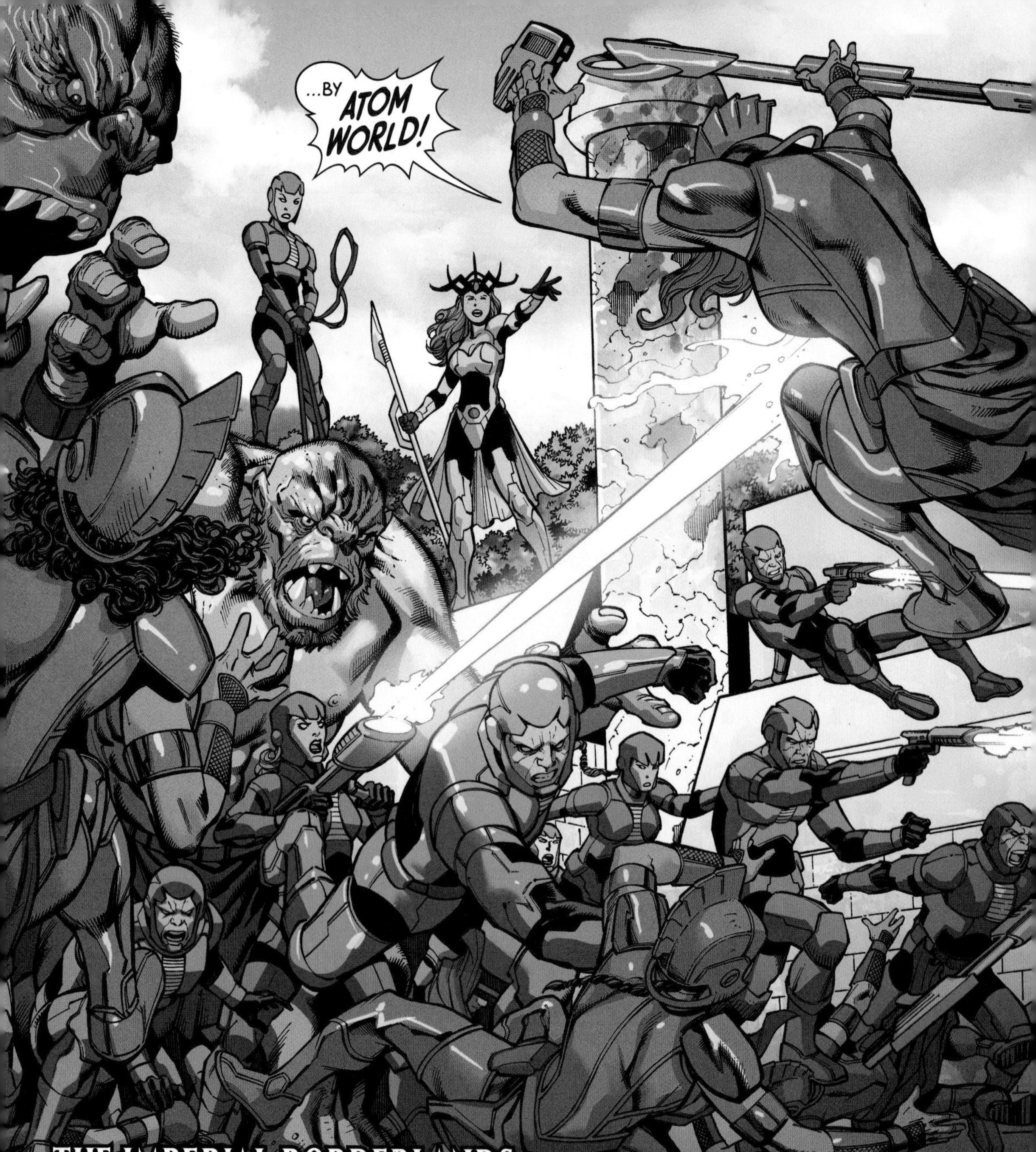
...BY ATOM WORLD!
THE IMPERIAL BORDERLANDS.

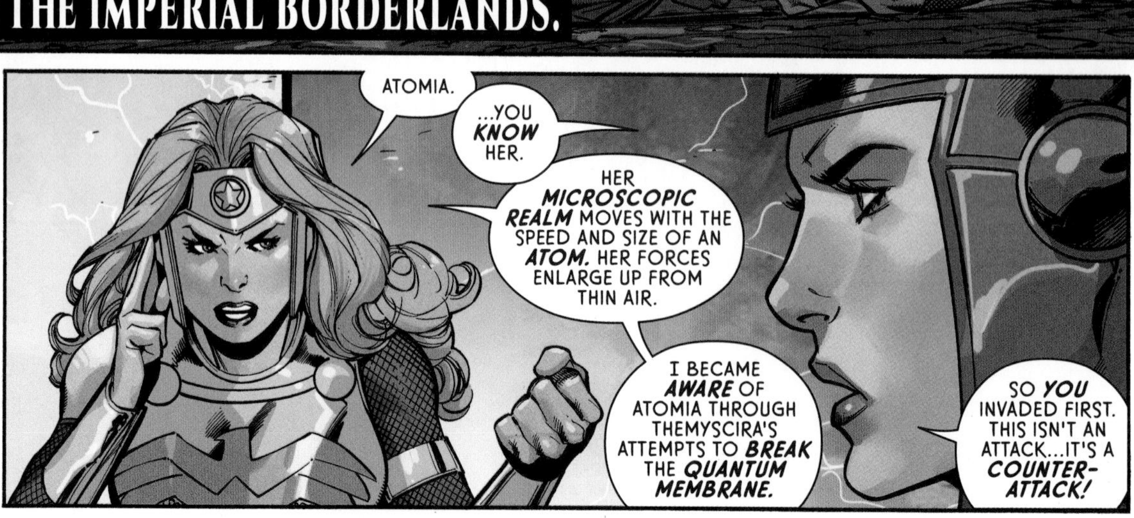
ATOMIA.
...YOU KNOW HER.
HER MICROSCOPIC REALM MOVES WITH THE SPEED AND SIZE OF AN ATOM. HER FORCES ENLARGE UP FROM THIN AIR.
I BECAME AWARE OF ATOMIA THROUGH THEMYSCIRA'S ATTEMPTS TO BREAK THE QUANTUM MEMBRANE.
SO YOU INVADED FIRST. THIS ISN'T AN ATTACK...IT'S A COUNTER-ATTACK!

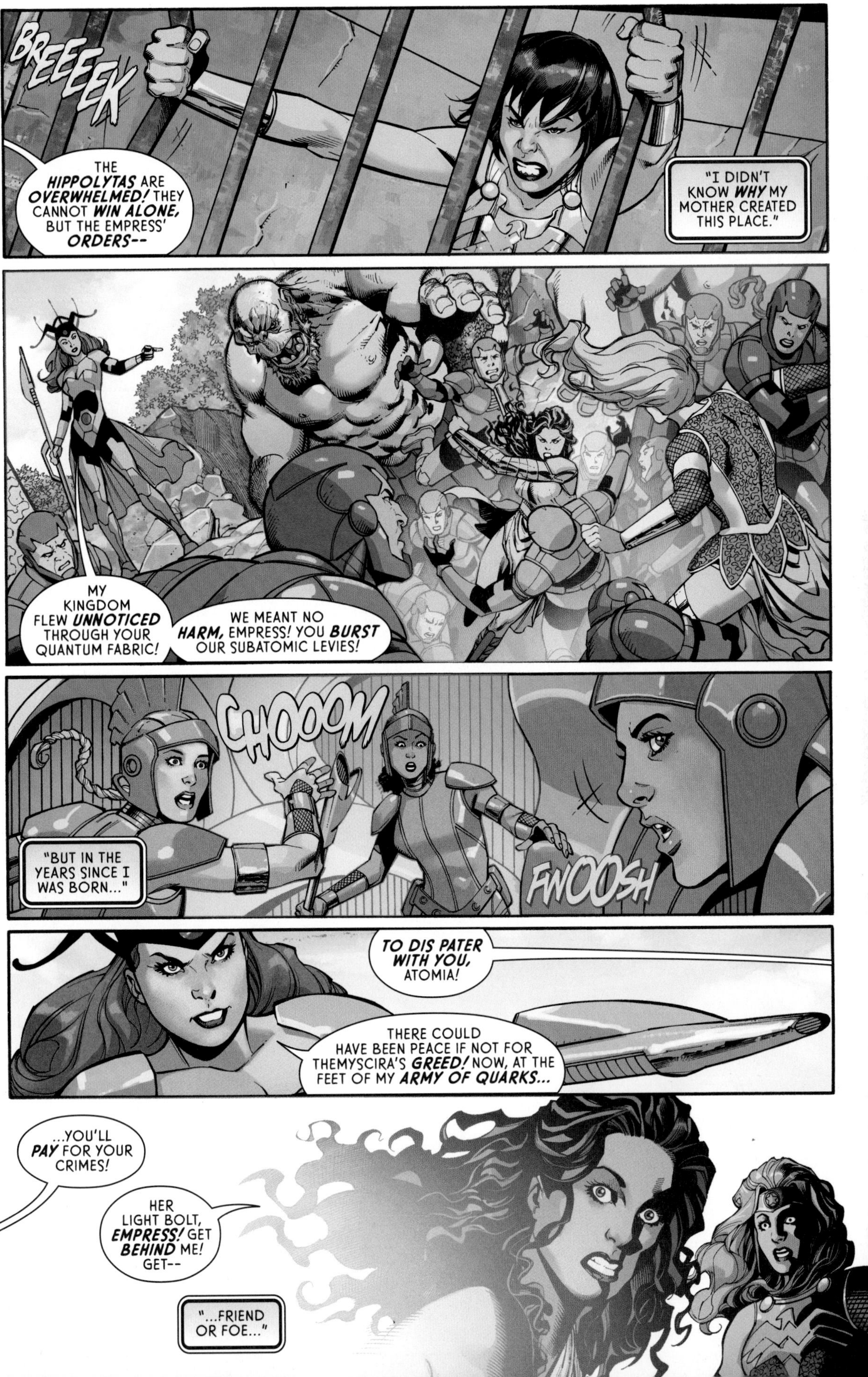
BREEEEK
THE HIPPOLYTAS ARE OVERWHELMED! THEY CANNOT WIN ALONE, BUT THE EMPRESS' ORDERS--
"I DIDN'T KNOW WHY MY MOTHER CREATED THIS PLACE."
MY KINGDOM FLEW UNNOTICED THROUGH YOUR QUANTUM FABRIC!
WE MEANT NO HARM, EMPRESS! YOU BURST OUR SUBATOMIC LEVIES!
CHOOOM
"BUT IN THE YEARS SINCE I WAS BORN..."
FWOOSH
TO DIS PATER WITH YOU, ATOMIA!
THERE COULD HAVE BEEN PEACE IF NOT FOR THEMYSCIRA'S GREED! NOW, AT THE FEET OF MY ARMY OF QUARKS...
...YOU'LL PAY FOR YOUR CRIMES!
HER LIGHT BOLT, EMPRESS! GET BEHIND ME! GET--
"...FRIEND OR FOE..."

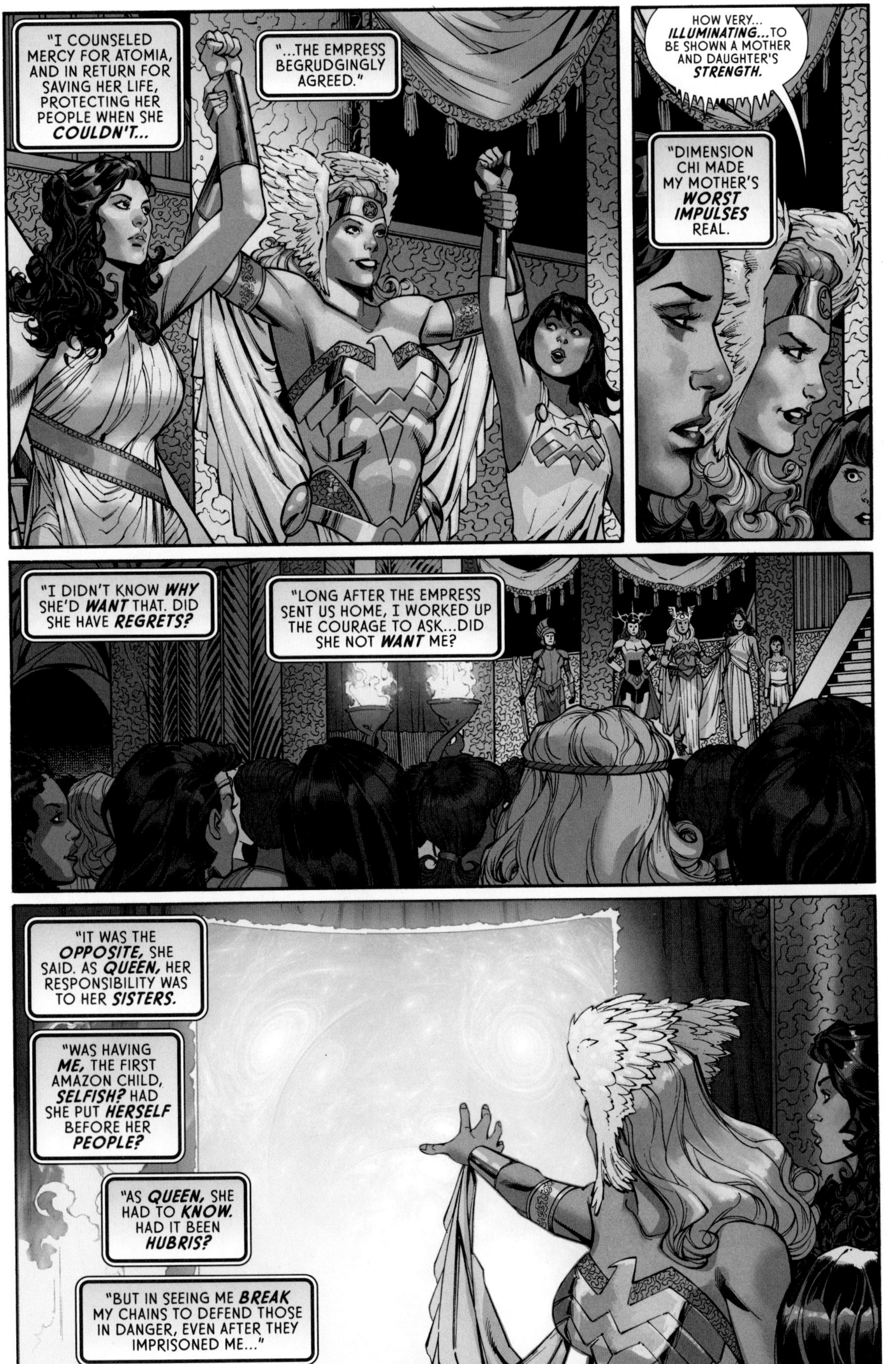
"I COUNSELED MERCY FOR ATOMIA, AND IN RETURN FOR SAVING HER LIFE, PROTECTING HER PEOPLE WHEN SHE COULDN'T...
"...THE EMPRESS BEGRUDGINGLY AGREED."
HOW VERY... ILLUMINATING...TO BE SHOWN A MOTHER AND DAUGHTER'S STRENGTH.
"DIMENSION CHI MADE MY MOTHER'S WORST IMPULSES REAL.
"I DIDN'T KNOW WHY SHE'D WANT THAT. DID SHE HAVE REGRETS?
"LONG AFTER THE EMPRESS SENT US HOME, I WORKED UP THE COURAGE TO ASK...DID SHE NOT WANT ME?
"IT WAS THE OPPOSITE, SHE SAID. AS QUEEN, HER RESPONSIBILITY WAS TO HER SISTERS.
"WAS HAVING ME, THE FIRST AMAZON CHILD, SELFISH? HAD SHE PUT HERSELF BEFORE HER PEOPLE?
"AS QUEEN, SHE HAD TO KNOW. HAD IT BEEN HUBRIS?
"BUT IN SEEING ME BREAK MY CHAINS TO DEFEND THOSE IN DANGER, EVEN AFTER THEY IMPRISONED ME..."

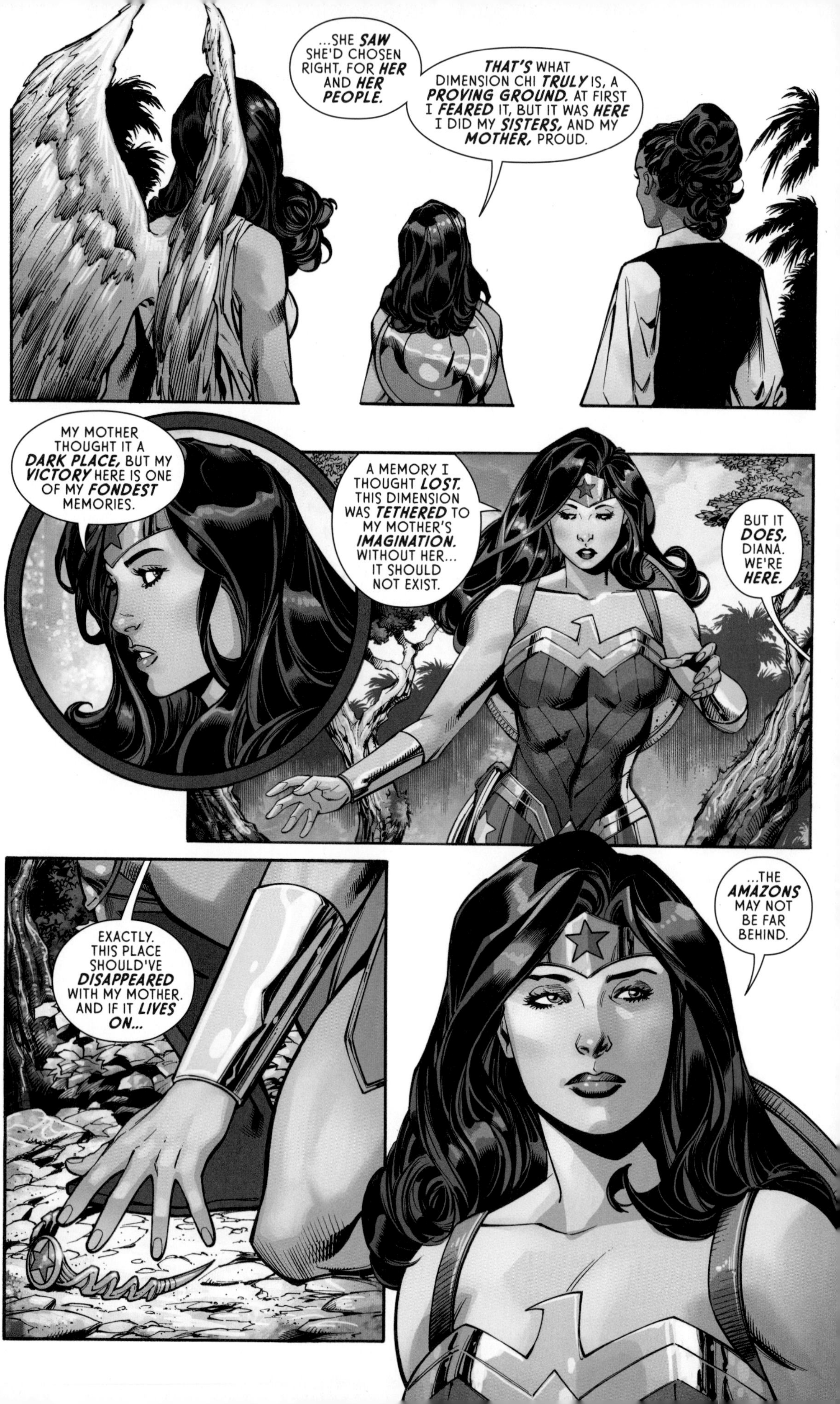
...SHE SAW SHE'D CHOSEN RIGHT, FOR HER AND HER PEOPLE.
THAT'S WHAT DIMENSION CHI TRULY IS, A PROVING GROUND. AT FIRST I FEARED IT, BUT IT WAS HERE I DID MY SISTERS, AND MY MOTHER, PROUD.
MY MOTHER THOUGHT IT A DARK PLACE, BUT MY VICTORY HERE IS ONE OF MY FONDEST MEMORIES.
A MEMORY I THOUGHT LOST. THIS DIMENSION WAS TETHERED TO MY MOTHER'S IMAGINATION. WITHOUT HER... IT SHOULD NOT EXIST.
BUT IT DOES, DIANA. WE'RE HERE.
EXACTLY. THIS PLACE SHOULD'VE DISAPPEARED WITH MY MOTHER. AND IF IT LIVES ON...
...THE AMAZONS MAY NOT BE FAR BEHIND.

VARIANT COVER GALLERY

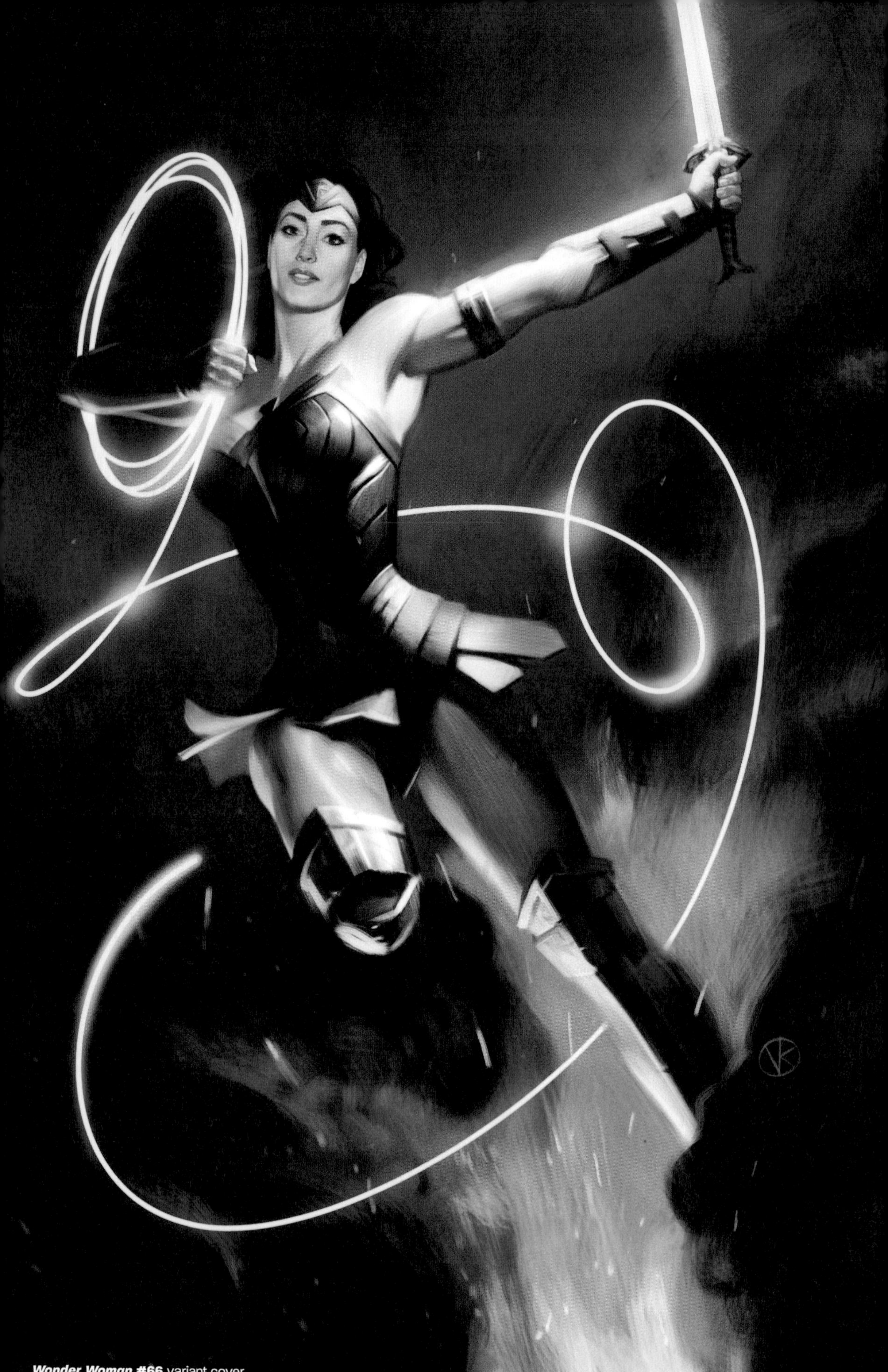

***Wonder Woman* #66** variant cover
by **VIKTOR KALVACHEV**

***Wonder Woman* #67** variant cover
by **ESTEBAN MAROTO & SANTI CASAS**

Wonder Woman **#68** variant cover
by **KAARE ANDREWS**

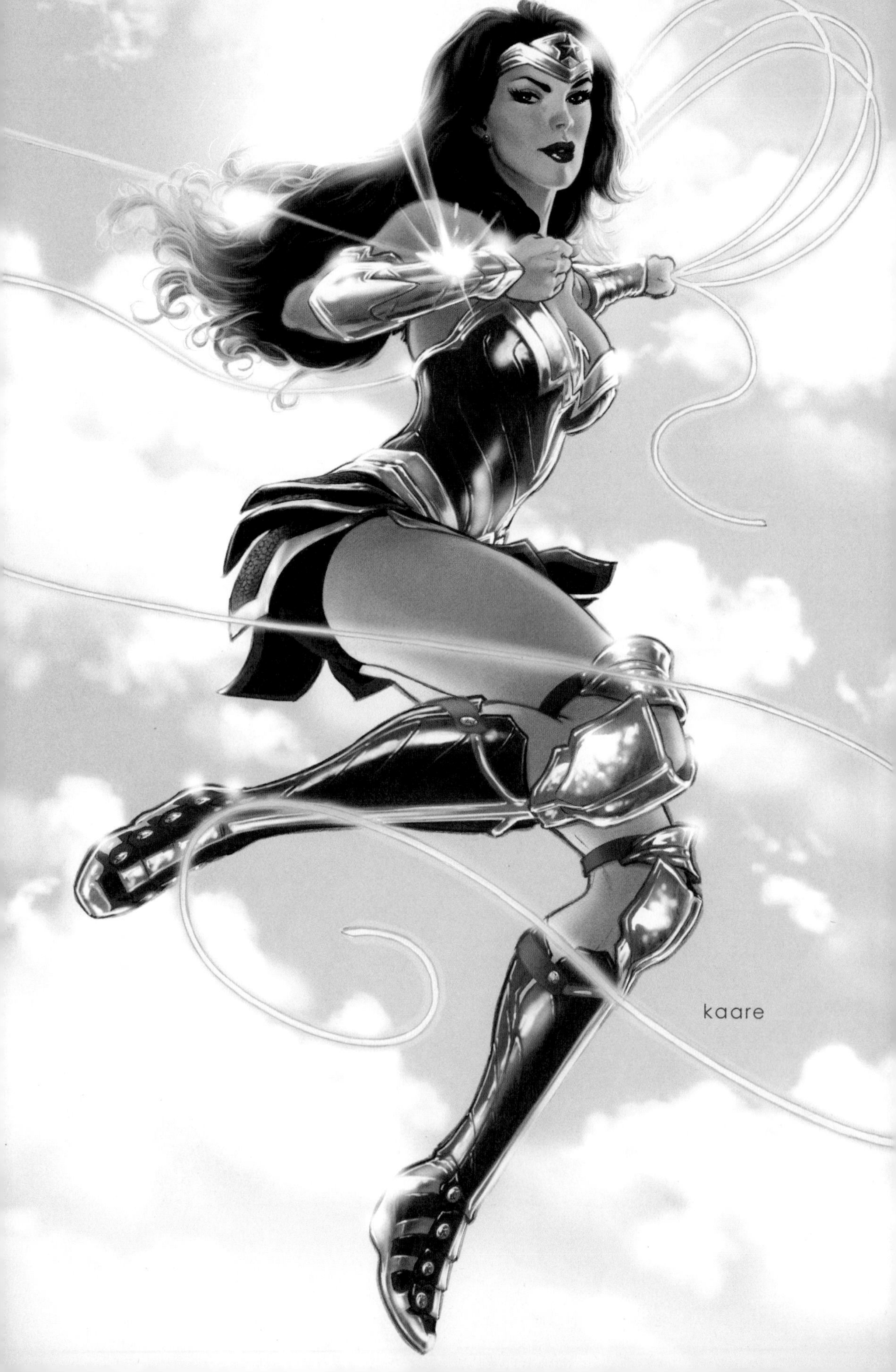

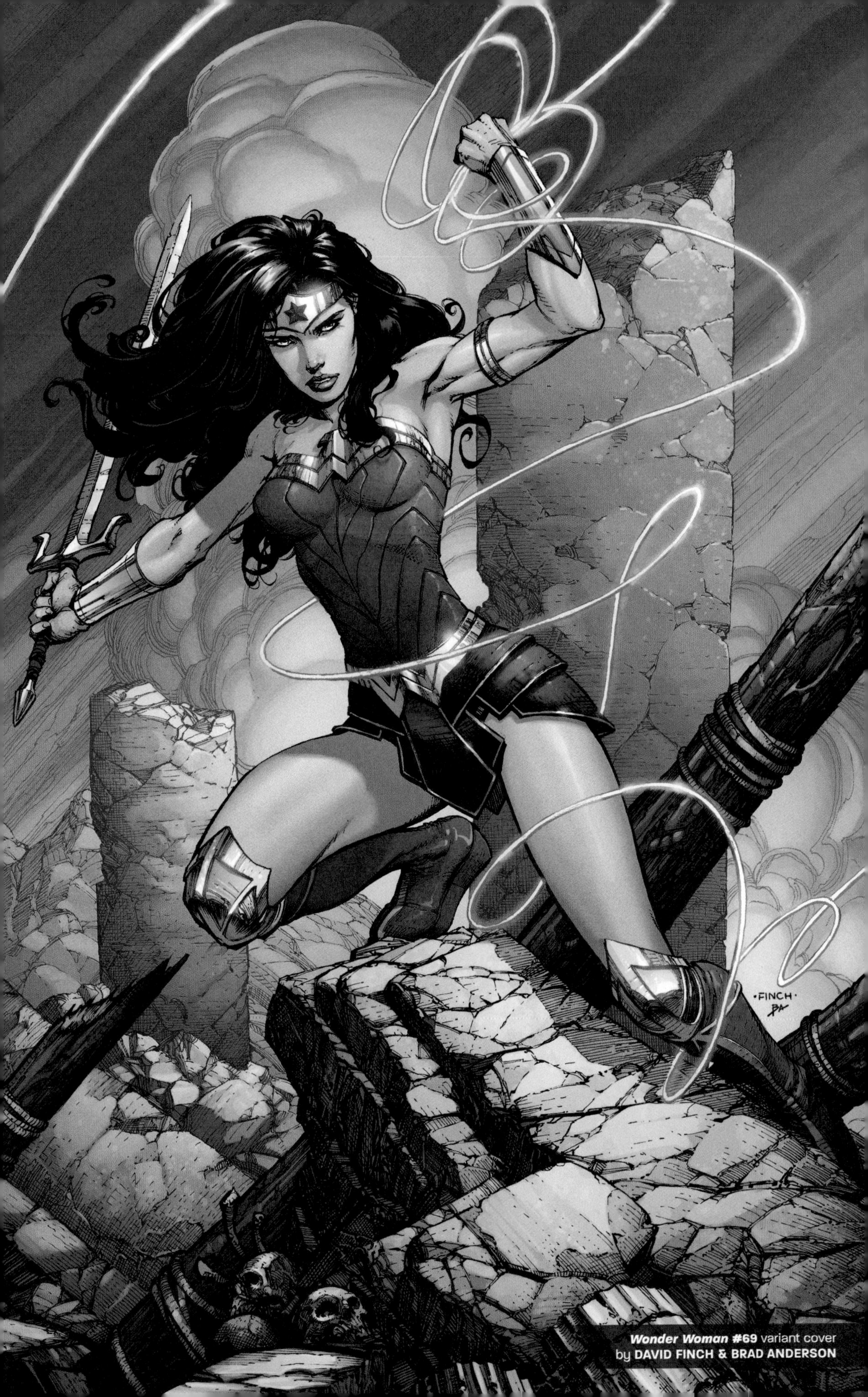
FINCH

***Wonder Woman* #69** variant cover
by **DAVID FINCH & BRAD ANDERSON**

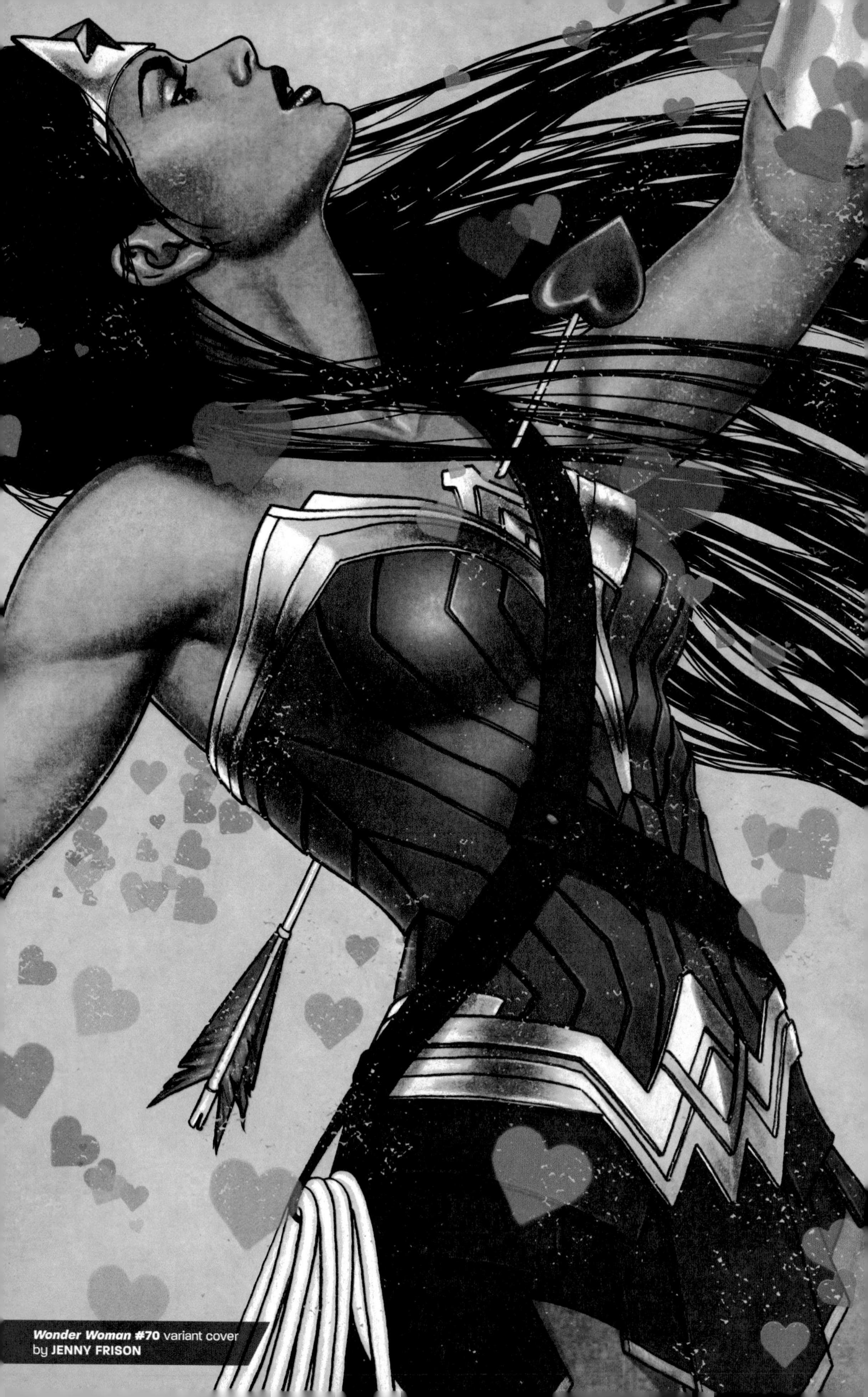

***Wonder Woman* #70** variant cover
by **JENNY FRISON**

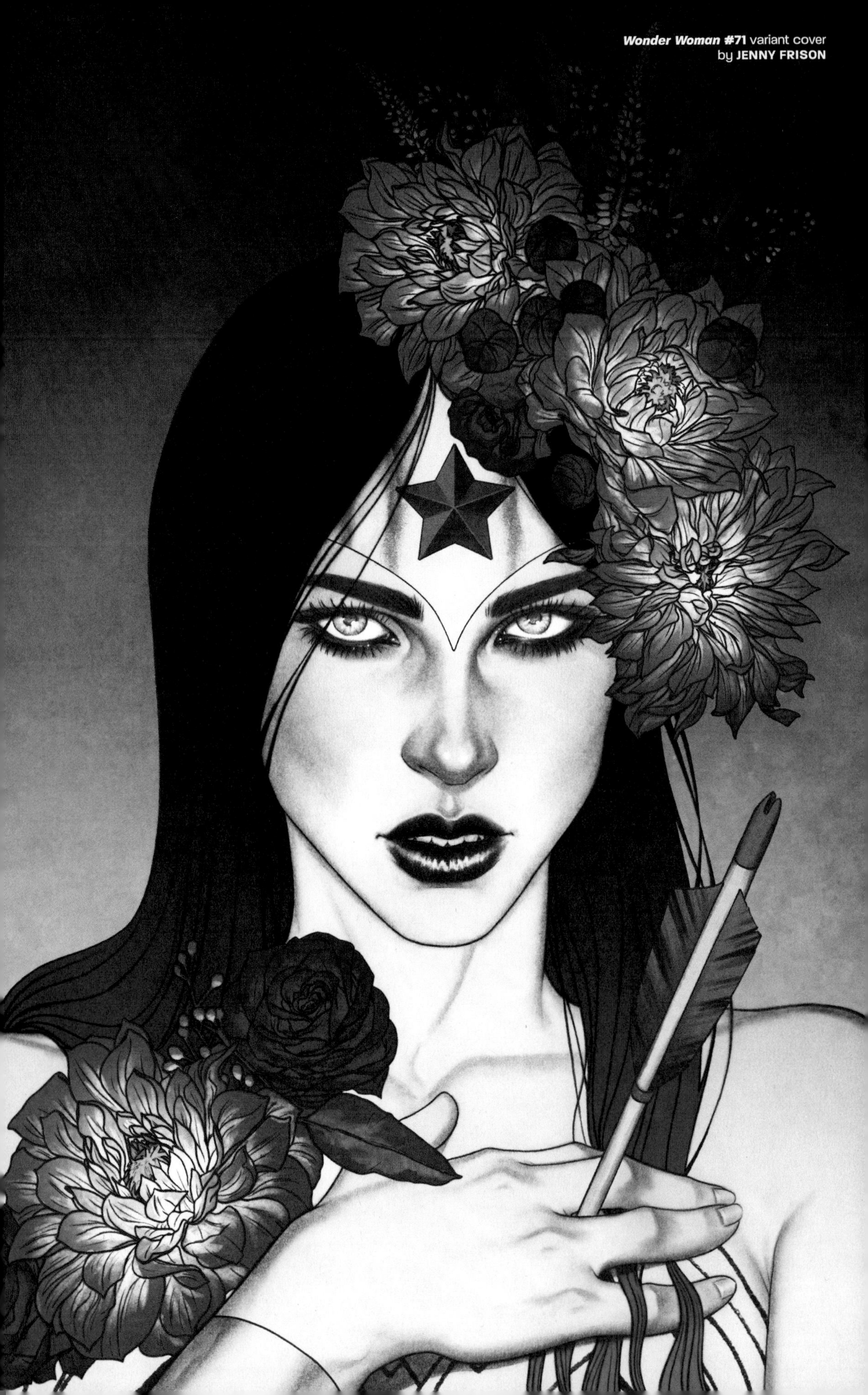

***Wonder Woman* #71** variant cover
by **JENNY FRISON**

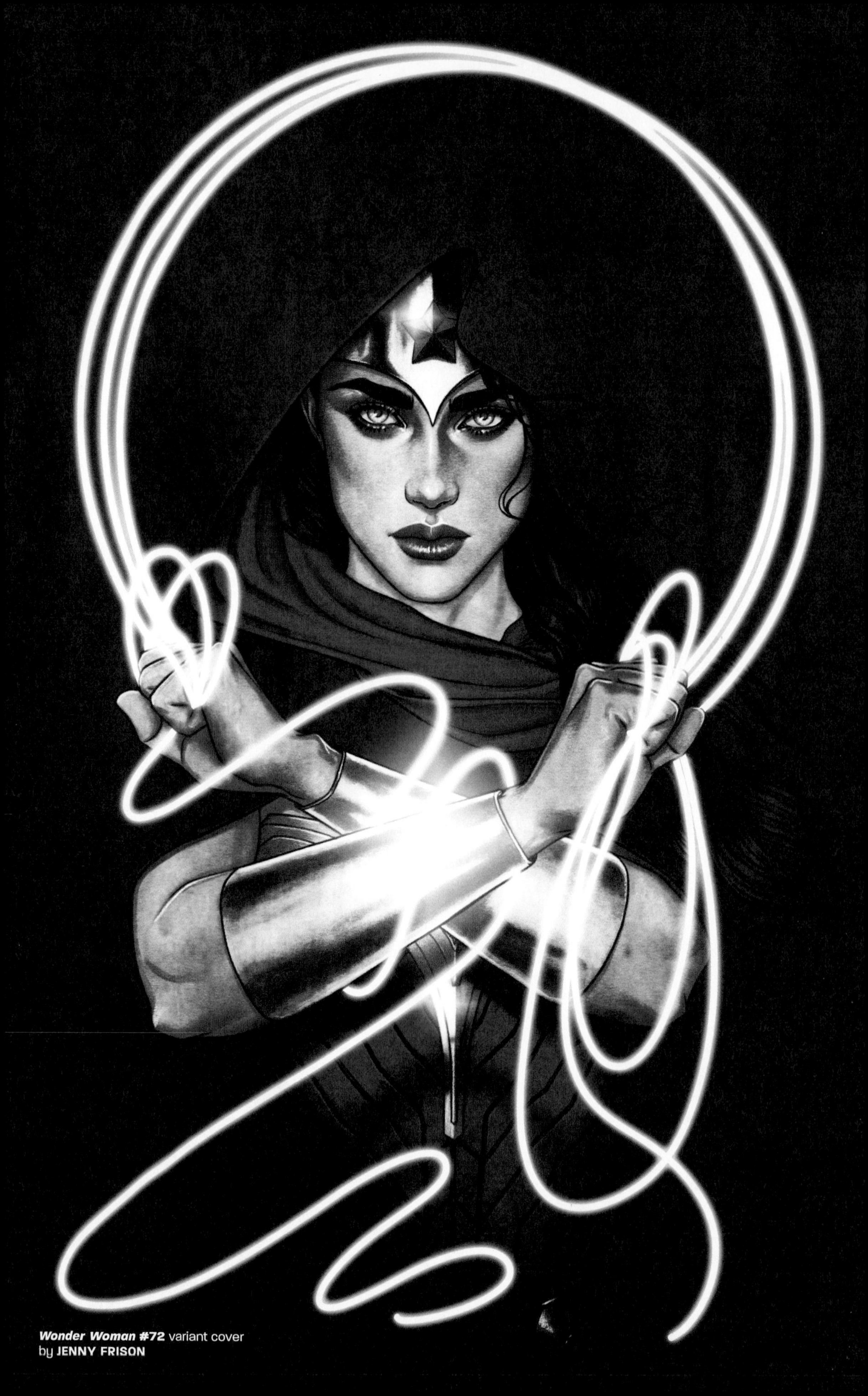

***Wonder Woman* #72** variant cover
by **JENNY FRISON**

***Wonder Woman* #73** variant cover
by **JENNY FRISON**

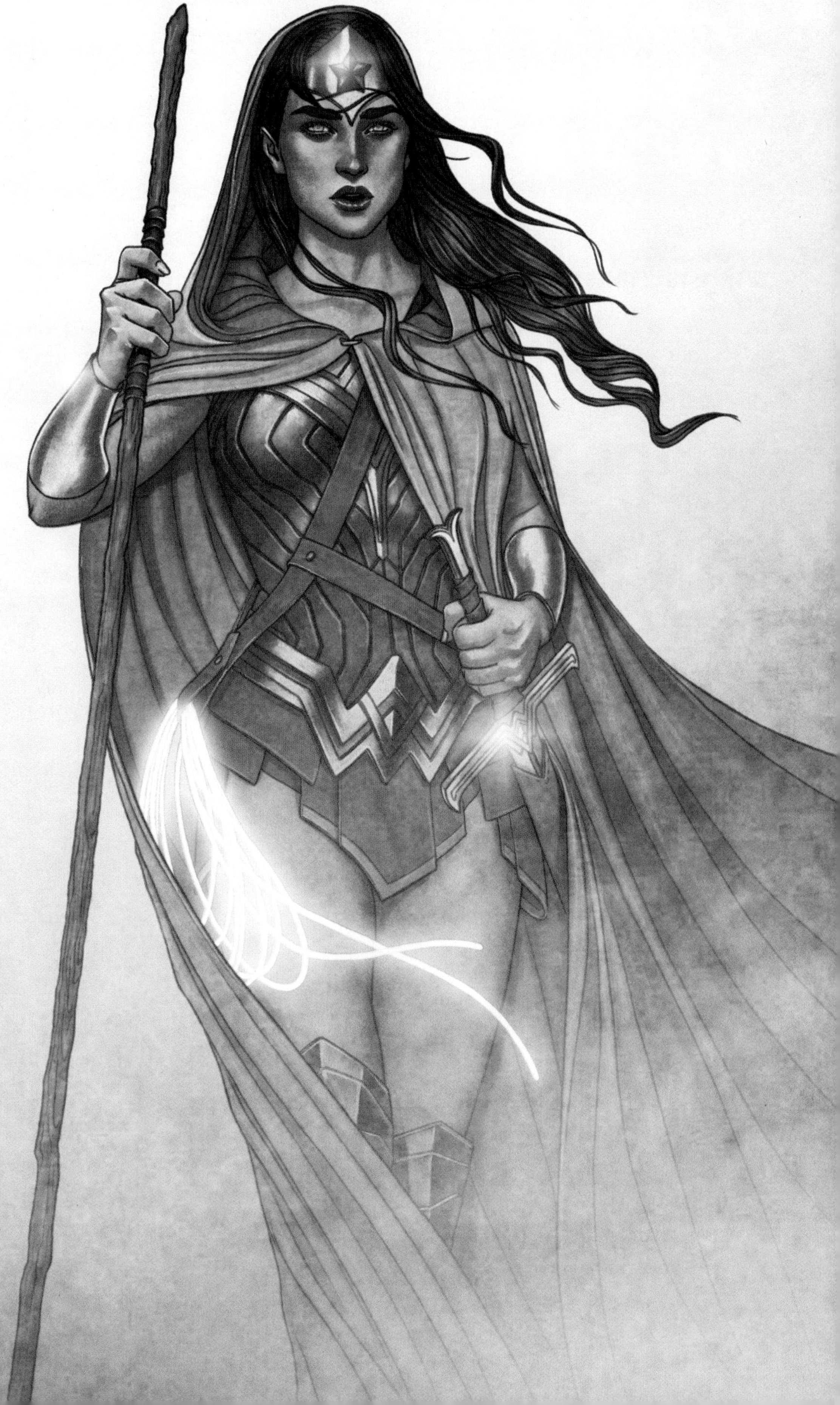

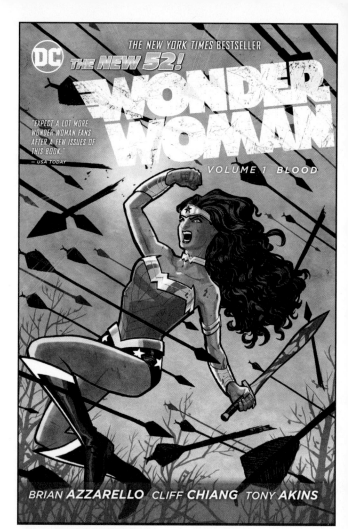
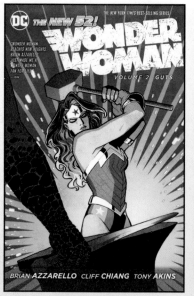

"One of the best writers for Wonder Woman in the modern era."
– NERDIST

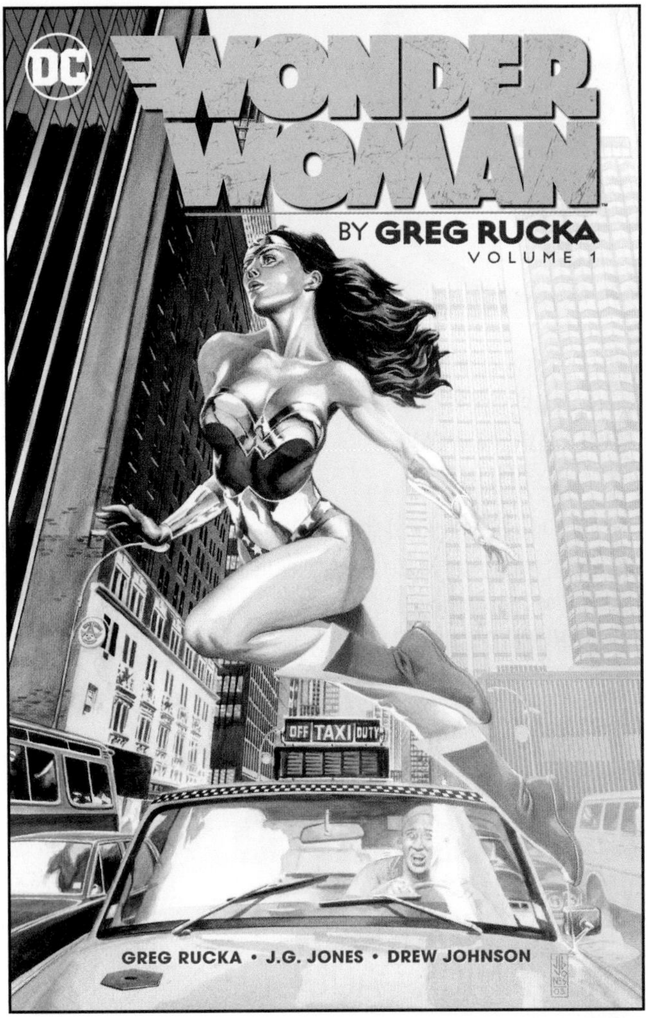
DC
WONDER WOMAN
BY GREG RUCKA
VOLUME 1
OFF TAXI DUTY
GREG RUCKA • J.G. JONES • DREW JOHNSON

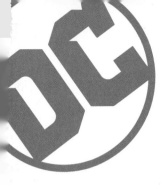

WONDER WOMAN BY GREG RUCKA
with J.G. JONES & DREW JOHNSON

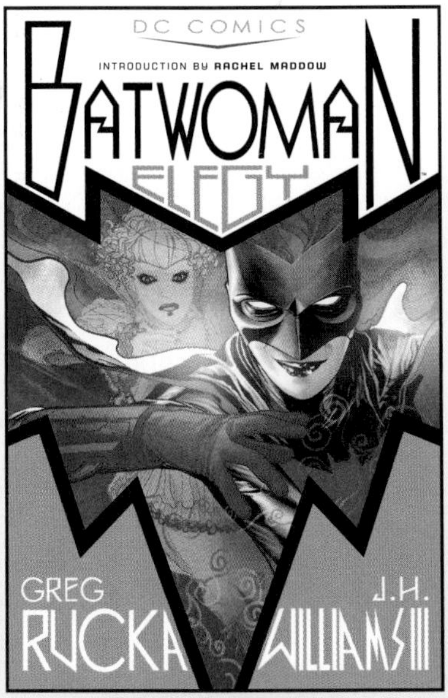
DC COMICS
INTRODUCTION BY RACHEL MADDOW
BATWOMAN
ELEGY
GREG RUCKA
J.H. WILLIAMS III

BATWOMAN: ELEGY with J.H. WILLIAMS III

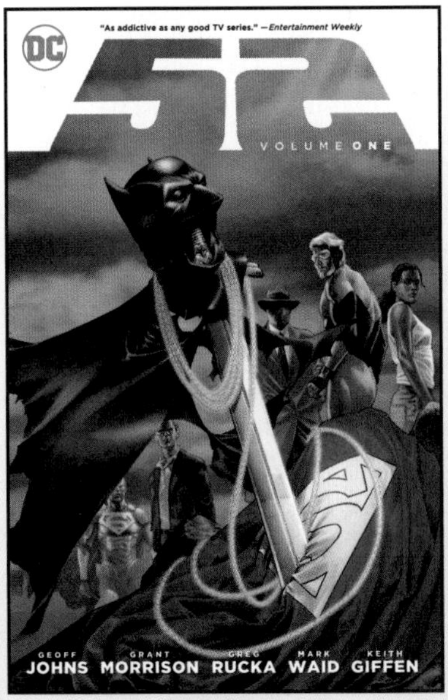
"As addictive as any good TV series." —Entertainment Weekly
DC
52
VOLUME ONE
GEOFF JOHNS
GRANT MORRISON
GREG RUCKA
MARK WAID
KEITH GIFFEN

52 VOL. 1 with VARIOUS ARTISTS

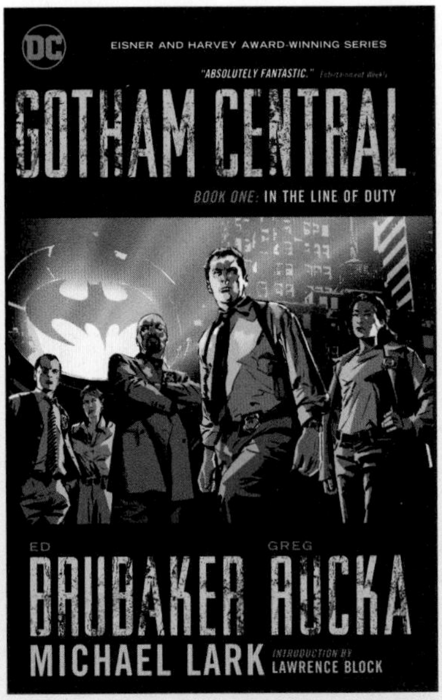
DC
EISNER AND HARVEY AWARD-WINNING SERIES
"ABSOLUTELY FANTASTIC."
GOTHAM CENTRAL
BOOK ONE: IN THE LINE OF DUTY
ED BRUBAKER
GREG RUCKA
MICHAEL LARK
INTRODUCTION BY LAWRENCE BLOCK

GOTHAM CENTRAL BOOK ONE with ED BRUBAKER & MICHAEL LARK

Get more DC graphic novels wherever comics and books are sold!

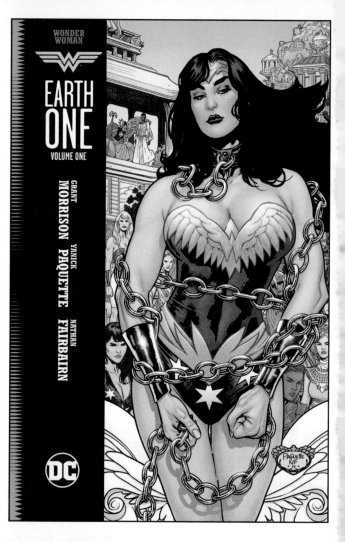